RECOLLECTIONS OF WILLIAM ARNOLD

RECOLLECTIONS OF WILLIAM ARNOLD

Edited with an Introduction by Keith Brooker

Victor Hatley Memorial Series
Volume 4

Northamptonshire Record Society
2014

ISBN 978 0 901275 71 4

Published by the Northamptonshire Record Society
Wootton Hall Park, Northampton, NN4 8BQ

*This is the fourth in a series of soft-backs published to commemorate the life
and work of the late Victor Hatley. Victor was for many years a member of the
Record Society Council, and published numerous articles and booklets on
Northamptonshire. He was honorary editor of two volumes in the Main Series
of the Society's publications.*

Typeset by John Hardaker
Wollaston, Northamptonshire

Printed and bound in Great Britain by Short Run Press Limited,
25 Bittern Road, Sowton Industrial Estate, Exeter EX2 7LW

CONTENTS

ILLUSTRATIONS

TABLES

Abbreviations and bibliography

Autobiography	J. W. Arnold, *Recollections of William Arnold* (1915)
A.H.R.	*American History Review*
B.P.P.	*British Parliamentary Reports*
B.U.S.M. Co	*British United Shoe Machinery Co Ltd*
B.S.T.J.	*Boot & Shoe Trades Journal*
C.R.O.	*Companies Registration Office*
D.B.B.	*Dictionary of Business Biography (1984-86)*
Ec.H.R.	*Economic History Review (2nd Series)*
E.J.	*Economic Journal*
F.O.	*Footwear Organiser*
J.B.B.S.I.	*Journal of the British Boot & Shoe Institute*
J.E.B.H.	*Journal of Economic and Business History*
J.E.H.	*Journal of Economic History*
J.R.S.S.	*Journal of the Royal Statistical Society*
K.C.	*Kettering Circular*
K.L.	*Kettering Leader*
K.O.	*Kettering Observer*
L.T.C.	*Leather Trades Circular & Review*
M.R.C.	Medical Research Council
N.A.	National Archives
N.U.B.S.O.	*National Union of Boot & Shoe Operatives*
N.U.B.S.R.F.	*National Union of Boot & Shoe Riveters & Finishers*
N.C.E.	*Northampton Chronicle & Echo*
N.C.M.	*Northampton County Magazine*
N.D.R.	*Northampton Daily Reporter*
N.H.	*Northampton Herald*
N.I.	*Northampton Independent*
N.M.	*Northampton Mercury*

N.P.L.	Northampton Public Library
N.R.O.	Northamptonshire Record Office
N.R.S.	Northamptonshire Record Society
N.P.P.	*Northamptonshire Past & Present*
O.D.N.B.	*Oxford Dictionary of National Biography (2004)*
P.P.	*Past & Present*
S.L.N.	*Shoe & Leather News*
S.L.R.	*Shoe & Leather Record*
S.L.T. Supplement	*Shoe & Leather Trades Supplement of 1916*
T.L.A.H.S.	*Transactions of the Leicestershire Archaeological and Historical Society*
V.C.H.	*Victoria County History*
W.N.	*Wellingborough News*

K. B. Brooker, *Change of the Footwear Industry: Major Technical & Organisational Developments 1857-1914* (1985); copy at Northamptonshire Record Office.

K. B. Brooker, *The Transformation of the Small Master Economy in the Boot & Shoe Industry 1887-1914; with Special Reference to Northampton* (unpublished PhD thesis, University of Hull (1986; available on the University Website).

PREFACE

During the Great War there appeared in Northampton a slim volume of reminiscences that is a unique published record of a successful footwear manufacturer's life in Britain in the last sixty years of the long Victorian period. The subject of this book is James William Arnold (always known as William Arnold), who rose from the shoe workers' ranks to occupy a position of authority and respect in the county town's premier industry: for a working man born into a poor home to attain success as a manufacturer was unusual; despite popular assumptions to the contrary.[1] He belonged to that generation of influential manufacturers that fashioned the industry during its final transition between 1887 and 1905 from a handwork-dominated outwork trade to a fully mechanised, factory-based industry. The production and retail structure introduced at that time was to last into the 1950s, when further seminal change overtook the industry driven by a new set of economic circumstances.

The book's interest and value rests upon two elements. First, it is a very human story of one man's achievement, and of the rewards that enterprise held out to Victorian men and women through the mantra of self-help: rewards often driven simply by family want rather than

---

1 Many Northampton manufacturers laid claim to this social transition, but few deserve this accolade. For example, H. E. Randall claimed lowly origins, but in fact this was not the case. Like many successful people contemporary biographies stressed his humble origins: "...A native of the town, he has risen from the ranks (and) by sheer grit carved his way to the front until today he is the head of one of the most important boot manufacturing and distribution companies in the country..." (N.M. 9/12/05 p. 4; c.f. E. Gaskell, *Northamptonshire Leaders: Social & Political* (1907) p. 36, "Sir Henry is one of those forceful determined Englishmen who would carve their way to the front in any sphere and in any circumstances of life, who are the builders as well as the architects of their own fortunes". But reality shows him as the son of a successful draper: the only son of Henry Ross Randall, of Bridge Street, Northampton (B.S.T.J. 28/6/1901 p. 900) died on 20 June 1901 aged 80 at Brixton), and Elizabeth, a daughter of Stephen Dickens Esq., farmer of Wootton Grange. His education was probably superior to that of most shoe workers. After attending a private school in the town (N.M. 25/7/1930 p. 2), St. Gregory's School, described as 'dilapidated', where the schoolmaster was the Rev. Charles Lutterwell-West, Vicar of Upton, Northamptonshire), he went briefly to Northampton Grammar School, before completing his education privately at Coventry. At 14 he was apprenticed, at 2/6d a week, to William Jones J.P., his uncle (1815-1889), a prominent manufacturer of Newland who founded an export-only business in the late 1840s and which failed in early 1894 some years after his retirement. A prominent local figure, he was elected Mayor in 1872. He died at his home Sidney House, Billing Road, aged 73 on 14/4/1889, leaving £32,066/0/6d. Jones, though married, had no children and Randall's apprenticeship was probably like that given to a manufacturer's son and not that of a working apprentice.

any higher motivation. William Arnold's story tells of one man's battle against his own frailties to provide a better life than he had enjoyed as a child for both his family and for himself. He is one of the few truly poor shoe workers turned successful footwear manufacturer in the industry between 1887 and 1914. Additionally, he provides an insight into Victorian business behaviour, and particularly about business failure of which little is written, and rarely available to us.[2] And as such, his story has come down to us as a local manufacturer we can know and understand more completely and personally than is the case of many of his fellow footwear manufacturers.

Secondly, the *Autobiography*'s uniqueness as a historical record enhances its value. Although there is a relative abundance of biographical material about leading, elite footwear manufacturers, albeit in scattered sources, this is the only complete published autobiography of a smaller British Victorian footwear manufacturer. The book provides an opportunity to learn about a second rank footwear manufacturer for whom there is little accessible and published information. Despite the commercial importance of these men, they are difficult to assess historically because of the paucity of personal written records they have left to posterity. The *Autobiography*, therefore, provides some unique insights into the trials and tribulations facing a working man and his family in building a new business from inauspicious beginnings. Issues of finding credit; of establishing a customer base; of overcoming failure and building success: all find a place in this book. It also provides a telling account of his personal journey in coming to terms with both his background and personality, and offers some understanding of the ways he builds a position for himself in his community. By birth and upbringing he was a working man and in many ways he remained emotionally attached to that inheritance throughout his life.

Working class autobiographies and oral testimony[3] have been used by commentators and historians for many years, but in the 1970s and 1980s such sources were more systematically utilised to illustrate and deepen our understanding of various aspects of the past. John Burnett, David

---

2 V. M. Lester, *Victorian Insolvency* (1995) is a recent summary of the financial, legal and administrative structure of insolvency in nineteenth-century England. On the use historians can make of deeds of arrangement and compositions, see K. B. Brooker, "Some Approaches to the Study of Small Scale Industries in 19th Century Britain," *Business Archives* n.s Vol. 4 No. 3 (1981) p. 7-17, and K. B. Brooker 1986, chapters 4 & 5 on the extent and effects of business failure on the nineteenth-century footwear industry.

3 An early example is the use made by George Sturt of biographical recollection. His letters give interesting insights of the use he made of such testimony. See E. D. Mackerness (ed), *The Journals of George Sturt 1890-1927*, (1967) 2 volumes.

Vincent and David Mayall's[4] study was able to demonstrate how the systematic use of working-class autobiographies can help historians to access a fuller human narrative of the past. More recently, two historians have added to our understanding about these valuable sources.[5] Where Burnett, Vincent and Mayall adopted a literary approach, Jane Humphries has subjected her material to both qualitative and quantitative analysis in recreating the life experiences of her subjects. Her book uses over six hundred autobiographies written by eighteenth and nineteenth century working men to analyse the harshness of childhood for many working people in a way not possible using conventional sources like demographic, social mobility and apprenticeship and school records. This has enabled her to gain insights into the family and early working lives of children drawing on working people's own accounts of their lives.

Of course there are some very clear pitfalls in the use of autobiography as an historical narrative, and so this introduction will subject William Arnold's recollections to a critical gaze. Statements he makes have been reviewed and corroborated where possible, and some additional evidence used to give both credence and an occasional word of caution about his written memories of pre-1914 Northampton and the wider county. William Arnold's story is both a record of the experience of running a business during a period of industrial and commercial change, and holds up a mirror to the differing fortunes of footwear manufacturers in the east Midlands. The introduction will also serve to place his story into the context of both the business and industrial world in which he rose to prominence. It will also expand upon and supplement William Arnold's text, giving additional information both about his family background, and the family business.

This *Autobiography* was ghost-written following a series of discussions between William Arnold and some army friends in early 1915: they were Territorial soldiers, teachers from London, billeted in Northampton. Although this book has been a valuable resource for the careful student of Northamptonshire history and its staple industry for some years, it has not been the subject of wide use and comment in historical

4 J. Burnett, D. Vincent & D. Mayall, *The Autobiography of the Working Class (1984-1989)*, a three-volume annotated bibliography of all known examples of material written by English working class authors. John Burnett wrote widely on ordinary people's lives. In this context, see *Useful Toil: Autobiographies of Working People from the 1820s to the 1920s* (1974); *Destiny Obscure: Autobiographies of Childhood, Education and Family from the 1820s to the 1920s* (1982), and *Idle Hands: Experience of Unemployment, 1790-1990* (1994); David Vincent provides useful discussion about the use of working people's reminiscences, see, for example, *Bread, Knowledge and Freedom* (1981) and *Literacy and Popular Culture: England 1750-1914* (1993).

5 J. Humphries, *Childhood & Child Labour in the British Industrial Revolution* (2010); E. Griffin, *Liberty's Dawn: a People's History of the Industrial Revolution* (2013).

writings. Still less, few regional or national historians have used this unique and valuable record.[6] Biographical information, some published some not, of leading elite manufacturers is available, but published autobiographical writings concerning the smaller footwear manufacturers are rare.

The book was privately published in Northampton with a small print run and has never since been re-issued. It is in boards measuring six by eight inches and contains seven pages of introduction and eighty-six of text. There is a monochrome portrait of William and seven other monochrome photographs through the text. In terms of editing, this new edition has been annotated to make the text readily comprehensible to the reader. The transcription of the text for preparation for publication in this reprint has been carried out electronically and in doing so there has been a loss of the original pagination and layout. Also, the opportunity has been taken to correct some minor typographical errors and English usage where it is felt that this does not spoil the original text. The original photographs have been digitally copied into this edition. Nevertheless, in all other essential respects the text presented here is an accurate reproduction of the 1915 edition.

Copies of the book are today hard to find outside of a small number of libraries: within the second-hand book market copies are difficult to locate. This makes the Northamptonshire Record Society's reprint of Arnold's *Autobiography* particularly welcome. It is hoped that this new edition of the now scarce *Autobiography* will go some way to bring the book to the attention of a wider audience, and give it wider prominence to those studying consumer industries, to Northamptonshire historians, and to the general reader.

Aylsham, Norfolk   Keith Brooker
St Alban's Day 2013

---

6 A recent welcome exception to this comment is the inclusion of extracts from the book in *Jane Humphries* op. cit. especially at p. 74-5.

ACKNOWLEDGEMENTS

In preparing any book for publication one inevitably incurs a number of debts. In this case, the foremost of these debts is the one owed to the late Victor Hatley. Like many historians who have researched the history of Northamptonshire and its county town in the forty years prior to his death, I was lucky enough to be touched by Victor's conscientious professionalism, his courtesy, and his friendship. His preparedness to offer advice and comment to all who contacted him about his deep historical knowledge of his adopted county, remains a testament to his open generosity and delight in historical scholarship.

No less important is the debt owed to my colleagues Geoff Crossick and the late Keith Nield. Over many years, Keith Nield provided much unselfish advice and guidance concerning my study of the economic and social transformation in the footwear industry and much else. This book provides me with an opportunity to record the unstinting support he gave to me. My warm thanks are also extended to Geoff Crossick. It was he who first opened up the world of the small master. He gave generously of his time to discuss the character and nature of nineteenth-century shoemakers and shoe workers. It is thanks to his insights that I was able to sort out some of the complexities surrounding shoemaker small masters, and the employer class that emerged during the industry's transition to factory working. My colleagues Ron Greenall and Mike Turner were kind enough to discuss and read an earlier draft of this introduction and offer insightful comments that saved me from a number of errors. My thanks must also be recorded to Duncan Bythell, Phil Cottrell, David Rubinstein, the late John Saville, and Rob James, who in different ways have added to this study and helped nurture my interest in history. David Hall, the editor of this series has eased my path through the publishing and production stages of this book with kindness and patience.

The librarians and keepers of records on which this introduction is founded have answered queries promptly, given me some interesting leads, and made available materials in their care with unflagging speed and professionalism. And lastly, I would like to thank Margaret, who persevered and gave help and succour in many ways.

Of course, it goes without stressing that the views expressed in this introduction, together with any remaining errors, are entirely my own.

Figure 1: James William Arnold (1927)

William Arnold's grandparents	William Arnold's Father's Siblings	William Arnold's Siblings	William Arnold's Children
William (born 1803) marr. Ann (born 1809)	Eliza (born 1836) **Matthew (1838-1911) marr. Ellen Isham (born 1839)** William (born 1840) James (born 1842) Anthony (1849-1919) Mary (born 1853) Other issue?	**James William (1860-1945) marr. 1st Elizabeth Harriet Walker (1860-1922)** Ann (born 1862) Henry (1864-1890) Albert (1867-1950) Matthew Anthony (1871-1942) Abigail (born 1873) Mary Rose (born 1873) Tom Austin (1875-1947) Signor Austin (1877-1881) Flora (born 1880) Sarah (born 1883) James (born 1886)	William jnr (1886-1978) Matthew (1887-1963) Thomas (1889-1940) Harriet (born 1890) Harry (born 1892) Alfred Walker (1893-1955) Annie (born 1896) James (1896-1969) Grace (born 1890) Ellen Joy (born 1903) An infant died

Figure 2: The Arnold Family

INTRODUCTION

William Arnold's *Autobiography* is a story of one man's successful struggle against business adversity to establish a thriving business, despite the exacting competitive and trading conditions of his day. But, additionally it tells of his successful fight against personal weakness and his commercial emergence from business failure.

This book gives the portrait of a rumbustious man, who took charge of his life. His published record is uncompromisingly frank and refreshing for a man of his generation. Absent in this memoir is the careful sanitised recapitulation of life's choreographed successful progression common of so many contemporary biographies. In its place, we are given a frank, almost raw memory. Here we learn not only about the vicissitudes of his business life, but also of his rough drinking and fighting ways and his desire to help his family. He lays out his story in an uncomplicated way: this is no old man's whimsical embroidering of his life. Instead, the country lad shines through. He appears never to have lost some of the uncomplicated ways of the rural outwork shoe worker he began life as, despite the success and prosperity that came to him in later life. These matters will be dealt with in their place in the narrative below. But also within this autobiography there is another dimension, for it shows us some of the strands of commercial endeavour that lies at the core of the footwear industry's development in the late nineteenth century. Sufficient of these elements find an echo in this intriguing account to enable the reader to begin to understand something of the nature of the economic and commercial changes that the industry was going through at this time. This detail helps us to understand William Arnold, but in order that it should not unduly complicate the dialogue the detail has been placed in an Appendix.

This revealing memoir awaits, but first some questions should be asked. How typical was he of his class? How typical is his story? What sort of manufacturer do we find here? To what extent is this book merely a fascinating insight into the life of a single late Victorian small manufacturer, and to what extent can it be regarded as an accurate portrait of this class of manufacturer? How typical was William's business experience and how typical was he as a businessman in the footwear industry of this period? This edited version of the book sets out to discover answers to these questions: to put the man and his firm into the context of the footwear industry of the period. Arnold's firm was part of a group of second rank companies that grew to prominence during an extended period of fundamental change in the industry. It will be one of the tasks of this introduction to locate Arnold and this group within this broad sweep of change that assailed not only the footwear industry but also many consumer and service industries of the period besides.

And lastly, in tracing Arnold's life story against the wider backdrop of industrial change, it is inevitable that we should ask the questions: how typical was Arnold's experience and how typical a manufacturer was he? At one level there is uniqueness about each person's life, but equally there are parallels and conclusions that can be drawn from one life experience to help us understand the broader sweep of entrepreneurial endeavour in an industry. The assessment that follows has been set out in a way that seeks to help the reader find some answer to these questions. From a consideration of the business world William Arnold lived in, this introduction will investigate Arnold the man, and finally his social position by comparing this against the social characterisation of his fellow manufacturers.

William Arnold's Business World

The starting point is to look at the overall business experience of the industry in the years between 1887 and 1914. What sort of industry did William Arnold work in, first as an outworker, working by hand, and later as a manufacturer utilising machinery to manufacture ready-made footwear? His years of progression from shoe worker to a successful manufacturer cover exactly the years of the transformation of the industry from an outwork dominated industry to a factory-based one. This transformation can be broken into three periods of development:

> 1857-1887: Development of distribution and retailing capability
> 1887-1895: Development of integrated machinery production capability
> 1895-1905: Development of manufacturer control over production capability

Each period had its own distinct focus and internal logic, and together represented the pathways of modernisation of the industry.

By 1857, the identification of the footwear industry with Northampton was already well defined. It had been built on a century long relationship between the town and the metropolitan market. It was a dependent relationship controlled by London merchant manufacturers and built upon cheaper production costs and the high skill base to be found in provincial centres like Northampton, which gave the high quality product required in metropolitan markets.[7] Giorgio Riello's book on the eighteenth-century development of the London footwear trade looks at the relationship between the capital and Northampton. It provides the latest in a long line of summaries of the Northampton footwear trade and tends to reinforce what we know of that trade at the mid-century.[8] He suggests that cost and product quality advantages are a sufficient explanation for late industrialisation in the footwear industry. But there were also to be persistent and long-standing technical issues hindering quick modernisation within the medium and above quality grade market segments that Northampton specialised in. Being able to produce an economically sustainable quality product using machine techniques, and to do this at an effective cost by adopting synchronised production, rather than the mixed machine and hand-work processes offered by early machine solutions, would take several decades of engineering endeavour. Closely linked to this were to be the tensions between master and man relating to embedding synchronised production into a workshop culture founded on patterns of craft working and social association at work.

The long first phase to 1887 witnessed wholesale manufacturers' development of wider distribution networks to assure their product got to market. Many adopted new merchandising techniques, and the most enterprising emerge as progressive, leading chain retailers. The available improvements to production methods tended to encourage these changes in distribution in order to absorb growing capacity: mechanisation in this early period may be viewed as a long transition period. The footwear industry had a wide ranging product base which was difficult to subject to efficient mechanised processes. And so, the development of a modern industrial landscape from hand working to machine work was achieved incrementally, both in Northampton and eastern parts of the county.[9] Many of the changes in this transitional phase involved the adoption of machines, few of which were powered, and so fitted into the existing production structure of the industry. Many

7 L. D. Schwarz, *London in the Age of Industrialisation 1700-1850* (1992) p. 197-8: This relationship developed from the 1760s at both Northampton and Stafford. The competition of provincial centres, particularly Northampton was to exacerbate the use of sweated labour in the capital and result in an absolute loss of trade from the 1860s.

8 Giorgio Riello, *A Foot in the Past (2006)* p. 221-32, which treats the development of the Northampton industry up to 1870.

9 On the early development of the footwear industry in the county see Keith Sugden, *The Occupational and Organisational Structures of the Northamptonshire Worsted and Shoemaking Trades c. 1750-1821*, University of Cambridge Master of Studies in Local & Regional History (August 2011); See also H. A. Randall "The Kettering Worsted Industry of the Eighteenth Century", *N.P.P.* Vol. VI, No. 5 (1970) and No. 6 (1971). V.C.H Northamptonshire Vol. 7, *Modern Industry* (2007) has a section on the footwear industry that also provides a familiar summary of industrial transition from outwork to mechanised factories.

of these machines both required the support of hand and perpetuated hand processes.[10]

It was only the second and third phases of change from 1887 to 1905 that witnessed the putting in place of the necessary technology and management structures to give cost-efficient production within an integrated factory setting. These changes ranged across the installation of integrated machinery systems, the shift of work processes towards managed teamworking, and the closer supervision and management of employees' productivity and conduct at work. It was in this short, intense period that the final impediments preventing fully integrated machine systems in factories were broken down; systems that were to dominate industrial methods and organisation throughout the first half of the twentieth century.[11]

Essentially the years 1887 to 1895 found manufacturers and their workers engaged in a struggle for the control of the workplace. For the manufacturer it was a fight to be able to bring footwear to market at an economic price that would ensure success. By contrast, many shoemakers and shoe workers viewed modern factory working as an unwarranted assault upon customary ways of working that gave them social independence through control of the work process.[12] And it was a fight that manufacturers won in 1895. In the following ten years they were able to complete the process change. The decade after 1895 witnessed the final putting in place of modern factory working in the industry. By 1905 the long journey from 1857, when Northampton shoemakers staged their first opposition to machinery, came to an end.

The modern integrated factory had arrived.[13] Economic competitiveness of the industry post 1895 was achieved, in broad terms, by virtue of the

10 K. B. Brooker, (1985) *passim*.
11 Idem.
12 In the course of pursuing their change agenda, a number of manufacturers followed welfare and conciliation policies within their organisations. Foremost amongst these were C. & E. Lewis, J. H. C. Crockett, and William Barratt. This period witnessed a country-wide labour management and industrial welfare movement in British industry. During the twentieth century, the employment and corporate welfare schemes which replaced owner paternalism also expressed a sense of mutual obligation between company and employee, but began to incorporate a new managerial philosophy. By the 1920s, large-scale organization and planning were being equated with higher wages, social security, and, ironically, stability of employment, and it was argued that only "human values" in industry could overcome class divisions (L. Hannah, *The Rise of the Corporate Economy* (1983), p. 32-3). On paternalism and industrial welfare generally, see, P. Joyce, *Work, Society and Politics: the culture of the factory in later Victorian England* (1980), chapter 3 and 4 *passim*, and R. Fitzgerald, *British Labour Management and Industrial Welfare, 1840-1939* (1988), chapter 3 *passim*).
13 For a more detailed account of modernisation of the footwear industry, see Appendix, 'The Footwear Industry of Northampton', below.

scale economies achieved in production and distribution, as a result of the efficient use of machines, and the eclipse of small order working by batch production utilising embryonic flow production techniques and in-stock systems of distribution. By contrast, some average practice British shoe manufacturers clung longer to outmoded hand processes, poor machine discipline, and small order working, partly as a result of demand side need, partly due to absence of comprehensive machine solutions to mechanised working in medium and high grade footwear, and partly due to attitude.[14]

William Arnold's entry into the industry in 1889 coincided with these radical changes in production. As he and his partners were learning to make their way, this second step change was underway and had begun to dramatically alter the wholesale footwear industry's scale and

14 *Small order production*: At one end of the spectrum was bespoke work, the essential feature of which was the production of single parts, one-off items; i.e. jobbing production. Such production did not necessarily use factories in the most efficient way. It did not admit standardisation, demand was unpredictable, and it required a workforce with a wide range of skills, and equally adaptable, skilled supervision. Such working made the planning or production difficult, and inevitably involved idle time for shoe workers. This was overcome by the outwork system and the presence of a pool of surplus labour to cope with seasonal fluctuations in demand. At the other end of the small order production spectrum, was the ability of pre-1860 manufacturers to execute the production of small batches to customer requirements. At this point, small order production quickly merges into batch production, and this mode of production was to persist through to and beyond 1914.

Batch production: However, what also clearly occurs in our period is the production of large batches, now in factories, with some early steps being taken in best practice factories to introduce batch production using synchronised flow/assembly-line techniques, although the use of conveyors etc. was not introduced until later in the twentieth century. Batch production, therefore, was the production of standardised units in small/large lots. It represents a halfway position between jobbing production and mass production. The main distinction between batch and jobbing production lies in the standardised nature of the former. Unlike the varied operations found in bespoke work, the products of batch production are dealt with systematically in lots, only moving on to the next operation, when each lot has been processed in the current operation. Such batches could either be made to fulfil a customer order or made for stock. Shoe factories were split in different departments, and the batches of shoes processed through each one. Here the emphasis was placed upon production planning, a staff with a narrow skills range, and relatively short production runs. The tendency in many shoe factories was to sub-divide orders into groups of *c*. 24 pairs. J. Gouldbaum states that the reasoning was "...to keep track of the shoes in process and of the work done by each operator for piecework payments. Each group passes through the factory from one operation to another to consecutive orders...the smaller the unit the fewer shoes there are in process; therefore a smaller quantity of lasts are required; also, small orders can be handled readily and quickly..." ("Principal Types of Shoe Construction..." *Coventry Engineering Society Journal* (1935) VI:4 p. 132). Work was conveyed on movable racks.

Although a general shift away from jobbing production to batch is discernible in the nineteenth-century shoe industry, even progressive firms retained a bespoke function and most were prepared to satisfy any size of order: see the pattern of small orders featured in the A. & W. Arnold Order Book 1907/09 (p. 31-2; 141; 157).

It should be noted that a recent trend in writings that describe this period in the industry's history witnessing the introduction of mass production is not accurate.

character of operations: the move from outworking to a factory-based industry. The industry he entered was a complex and diverse one. From an industry reliant upon small masters and small units of production, there had emerged a small elite group of dominant oligopolistic firms, who led transformation. A measure of their success was the rise of second-generation owners amongst the leading manufacturer families, and the emergence of identifiable captains of the industry. Nevertheless, enterprising workmen like William Arnold continued to enter the manufacturers' ranks; there was no inevitability about the terminal decline of the smaller manufacturer in this highly seasonal industry with a wide-ranging product base of good quality footwear. North-ampton's business community was made up of all sorts and conditions of businessman at this time. Smaller firm survival was due in large measure either to their role as sub-contractors or component makers, or their ability to exploit niche markets. But increasing credit and capital needs, together with the strong competitive pressures in footwear markets, assured that the dividing line between business success and business failure was a fine one.

Indeed, William Arnold's business life aptly reflects this complexity. From tentative beginnings as a new, small producer, through a suspension of trading, and the move to success; his autobiography well illustrates the career path mix of fellow manufacturers of the time. The changes outlined above brought with them the failure of many footwear manufacturers not able to cope, and an important accolade for William Arnold that he survives early business difficulties and challenging trading conditions as he built his business and shared in establishing his elder sons' firm. His was just one of seventy six wholesale firms left standing in 1914.[15] Unfortunately, too few of the existing historical studies of the industry reveal the rich diversity of businessmen, large and small, active in Northampton and other production centres in the latter part of the nineteenth century. To understand more about the changing business position of Arnold's business career and the footwear manufacturers that he represents, it is instructive to further explore the character of the town's prominent premier business community and William Arnold's position in it.

15 An analysis of successive editions of Kelly's and other directories for Northampton between 1884 and 1914 reveals the extent of this shake-out of firms. Whilst the period after 1884 witnessed a continuance of the secular rise in the number of firms trading; that trend was reversed after 1893. At least 533 wholesale manufacturing firms entered the industry in these years, in addition to the 110 already present in 1884: a total of 643 firms. 195 were present in the amended directory list of 1884, in contrast to 76 a generation later, in 1914; a reduction of 61%. In all, 567 wholesale firms ceased trading.

16 Since Alfred Marshall's work on the nature of the firm, economists have repeatedly come back to the notion of the life cycle of the individual firm. From its precarious start period of initial development, followed – if it survived – by a period of successful mature trading,

William Arnold's Transition from Shoe Worker to Successful Businessman

This vibrant period of change in the wholesale industry at Northampton and other centres provided opportunity for the energetic and resourceful to carve out a position as a manufacturer. But this goal of business success was not achieved without difficulty and risk for the individual manufacturer. As happens today, many Victorian firms revealed a change in size and function as they developed over time. Two observed patterns of change behaviour amongst owners can help us to follow the business career of a man like Arnold. It is well understood that new infant firms went through a start-up period of about five years. These early years tended to be dominated with building up internal business operations and organisation, and struggling to establish an external stable trading position in the marketplace. Such infant firms were particularly liable to cease trading through either personal choice or being forced by the external pressure of creditors. All manner of issues were to cause such business failures. There were the general commercial pressures of establishing markets, and securing suppliers; financial worries about obtaining sufficient working capital and investment money; in addition to the more individual issues of making the personal transition from being a work person to manufacturer and employer. Many floundered simply because they lacked basic business skills and prudence. Once established, firms enter a period of greater stability when, despite continued external pressures, they are able to enjoy levels of business success. This success, however, can ultimately be compromised by a growing failure to face change.[16]

In the quarter of a century from the foundation of his firm in 1889 to the publication of his *Autobiography* in 1915 William Arnold progressed through several developmental stages within the business class. His development as a businessman stands not just as a personal testament, but helps the reader to understand something about the complex internal structure within the contemporary footwear business community of this period.[17] His business development stages can be

before experiencing difficulties of adapting to a changing situation as an old firm that often leads to its demise. Marshall somewhat colourfully describes this as the trees of the forest analogy.

17 Within this community were to be found both the dominant, elite group of large manufacturers, together with related groups of volume wholesale producers and of small producers comprising both makers of high grade footwear and marginal producers. In total, these people made up the prominent members of the wholesale footwear business community of the town. Allied to this was a further group of ancillary producers and of sub-contractors, who provided a range of process functions and industry services to the town's main production group, the wholesale manufacturers. For more details, see Appendix, "Northampton Footwear Business Community 1840-1914", p. 159 and 167.

stylised as follows:

> as a new, small scale wholesale producer
> as a failed businessman
> as a mature prominent and successful manufacturer

Although he was ultimately to become a successful man of probity and reputation in the town, this was only attained after both personal hardship and trial. These stages in his business development will be outlined below. But first, it is important to look at his life as a working man. Like so many of his contemporaries, before venturing out as a businessman, Arnold had been employed in the trade: in his case a period of nearly twenty years: it is necessary to chronicle briefly this part of his life.

William Arnold's life as a Shoe Worker.[18]

William Arnold was the son of "a poor working man, a typical old-fashioned English village shoemaker",[19] who, the *Autobiography* informs the reader, was employed by C. Rodhouse as an outworking shoemaker.[20] A practical riveter, he learnt his trade from the age of eight years in Daventry, daily walking the eight miles each way from Everdon. At this time, this was a usual age for rural children to commence work, although his undertaking farm labour from around

18 In the first years of industrial change in the industry, as machine working gradually increased the sub-division of labour in the industry the shoemaker, a man who make a pair of shoes throughout, lost ground to men and women whose working life was spent working on one of the divided processes into which footwear manufacture developed. Relatively quickly contemporary sources begun to refer to shoe workers; a collective phrase for those employed in these various sub-divided processes. Some of these process workers used machinery, others retained hand work for a longer period, according to the ability of engineers to mechanise a process. William Arnold was a riveter, a process used to fix the upper of a shoe to the sole: it was an alternative to sewing these components together.

19 *Autobiography* p. 90.

20 The **Rodhouse family** in fact traded across three generations and was a prominent Daventry shoe manufacturing family. Charles was of the second generation and in age contemporary with Matthew Arnold senior. If Matthew worked for them over time, as the Autobiography suggests, he worked initially for John Marriott Rodhouse, Charles's father. John was born in 1812, lived at 34 Waterloo Street Daventry, maintained by a servant, and had six children from two marriages. He died in 1866 aged 54: probate was granted to his sons with effects valued at under £4,000. Both Charles and John Edward Rodhouse and later their sons continued shoe manufacture in Daventry into the twentieth century: circumstantial evidence suggests that they took over their father's business. Both men had trained as clickers prior to becoming manufacturers. Whereas 50 people had been recorded as being employed in 1851, by 1870-1890 employment levels had risen to about 10 indoor workers and 190 outdoor. Charles lived at 38 Oxford Street Daventry with his family for many years. He died in 1920 aged 80: probate was granted and his effects were valued at £13,180. He held a number of public positions in the town: these included being a J.P. and a member of the local Board of Guardians. John's married home was at 1 Waterloo Street Daventry. He died in 1892 aged 51: probate was granted and his effects were valued at £4,039.

six years old was less common.[21] Like many rural industrial workers at this time, he had experience of rural work too. He was initially employed on farm work and had a brief spell as a cattle drover's boy. In between times his father had taught him the rudiments of hand-sewn work before he migrated to Northampton at thirteen to live with his uncle Anthony.[22] There he worked for Joseph Gibbs & Co,[23] and later for J. Laycock & Co.[24] When the Northampton trade worked short time,

21 In 1868 it was noted that "…all boys in the agricultural villages…begin to work about the age of 8, a few as young as 7; and almost of them have been to work before they are 10… after the age of 10 or 11 they are usually employed continuously throughout the whole year…" *First Report of the Royal Commission on the Employment of Children…in Agriculture"* B.P.P. (1867-68) XVII, report by F.H. Norman on the county p. 111. Quoted in P. Horn "Child Workers in the Victorian Countryside: the Case of Northamptonshire" *N.P.P.* VII, 3 (1985-86) p. 173. She notes that "In country districts for much of the nineteenth century it was the custom for labouring families to send their children to work from an early age…" This essay gives a useful picture of parents' functional attitudes to education and child labour: the former provided care facilities and the latter additional income for the family. The 1867 Factories & Workshops Act set the minimum age for children's work at 8 years.

22 In fact William Arnold initially moved between Northampton and Daventry according to where he could find work. When at Daventry he lived in the family home; when at Northampton in lodgings. An early lodging was taken with his uncle William, and then with George Baker, a commercial traveller and his family, at 41 Victoria Road, Northampton. At a later stage he boarded by turn with uncle William and uncle Anthony at 47 Lorne Road, Northampton and 109 Hunter Street.

23 **Joseph Gibbs** was born into a Northampton shoemaking family in 1842, two years before his brother William. His father George was a shoemaker born at Little Houghton and his mother Emma was born in 1828 at Hull. The family was deeply influenced by religion and were members of the Kettering Road Church for many decades. We will return to this aspect of their lives later in this introduction. Joseph followed his father into the footwear industry. But before becoming a manufacturer in his home town, he worked as a shoemaker in Stafford and Manchester: the 1861 census finds him lodging the home of a shoemaker at 28 Royton Street Manchester. His business was founded shortly after that at Northampton and by 1871 employed 30 indoor workers. In 1863 he married at Northampton, Eliza Britten, born at Stanwick in 1836. There were six children of the marriage. At this time the family was at Cyril Street, where a female servant was employed. In the late 1880s the family home was moved to Cliftonville (in the 1891 Census the house is identified as "Mr Gibbs" The house on one side was occupied by Henry Mobbs and on the other M. P. Manfield. There were two indoor female servants). Following the death of his first wife in 1890, he married secondly Emily Payne (1865-1938). He died in March 1893. Probate of his will was granted to Thomas Britten (his brother-in-law and foreman) and James Giles cashier: his effects were valued at £13,935, but re-sworn in 1894 at £1,402 (this no doubt related to dividing business monies for personalty). His executors took over the management of the firm. The bulk of Gibb's effects were used to settle business debts, enabling his executors to take the firm free of debt (*The London Gazette* 5/10/1894 p. 5,652 and 9/10/1894 p. 5,712). The firm was taken over by Charles E. Gubbins in 1899; he was a former manager at Manfield's and at Kettering Boot Manufacturing Co Ltd. From 1912 it traded from Queen's Park and was subsequently taken over by his sons when he retired in 1923: by 1935 it was trading as W. Gubbins & Co.

24 **Thomas Laycock** employed William Arnold at a time when he had become the sole owner of J. Laycock & Co. This was a prominent Northampton footwear firm founded by Thomas's father. Thomas was born at Skipton in 1850 to John Laycock (born in Lumb Mill, Cowling, Yorkshire in 1815), a master shoemaker, later manufacturer, and Mary Riley (born in Malham Dale, Yorkshire, in 1812). There were at least three children of the marriage. As

he returned to Everdon and worked for William Dickens.[25]

The autobiographical account of his early Northampton years provides one of the few published, personal insights into the life of an outworking shoe worker in the late Victorian period. Historically, shoemakers were known as independently-minded artisans and politically radical. But changing patterns of work in the industry's transitional period witnessed the meeting of two workplace cultures, when the older craft-based artisan world clashed with that of the new evolving semi-skilled process worker. Over several generations from the 1860s the Northamptonshire shoemaking workforce became split between skilled craft artisans able to make footwear right through, and new grades of shoe workers, like William Arnold, working wholly within a small, sub-divided portion of the production process. After 1887, there was a progressive shift of both parts of the workforce towards their mutual de-skilling into semi-skilled factory workers. The older craftwork traditions, however, had been taken up by the new generation of shoe workers and not finally breached by employers until factory working became a final reality early in the Edwardian period. Thus, all those working in the industry, whether as outworker or on an

a child and young man he spent time in Clitheroe with relatives. In 1851 he was in residence there with an uncle, James (born at Kildwick in 1822), a clog & patten maker: he shared the house with two sisters and a niece, all of whom were employed as cotton power loom weavers. Again, in his early twenties he resided with his uncle Matthew Riley and his family. He was listed as a footwear manufacturer presumably being trained by his uncle. At this time his family's home was at Sheep Street, Northampton, where his father had established the family footwear manufacturing firm in the 1850s: there was a female servant in the home. Thomas returned to Northampton in the 1870s to take over the family firm, which at this time employed 125 men. Late in that decade he married Emily (born at Wellingborough in 1847): they were to have at least eight children. In the 1880s the family home was at 9 Billing Road, and was shared with three indoor female servants. However, in the early 1890s his firm suspended trading. A composition was arranged and a son, Henry, took over the firm and run it until 1905, when it again failed and closed. Thomas and the family moved to Wellingborough in the early 1890s following the first suspension, where he set up as a boot upper and legging manufacturer until his retirement in around 1905. He lived in Wellingborough Park Road, and in retirement at Bengeworth Road. Thomas died at Wellingborough in the spring of 1918: there was no published probate will.

25 **William Dickens** was associated with the footwear industry throughout his life. He worked in Coventry in the 1840s before setting up as a manufacturer at Daventry in the early 1850s. Initially he employed 30-35 men and boys (1851/61 Census Enumerators' Return for Daventry), but by 1871, his workforce had grown to 179 men, women and boys. He traded as a manufacturer and leather factor in the town until his death in 1893: there is no trace of either a will or probate. For much of that time his warehouse premises were at Staverton Road, Daventry. In 1890 he also acted as a shoe agent for the London firm of Samuel Smith & Co, who had a branch factory at Long Buckby (S.L.R. 13/9/1890 p. 340). He was born at Kilsby, Northamptonshire in 1817 and married Eliza, born at Daventry in 1819: they had three children. The family home was at Oxford Street, Daventry. From the late 1860s, his daughters Martha (born 1845) and Clara (born 1849), and his sons William (born 1847) and Charles George (born 1853) were all assistants to their father: both sons had trained as clickers. The elder son later became a sewing machinist employer.

employer's premises, retained many of the customary work and social controls over the workplace that artisan shoemakers had enjoyed. Thus, all outworkers, regardless of their background, continued to enjoy the freedom of workshop life, both in terms of the pace and method of working and of social association at work, until constricting factory working gained full ascendancy.

As an outworker William Arnold would have worked in a workshop away from the control of his employer in just this way. The pace and the details of how work was executed would have been decided by those in the workshop rather than the employer. Beyond the fixed date for the return of finished materials, the outworker would have had discretion when and how he carried out the work. Life in the workshop would have been a blend of social and working activity. The need for a consistent application to work familiar to those working on an employer's premises would have been absent and alien. Above all, workshop workers like William Arnold would have been able to work around days when favoured events like horse racing or political elections were taking place. A weekly distraction was the need to take completed work to the employer's premises and the collection of more materials. The cost of the time lost was incurred by the worker, but in effect many turned this into a holiday. The day has become known as St Monday; a time for convivial drinking, socialising and discussion, as well as cleaning tools and workshop.[26]

Certainly independently-minded outworking shoemakers and shoe workers still worked in this way during William Arnold's early working life. They cherished what they perceived to be fixed customary work privileges; part of their work status. In Northampton the final attempts to enforce in-door working in the early 1890s brought about a series of work stoppages and of unofficial strikes of local union members. J. Greenfield reminds us that for the first time women workers in the industry were involved in these actions.[27] But historians have raised questions about the apparent contradiction of the enduring strength of such radicalism. In his study of the Leicester footwear industry[28]

---

26 *Autobiography* Chapters 5 to 8 *passim*: For a discussion of other contemporaries accounts of the outworkers life at this time, see K. B. Brooker "The Northampton Shoemakers' Reaction to Industrialisation: Some Thoughts" *N.P.P.* (1980) VI No. 3, p. 151-59.

27 J. Greenfield, *Task & Gender Divisions of Labour in the Boot & Shoe Industry 1851-1911* (unpublished PhD thesis University of Warwick 1998) especially Chapter 4. This active involvement of women in trade union disputes was part of wider unofficial stoppages and action, and of official union opposition mounted by both men and women in Northampton in the early 1890s. This rise of women unionism, of course, can be seen in other industries and localities following the formative events in the late 1880s like the famous London match girls' strike of 1886.

28 W. Lancaster, *Radicalism to Socialism: the Leicester Working Class, 1860-1906* (unpublished PhD thesis University of Warwick 1982).

W. Lancaster writes of an inexplicable divergence between the relatively weak trade union organisation of Northamptonshire workforce at this time and the continuance of the radical political tradition of North-ampton shoemakers.[29] Certainly during this period of industrial transition the Northampton shoemakers support for Bradlaugh as the town's M.P. continued. Radicalism of a different hue can also been seen in the emergence of the town as a significant national centre for the support of the Social Democratic Federation.[30] These two factors very strongly point to both a persistence and broadening of this radical tradition. But surely the reason for this continued radicalism, in spite of it not being reflected in higher levels of union membership, lies in the persistence of the small workshop culture in the town with its emphasis upon individual worker controls over the workplace, and of a production process that gave emphasis to a traditional status of independence. In an outwork culture, the dispersed working popul-ation was an added impediment to trade union membership. This narrative of a culture based on worker independence took time to break down and form itself anew as a factory worker culture. It is only as Northampton workers congregate in factories that local union membership rose appreciably.

By contrast, William Arnold's recurring memory of his days as a shoe worker centred on his success as an independent worker. At this stage in his life, the *Autobiography* portrays a figure without deep social roots in his new community. It focuses on his pride of his work speed and high productivity as a riveter; on the high pay he was able to earn (he was a piece worker); and on his ability to remain in work despite short time working locally. Added to this was the culture of drink and social conviviality that he enjoyed during his outworking years.[31] No space is given in his recollections to any political commentary about his position as a shoe worker, or to any wider treatment of contemporary political events or views in town or country.

As a small scale wholesale producer.
But this radical independence has another dimension: the underlying small-producer character of the industry. It was made up of a number of segments. There was a thriving small master base of high grade local retail master shoemakers in town and rural areas throughout the country. These were competent hand stitch producers, who made complete pairs of traditionally hand crafted footwear retailed from the

29 By contrast, the growth in trade union membership at Northampton in the face of industrial transition was both greater and sustained.
30 On Northampton Social Democratic Federation branch, see below, p. 80 and 81.
31 On this aspect of the town's working and employer antipathy towards such leisure in K.B. Brooker (1980) *op. cit. passim.*

same small retail workshop premises. Through to the mid-nineteenth century and beyond they remained the cornerstone of the industry nationally. But as the century progressed they were gradually marginalised by the growing dominance of wholesale centres of the trade of which Northampton was a dominant example.

Small producers were also to be found in wholesale centres like Northampton. Some were fledgling infant firms making the transition from employment to business ownership. Others were mature firms that gradually expanded their activities, whilst others again found small scale sub-contracting, component making, or the small production of high quality small order and bespoke work, or local retail trade, to be a sustainable, stable business solution. The presence of the wholesale trade in the town also enabled some retail makers to became wholesale manufacturers and for some wholesale owners to transfer into the retail trade: others again provided the wholesale trade with a sub-contract function during busy season trading periods and substantially retained their retailing trade.

Of the former category, many of these fledging, infant firms were unable to sustain business over time. As in any sector, the failure rate was high. Indeed many of these failures were of traders of no real business substance. Only 40% of start-ups reached maturity, with nearly one third failing in the first year of trading, and a further third thereafter. Some mature firms would expand their activities, but for others small production was a sustainable business solution, and they traded as either component makers, producers of high quality small order and bespoke work, or local retail makers.

The evidence from Arnold's time as a small producer provides a view of quite how small and insubstantial a scale this class of producer enterprise could be in the Victorian period. His *Autobiography* notes how an almost domestic scale of business was initially conducted:

> …We knew that £94 would not go far and we knew therefore that it was necessary to proceed in a very small way – as a sort of overtime employment for us. A man we knew, named Smith, who worked at Mr Manfield's was to do the pattern cutting and clicking for us. Uncle was to cut the sole leathers and I was to do the riveting. The finishing we could give out to work people. The other partner, Mr Flint, was to do the books and his wife the closing or stitching of the uppers. It all seemed very simple and we took a little place in Duke Street to start in, one room up some stairs…[32]

32 *Autobiography* p. 114: given that one person was to be employed on each of the four processes no more than five finishers would have been required.

Inevitably, William Arnold and his partners were by no means unique. The presence of small, insubstantial masters in the industry is starkly revealed in surviving business failure reports as well. This source provides systematic evidence that demonstrates just how small and commercially unviable some small producers could be. Table 1 provides a sample of the realisable assets of traders at the time of their suspension of trading and clearly demonstrates the small asset base some had. The very nature of the development, growth and culture of the industry in the transitional period encouraged this nature of small trading. Data from business failure reports starkly captures their often precarious financial state: an inconsequential asset base matched by unsustainable levels of operating debt. Yet, small firms were not necessarily an economic drag upon the industry as they did provide a competitive means of manufacturers buying components and getting seasonal orders completed. But trying to operate with unsustainably low levels of operating capital led many inevitably towards failure. This sample does not cover all small producers who went out of business; the records are not complete, and the people of this class who ceased trading were often able to wind up their affairs privately with the agreement of creditors and in some inevitably merely slipped quietly away.

The social impact upon people who worked for them was, however, potentially more damaging. There was a tendency for such traders to

Table 1: Declared realisable assets of Northampton wholesale footwear firms at the time of business failure 1884-1912

[1] All Firms

Period	£0-499	500-999	1000-1999	2000-2999	3000-3999	4000-4999	5000-5999	+6000
1885-1895 [135]	67 49.6%	32 23.7%	17 12.6%	10 7.4%	4 3%	2 1.5%	1 0.7%	2 1.5%
1896-1912 [141]	60 43.4%	27 17.4%	24 17.3%	9 6.5%	8 5.8%	3 2.2%	0 0%	10 7.2%
1885-1912 [276]	**127 46%**	**59 20.7%**	**41 15.2%**	**19 6.7%**	**12 4.5%**	**5 1.9%**	**1 0.4%**	**12 3.7%**

[2] Firms with assets between £0 and £499

Period	£0-99	£100-199	£200-299	£300-399	£400-499
1885-1895 [67]	17 12.6%	14 10.4%	18 13.3%	10 7.4%	8 5.9%
1896-1912 [60]	27 19.2%	11 7.9%	11 7.9%	8 5.9%	3 2.3%
1885-1912 [127]	**44 15.9%**	**25 9.1%**	**29 10.5%**	**18 6.5%**	**11 4.0%**

Source: business intelligence reports in *B.S.T.J.* and *S.L.R.* 1884-1912.

resort to sweated labour tactics in an attempt to make the business work.[33] This evil was concentrated predominately in the closing trade. Many closers to the trade were women, who conducted business in upstairs workshops attached to terraced houses. At the heart of this exploitation was the keen competition that existed.[34] Both factory inspector reports and local medical officer of health reports tell of both the poor structural state of many of the older workshops, and of the cramped airless condition of new workshops often built over back kitchens.[35] Both had an equally deleterious effect on worker health: on average these domestic workshops employed around eight workers.[36] But the evil of sweating was something that small masters could inflict upon their families and themselves too, as often as the labour they employed. But these component makers were not an exception, for when one looks at the realisable asset base of all firms that suspended trading this inconsequential economic character is again revealed. In part this is due to the high number of infant firms amongst the sample, but the continued small master base in the industry also reveals itself here.

At the time William Arnold set up on his own account he was employed by Manfield & Sons. It is interesting to ask about his motivation and suitability for taking such a step. As to motivation his reply was both prosaic and personal. With money short, the struggle to set up their first married home freshly in mind, and the looming financial pressures of a growing young family starkly in front of him and his wife, he simply states that he and his partners "would have a go." He notes:

> ...We kept struggling on and our second and third children were born. Of course our expenses were increasing and there never seemed to be enough trade to enable me to earn the large sums that I did when I was single. I was not satisfied, neither was uncle Anthony and

33 The classic work on sweating in this period is D. Bythell, *The Sweated Trades* (1978). On sweating in the London footwear industry, see G. Thorn (i) *The politics of trade unionism in a sweated industry: boot and shoemakers in late nineteenth century, London* (unpublished PhD thesis University of Warwick 1983), (ii) "London Bootmakers and the New Unionism", *London Journal*, vol.13:1 (1987); and for Leeds slipper makers, see J. Buckman, *The Economic & Social History of Alien Immigrants to Leeds 1880-1914* (unpublished PhD thesis Strathclyde University 1968).

34 *S.L.R.* 22/2/1890 p. 259 and *S.L.R.* 18/10/1890 p. 493. But there is evidence that sub-contractors also used these techniques too; see R. Rowe, "Toiling & Moiling: vi the Northampton Shoemaker", *Good Words* 1/11/1869 p. 16

35 N.A. *Annual Report of the Chief Inspector of Factories, year ending 31/10/1886 (c. 5697)* p. 83-4; and *Report for year ending 1890-91 (c. 6330)* p. 20-2: N.A. *MH12/8793/33736/84 Northampton Medical Officer of Health Report*, 1883 p. 5 and 12; *MH12/87935/25567/89 Northampton M. O. H Report* 1889 p. 21. For sweating in closing workshops a generation earlier, see V. A. Hatley, "St Giles' Shoe School", *B.B.S.I.J.* (1961) Vol. V, p. 619.

36 N.A. Census Enumerators' Returns for Northampton RG10/1481-84 and RG11/1547-54.

we talked of starting manufacturing ourselves. Others were doing it
and were getting on, why should not we...[37]

This reveals the extent to which family needs could intertwine and
dictate business ambitions and policies. Of course, what we will never
know is whether this prosaic explanation of his motivation to start in
business was not also nurtured by the prevailing tradition of
independence and of the customs of the outwork workshop; the
tradition of the ability of working men to become masters still
resonated. This, too, was an important influence over shoe workers like
William Arnold, who made the transition from the work bench to the
manufacturer's desk. As already noted, shoe workers absorbed at least
some of the cultural expectations of the artisan shoemaker. In the notion
that they "would have a go," can we not see a persistence of the
customary expectation for them to "rise from the seat"? In this are there
not echoes of past times; of the progression open to competent
journeymen, following a period of apprenticeship training and the
gathering of experience, to rise to be a master?

And what is more, this persistent custom of people seeking to enter
business on their own account was, with difficulty, still practically in
reach. Both the scale and nature of the industry, as well as prevailing
financial and business conditions, gave a basis for entry. The relatively
small resource requirements, the sub-divided character of manufacturing, and the seasonal character of the industry encouraged the wide use
of sub-contract arrangements and component making for established
firms. William Arnold started as a part-time sub-contractor; not severing
his employment as a shoe riveter until some business stability had been
established.[38]

Enthusiasm aside, equally important was the question of his suitability
and disposition to make the transition to operating a business. Although
a competent worker, that much we know, William Arnold's early adult
life prior to marriage was dominated by his growing liking of drink
made worse by a readiness to fight when in drink. It is here that the
Autobiography helps the reader to understand something, not just of his
business achievements, but of the development of the man as well. His
marriage in late 1886, together with the help of friends and a deepening

---

37 *Autobiography* p. 113.
38 The occupations given by the partners at the 1891 Census are revealing and suggest the
apparent caution they feel at this early stage. William enters that he is a shoe trade riveter
(employed), whilst Anthony opts for the anodyne Boot Manufacture (employed). Alfred
Flint, by contrast, returns Clerk in Boot Trade (employed) [Census Enumerators' Returns
for Northampton 1891]. However, the entry of the firm in local trade directories
presumably reveals a need to advertise for trade purposes?

religious faith enables him to confront these personal issues to emerge as a man of principle and honour. From this point, his adult life is marked by a growing confidence and sense of self-worth exemplified by his doggedness in paying his business creditors. This is the human story behind the man of business. And it is here that his *Autobiography* offers us a rare glimpse of the man: something not available for his business contemporaries.

And so in 1889, three working men founded Arnold & Co: William Arnold, a practical shoe riveter, together with his uncle, Anthony Arnold a shoe riveter[39] and Alfred Flint, a clerk and book-keeper and a relative by marriage of Anthony.[40] With minimal capital,[41] trading was started from a shoe worker's workshop in the garden of Anthony's home in Hunter Street (Figure 3). As trade increased, small premises in Duke Street, Northampton were taken,[42] with a move to larger premises in nearby Military Road taken as trade grew further.[43] Despite the retrospective colouring of events that William Arnold indulged in, his *Autobiography* well illuminates the anxieties and difficulties faced by infant firms.[44] Like many new small masters, the three partners began the business "as a sort of overtime employment for us", but their employers, the dominant firm of Manfield & Sons[45], soon learnt of the venture and dismissed them.[46] The months that followed were fraught with worry and low wages.[47]

39 **Anthony Arnold** was the fourth child of Matthew and Ann Arnold: he was born at Everdon in 1849. As an adult he worked in Northampton as an outwork shoe riveter. In the *Autobiography*, William Arnold refers to his uncle as a clicker, but in the light of Census Returns and other evidence to the contrary this is scarcely credible. Anthony married Betsey Thomason, a shoe fitter, (born at Daventry in 1844) in 1876. Her father was a shoemaker. There were five children of the marriage of whom two survived infancy: Bessy (born in 1880) a clerk in a shoe factory and Kate (born in 1882) a dressmaker, who worked "own her account at home". The family lived in the shoe district north of the centre of the town at 47 Lorne Road and subsequently 109 Hunter Street. The Hunter Street house had an outworker's workshop in which the business was started. By 1911, Anthony had retired from the business and lived in retirement for some years at Ivy House, Roade, Northamptonshire. It is probable that from the re-launch of the firm in 1892 that Anthony played a subordinate and marginal role in business affairs. He died at home on 13 October 1919. Probate was granted to his executors, William Arnold and Bessie Woodward. His effects were valued at £976/11/0d.

40 **Alfred Flint** was born at Braunston, Northamptonshire in 1840. His parents were Edward (born at Swinford, Leicestershire in 1810), a school teacher, and Mary (also born at Swinford in 1814). There were at least 7 children of the marriage. Alfred, the second born, spent his childhood in Leicestershire, before commencing work as a commercial clerk in Braunston, where he married, in 1862, firstly, Frances Douglas (born at Hardingstone in 1841). There were at least five children of this marriage. The family migrated to Derbyshire in the mid-1860s, living first in Litchurch and later in Chesterfield, before moving on to Leeds in 1870. At this point misfortune struck the family. Frances died sometime in the 1870s, and by 1881, Alfred is living at 46 Flousham Street, Northampton with only a younger daughter, Clara, and is working as a book keeper clerk there. Later in that year he married, secondly,

However, as was so often the case, from a promising start this new enterprise begun to flounder on the rocks of poor financial control and a lack of business acumen. The Arnolds were competent shoe workers and their production skills enabled them to build up a core of custom. But the business skills necessary to extend the firm's activities further were lacking: a common state of affairs amongst many small, infant firms. Business matters were left in Flint's less than capable hands, as both William and Anthony "entirely lacked all business training."[48]

Sarah Ann Bedford, a shoe closer (born at Daventry in 1839): she was a widow. They were living at 20, Bailiff Street, with a lodger, by the time he became a partner in Arnold & Co. Following the failure of the firm in 1892, Alfred appears to leave the town, possibly a consequence of the blame directed at him for the firm's suspension. In 1901, his wife was living at 25 Grey Street with her daughter, Emily, by her first marriage, and Emily's husband Fred, a commercial traveller. She is the head of the household, still married, and had retained her employment as a shoe closer, despite her advancing years. Alfred is not readily traceable by surviving records, but later in the decade appears as a pauper inmate in a Staffordshire lunatic asylum, where he remains until death in 1914 at 74: there is no published probate will. At the time of the firm's failure a large part of the trading difficulties were laid at Alfred's feet due to his lack of skill and his drink habit. Thus, are we seeing in these bare biographical facts some understanding of Alfred's position? Did the loss of his first wife and the loss also of his children give rise to his drinking? Or was the drinking the cause of his family splitting up at her death? Or, does his drinking start when he found himself responsible for the firm's books with a skill level that did not match the challenge before him (clearly William Arnold's view: *Autobiography* p. 114. Does his slipping under the radar of official records hint at his social disgrace? These questions must remain just that. The incarceration of habitual drinkers in lunatic asylums at this date was a not an uncommon course of action. Contemporary debates were taking place about the treatment of habitual drinkers, and much of that debate centred upon the different forms of institutional care with less attention paid to rehabilitation.

41 The *Autobiography* p. 114 quotes the sum of £94, *S.L.R.* 2/9/92 p. 591 stated that the figure was £105.

42 See *Autobiography* p. 114, where these clearly modest premises are tersely described as "one room up some steps."

43 Both the Duke Street and Military Road premises were converted dwelling houses. This type of premises was commonly used in the industry at this time. For some young firms this represented cost effectiveness and sufficiency, whilst for other manufacturers converted dwellings were an inadequate but convenient stop-gap measure (See Figure 4).

44 See *Autobiography* p. 125, "yes, our business is prosperous. When I think of it, I am astounded that the poor little village boy should reach where I am today."

45 On the founder, Philip, see K. B. Brooker, "Moses Philip Manfield" *D.B.B.* (1985) Vol. 4; M. Haynes "Sir Moses Philip Manfield" *O.D.N.B.*(2004) Vol. 36, p. 408-9.

46 See *Autobiography* p. 114.

47 Arnold, true to his desire to embellish his success, notes in his autobiography that their wages were initially £1 and rose to £1/5/0d after one year, and then to £1/10/0d. But a contemporary trade newspaper report tells a different story of wages commencing at £1/9/0d and rising quickly to £2/10/0d. This level of wages is in line with that earned by competent, trained workmen, whilst the latter represents a level earned by successful foremen and office workers in the town. As was noted, "...both could earn considerably higher wages than previous to starting in business on their own account." (*S.L.R. loc. cit.* p. 582).

48 See *Autobiography* p. 116: Despite this, William did bring to the business, beyond purely practical skill, an obvious facility to handle money. At several points in the autobiography he mentions his natural frugality, a residue of his childhood. In an industry racked with

William was barely literate; Anthony somewhat timid and diffident; whilst Flint's erratic drinking habit did nothing to lessen the firm's problems. Flint left the partnership within a short while, but continued to do their accounts.

In a real sense, the partners of Arnold & Co were very typical of those shoe workers who started as manufacturers in the long transitional period. But what was to set them apart from the many firms that were to fail was that William's tenacity and character enabled the firm to be re-launched.[49]

As a Failed Businessman.
Even a cursory reading of Victorian economic history at regional and local levels quickly leaves the reader with an understanding that the failure of businesses was part and parcel of commercial life. Modern studies[50] suggest that business failure was all too often the outcome for certain categories of business that are disproportionately at risk. First is the vulnerability of new infant firms. Their early years were absorbed in building a sustainable company. In the late nineteenth century, the

credit problems this facility was of inestimable value. "There is one thing about my business practice which I think important. No one ever suggested it to me, but somehow I saw it was a good thing to do. I have always had enough money at the bank or I have always been able to get enough to pay my biggest creditor instantly, if required – all that was owing to him." (*Autobiography* p. 125-6).

49 The sample study of Northampton's failed firms suggests that where firms re-start after suspension, they often trade on for a few years and then failed again; the lessons of the suspension not fully learnt. An example of this is **T. Laycock & Sons** (see p. 9 footnote 24). Few other Northampton firms that were able to achieve a long term recovery, but others than William Arnold achieved this. Successful manufacturers that overcame failure included John Sears, and William Barratt. A key difference, however, was that in these two instances the next generation of the family had taken charge of the post-failure revival: Arnold stands alone as a manufacturer in this period who takes charge of his reconstituted firm and makes a long term success of the re-launch. **Sears**: His father James Sears a leather seller and manufacturer, failed in September 1891: liabilities £739 against assets of £212 (*S.L.R.* 25/9/1891 p. 750 and 2/10/1891 p. 804). John made a private arrangement with his father's creditors and commenced, took over the stock, plant and trade customers and started manufacturing from the old premises in Derby Road (*N.D.E.* 19/2/1916 p. 5 and *S.T.J.* 25/2/1916 p. 246). Within a short while, he went into partnership with his brother W. T. Sears, a shoe retailer, who traded under the name True Form Boot Co. (*N.C.* 19/2/1916 p. 3. **Barratt**: William Barratt was a Manfield's shoe shop manager when, in 1901, acquired his father's failed retail footwear shop in The Drapery, Northampton. The total of his father's debts were not published at the time of his failure (*B.S.T.J.* 18/7/1902 p. 76). He entered a partnership with his brother in 1902 and they began manufacturing in 1905. They developed rapidly, including a mail order business, but they, in turn, failed as a result of undercapitalisation and high overheads. Liabilities were put at £9,610 against assets of £4,547. Out of this second failure, the famous limited company W. Barratt & Co. Ltd was born (*B.S.T.J.* 14/12/1906 p. 460, and *C.R.O.* 91791).

50 For example, J. Boswell, *The Rise & Decline of Small Firms* (1976). Note also the references listed in the section of business failure at p. 23 et seq.

Figure 3: Outworker's workshop in Northampton

Figure 4: Dwelling house converted to a small factory, Northampton

Figure 5: Factory in Louise Road, Northampton

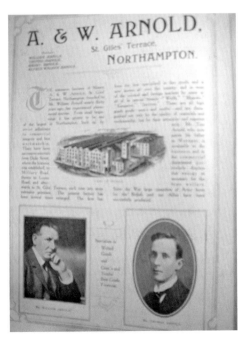

Figure 6: The A. & W. Arnold factory, St Giles' Terrace, Northampton

Figure 7: The site of A. & W. Arnold's St Giles' Terrace factory

Figure 8: View of Arnold Bros. Factory, Northampton, 1916

Figure 9: Henry Street frontage of Arnold Bros. factory

Figure 10: Arnold Bros. Factory frontage to Talbot Road

numbers of new business aspirants entering Northampton's wholesale manufacturing community were high. Usually in a small way of business, many were marginal producers and often under-capitalised and inexperienced. People started enterprises full of hope and expectation only to find either the current economic circumstances were against them or their business skills were insufficient to give them the success they were hoping for. Their business life was characterised by a very short period of trading that was full of worry, and ended in the disappointment of debt and failure. And yet historians, generally, give too little regard to this aspect of British business experience, focused as many remain upon understanding economic growth patterns in history. But part of that narrative of growth encompasses business failure.[51] And secondly, older, experienced but inefficient firms were equally at risk from a variety of situations. The retirement or death of an owner could signal not just the loss of expertise but also of capital as changing family circumstances and expectations might also require the liberation of company capital. Equally problematic was the older firm's failure to keep abreast of change. A step change in industrial techniques or changes in patterns of trading could quickly reveal an older firm's economic vulnerability. All of these factors were either singularly or in concert able to precipitate failure.[52] In addition, there was the constant ebb and flow in the headline level of business failure dictated by the cyclical strength or weakness of the national or the regional economy.

---

51 For more details about business failure and the research on the Northampton footwear industry between 1885 and 1914, see Appendix, p. 171 et seq.

52 The decade after 1895 witnessed the failure of many old established and well known firms in the town that had dominated the industry both locally and nationally earlier in the century. Individual details of their departure differed but the underlying cause and effect were the same. Despite a continuing good reputation enjoyed by many, they struggled from high costs because of the dead weight of dated production and wholesaling methods: the shift to new integrated machine system production did not happen. Often, too, family demands upon company income and capital had exacerbated overall business indebtedness. Invariably, they increased trade debts usually with either their leather merchants or their bank. The inevitable suspension was often precipitated by a set-back that led to debtors acting to protect their interests. In most cases the assets were only able to cover about 60% of the liabilities. Many still enjoyed a high reputation for their products. For example: [1] **William Hickson & Co. in 1909**, dated methods and much troubled by the financial burdens of a dependent family; [2] **Henry Marshall & Co. in 1909** following a ten year battle because of dated methods and high costs. Heavy trade debts incurred with leather merchants; a factory fire at the factory precipitated the suspension; [3] **Major, Howe & Co. in 1898** following the death of the owner and the subsequent break-up of his son's partnership. The paying out of a partner led to the suspension as the company was financially unsound; [4] **Robert Derby & Co. in 1900**. A manufacturer for fifty years, whose business faded away because of his old hand outwork methods. At suspension this once front-rank company employed only 35 people. Derby died two years later penniless, his fortune gone; [5] **Henry Harday & Co. in 1902**. A company of 50 years standing. Partly due to large sums being taken out to pay annuities on the death of partners, but principally because old modes of production and marketing were still being used – the press noted "the firm had got sadly behind the times". But the biggest casualty was **Turner Bros. &**

Certainly Arnold & Co, after a relatively short period in business, experienced trading problems on a scale that led to the need for a creditors' meeting. In this case, the trading suspension was resolved by creditors accepting an accommodation that allowed the firm to continue trading. This clearly had a salutary effect upon William Arnold personally, and fashioned the rest of his business career. Viewed against this background, William Arnold's suspension of trading was not unusual, but his successful re-launch and survival was. A sample study of 305 Northampton firms that suspended trading between 1885 and 1914 enables the typicality of this failure to be assessed, and helps the nature of business failure itself to be better understood. Not all published failure reports provided reasons for the suspension, but sufficient did to provide some compelling evidence of the reasons why firms got into trading difficulties. Brought together in tabular form this evidence provides in effect a definitive set of causes that explains why business Northampton footwear firms failed over time. This evidence has been assembled in Table 25, which lists the causes given for the failure of Northampton wholesale footwear manufacturers.[53] This information is arranged first as primary and secondary causes for failure, and, secondly, breaks down the evidence into external factors and internal factors. The list of external factors is as follows:

1 *Business too small*: insufficient turnover; want of capital
2 *Business activity change*: fall off in trade; competition
3 *Miscellaneous*: fire; strike; demise of owner; debtor suspension; "genuine failure"

And for internal factors:
1 *Failure of business probity*: poor costing; failure to keep records; bad debts; excessive credit; over reliance on borrowed capital; lack of fixed capital depreciation
2 *Errors of judgement*: knowingly selling below cost; knowingly insolvent; over extension/loss capital; recklessness; irregular bill transactions; no shoe trade experience; poor management; illiterate

---

Hyde. The company was once one of the largest employers of shoe workers in the world. From around 1895 the firm increasingly struggled and in 1904 closed. In 1897 it was reported: "...one old established firm discharged a great number of hands on Saturday. They are finding out that things have changed from what they were twenty years ago... For some time past, they have found their trade gradually drifting away into more energetic hands..." (*B.S.T.J.* 16/1/1897 p. 63) This was a voluntary closure of a solvent company and the second and third generation owners moved into a number of other smaller enterprises providing equipment and materials to the trade. All of the other firms cited failed and the assets were sold. Some ended up being taken over; for example Major, Howe & Co was purchased by H. E. Randall Ltd.

53 For Table 25, see the Appendix p. 178.

Collectively, then, the judgements of creditors' meetings build over time to provide a ranking of the common issues that led to suspension. In the most general of terms the study shows that of total judgements made, 19.8% related to external factors and 80.2% related to internal factors. Thus, like Arnold & Co, most footwear firms failed because of issues relating to the way the firm was being managed rather than issues relating to external trading factors. There is an element of overstatement in these conclusions, as some of the reports apportion reasons to both external and internal factors. But this does not alter the balance of the outcome between external trading factors and internal management factors. On balance this study suggests the failings amongst footwear manufacturers related to some lack in the business skills they brought to manufacturing. 56% of all reasons for failure related to inadequacies in basic business administration that prevented firms from understanding their true trading position: poor costing, failure to keep records and bad debts. This area of work in Arnold & Co fell primarily to the hapless Alfred Flint. And, in addition, there followed errors of judgement. Here reasons relating to knowingly trading when insolvent and selling below cost amounted to 13% of all reasons in the sample study.

Arnold & Co's first years of trading follow a recognisable trend. As has been observed, they initially conducted business on an after-work basis in a backyard workshop making goods for Manfield & Co. Such levels of entrepreneurial initiative fade quickly into marginal production. This adds a further dimension to a wider contemporary narrative of sweated labour within the town and puts William Arnold's early business life into a sharper perspective, dealt with elsewhere in this introduction.[54] Heavy reliance was placed on the principals' active involvement in production using sub-contracting as a basis for trading. Anthony did the pattern cutting, a work friend called Smith the clicking, Alfred Flint's wife the closing, and William and Anthony the riveting. The work was then sent out to finishers for the final processes before distribution: given the probable level of production about five finishers would have been required. After some years of trading in this way, the physical pressure on partners and the precarious financial basis of the business became unsustainable. Moreover, broader current trends within the industry were unfavourable. When the levels of business starts and business failures for the town's footwear trade are investigated, it is apparent that as trading conditions generally became tougher from 1887, so the volume of failures increased and Arnold & Co was amongst this number. In 1892, the firm suspended trading

---

54 For sweated labour in the Northampton industry, and the sweating imposed by manufacturers both on workers, on themselves and on their families, see p. 14-15.

following a "domino" failure caused by the insolvency of a principal customer, who owed £1,000.[55] The *Autobiography* captures the mood of the partners at this stage:

> …We had to call a meeting of the creditors and explain to them the whole position. Well, working in the factory all day, struggling and worrying, was bad enough, but it was nothing to those awful days before the creditors' meeting. The factory was closed because there was no money for wages and I thought everyone I met was talking about us, calling us thieves, which we were not. I was ashamed to be seen, so was my uncle and we used to get up early in the morning and go out into the country for the day, returning only at night, when dark. My wife suffered the same: it was a terrible time. It settled me: I decided that I would never have anything to do with business again, but would go back to the bench and be a workman…[56]

The total liabilities were assessed at £2,831/14/3d against assets of £686/7/5d. In three years turnover had been £15,350 and gross profits £767.[57] But as was so often the case in these matters, their creditors preferred to keep their customer in business rather than lose the firm through a suspension of trading, and they finally offered a settlement of 4/- in the pound, which was accepted.[58] It was recognised by the creditors that the nucleus of a good business had been developed; that the suspension was unfortunate and that trading should be allowed to continue. Despite no legal obligation to do so, between 1892 and 1915 William Arnold gradually repaid, in full, all debts resulting from this suspension. This can be seen as the measure of the man. He makes it clear what his motivations were in the following words:

> …ever since the old firm of Arnold & Co had the misfortune to call its creditors together, it has been my great desire, my chief ambition, to reach a position so that I could repay all who lost money by us. The failure was owing to no fault of mine and the creditors were all

55 *S.L.R. loc. cit.* p. 583 where it is stated that "…the immediate cause of the stoppage was the heavy loss through the failure of A. & J. Amsden, the debtors' claim being £998…" A domino failure is where the failure of one firm has a knock-on effect on other firms whose trading position often itself precarious. In this instance a local leather firm precipitated the failure by its habit of extending favourable credit terms to weak firms.

56 *Autobiography* p. 116.

57 *S.L.R. loc. cit.* p. 583.

58 This arrangement was made under a composition or scheme of arrangement, which was sanctioned by a court. The composition itself was a meeting between the debtor and the creditors that did not directly involve the court. At the meeting an agreement was reached for the pay portion of the debt and to let the debtor to continue trading. Bankruptcy proceedings could be used against a trader as an individual, but this would mean that trading would have to cease and that was often not in the interests of either the debtor of the creditors.

kind and were quite prepared to put down their losses to the ordinary
hazards of business. But I have always felt that it would be my duty
to repay them every penny. I am thankful to say, that by the goodness
of God, I believe I am within sight of the ability to do this and I have
every hope of repaying all claims against the old firm, with interest,
at the end of this year [1915]...[59]

Following the resolution of the firm's suspension, the creditors' meeting
recommended the firm should be reconstituted as a new partnership
between William and his uncle, Anthony.[60] It was unusual in itself for a
small infant firm to survive a suspension and to re-emerge, ultimately,
as a successful firm. But when this is set alongside the major internal
and external business threats and challenges facing the firm at this time,
that re-emergence takes on a new significance. It was equally unusual
for a firm to decide to re-pay all debts to creditors of the suspension: it
was William Arnold's personal decision. This decision had immediate
repercussions for the firm's financial management for it went beyond
the requirements of the agreed composition. Although having a positive
effect on the firm's business probity and its working credit rating in the
market, the money diverted to meet this decision would have tended
to affect short term cash flow and longer term investment to some
degree.

However, a major challenge arose within two years of the start of the
new partnership that again changed the profile of the firm. The ending
of the national lockout of 1895 led to a rapid move within the industry
towards the final complete mechanisation of footwear manufacture
inside factories. This required a major re-structuring of production
needs. Larger premises were sought by the company in order to comply
with the "indoor working" agreement (Figures 5, and 6 and 7).[61] This
caused a renewed anxiety for the partners as they struggled to re-equip
and remodel their factory in a bid to comply with the decision to end
outwork and bring their employees into the factory. Of this period
William later reflected:

> ...This time, like all that had gone before, was one long struggle. All
> who are in business will understand, when I say that for a long time
> there was nothing but work and worry, planning and scheming,
> pinching and saving, forecasting and grinding, to hold our own and
> make just a little headway. Practically everything depended upon the

---

59 *Autobiography* p. 131.
60 When Anthony retired in 1897, William continued in business on his own account until, in
   1909, he entered into partnership with three of his sons.
61 On employer-trade union struggle in early 1890s see A. Fox, *History of NUBSO* (1957)
   chapter 14, *passim*; K. B. Brooker (1981) p. 157.

energy of one pair of hands and every week brought its crop of difficulty and care. The struggle in the home, with a growing family, was quite as great as our fight to keep the doors of our factory open and I remember my pleasure and my wife's relief when I began to draw £2 a week from the business instead of 30/-...[62]

Along with many other average practice firms[63], A. & W. Arnold shifted to modern machine working. This change required not just the purchase of new plant, but also required the putting in place of work practices and workplace supervision to assure the efficient operation of that plant. His recollection of that time is again coloured by the risk element that surrounded a significant change in business practice:

…I could see that if I did not go in for machinery I should be quickly left behind and go under. This was an important time in my life; I must make the change or lose my business. I made it a matter of prayer and, confident that I was doing the right thing, I speculated on thousands' of pounds worth of machinery when I had not a spare shilling. Happily I came through it. It was a great plunge that enabled me to keep up with the others…[64]

It is probable that Arnold and his growing family were able to weather the privations of this period not just because of his desire to succeed but also because of the nearness of their experiences as an outworking shoe worker family. As such a family, they would have been familiar with periods of straitened financial circumstances brought about by regular seasonal short order working, trade depression and the shoe workers love of St Monday.[65]

As a Prominent and Successful Manufacturer.
As already noted, if he was not unusual in succumbing to failure,

---

62 *Autobiography* p. 117. Contrast this with the initial carefree optimism that pervaded the partners thinking when the business was commenced: "…we discussed the thing all round and decided to make a start. Between us, we thought we knew a lot and that the three of us working together could almost beat creation making boots. As for capital, the two others had some money; I had little or none, but I was so necessary for the concern as an expert workman, that I believe they would have taken me in without any. Everything looked so rosy." [*ibid.* p. 114].

63 A best practice firm is one using the production methods considered to deliver the most efficient results that gives the firm a marked financial advantage in the market place. By contrast an average practice firms are those using median industry practices

64 *Autobiography* p. 125.

65 On the local situation in Northampton see comments in K. B. Brooker (1981) *op. cit. passim.* See also, D. A. Reid, "The Decline of Saint Monday, 1766-1876", *P.& P. 71* (May, 1976); D. A. Reid, "Weddings, Weekdays, Work and Leisure in Urban England, 1791-1911: The Decline of Saint Monday Revisited" *P.&P. 153* (Nov., 1996); W. Rybczynski, "Keeping Saint Monday" in W. Rybczynski, *Waiting for the Weekend* (New York 1991).

William Arnold could be regarded as unusual in successfully recovering from failure. And so the years after his failure in 1892 witness his struggle for business success. For several years he worked with a partner, Anthony Arnold, but he retired in *c*. 1897. From this time and until 1909 William Arnold was a sole trader. These years unfortunately receive little detailed coverage in his *Autobiography*: he leaves his stature and that of his company, well known to the largely local and trade readership of the book, to speak for itself. At one level this could be regarded as a form of conceit, for this approach has about it an expectation that the reader is inevitably going to see similar merit in his enterprise as he does himself. The book is certainly written as a conscious celebration of the firm's prominence and success. Although at another level, it is as much a celebration for William, of his drive to repay all his creditors in full, as it is about personal aggrandisement.

Be that as it may, what is clear is that William Arnold gradually eased himself out of the ignominious position of failed businessman towards a greater prominence in the trade and the town. As a mature and prominent player in Northampton's footwear trade he never completely left behind the rough diamond figure of earlier years, but gradually by 1915 there emerges a man who is well-respected; someone who is a force in the trade and so in the town. Whilst he never went on to become one of the elite, his energy and probity nevertheless assured his rise to a position as one of the respected middling rank members amongst the wholesale volume production firms in Northampton.

Volume producers formed part of the wholesale footwear manu-facturing firms of the town. As has been discussed elsewhere,[66] by 1914 there were 63 surviving mature wholesale manufacturing firms[67] of differing size and character. The economic characterisation of these firms is shown in Tables 18, 19, and 20,[68] which summarise their respective scales of economic activity. These mature firms compose themselves into three internal groups that operated at different levels of influence, output and success:

Elite producers, comprising 7 firms
Volume producers comprising 15 firms
Small producers comprising 41 firms.

The character and nature of firms in these three internal groups differs

66 See Appendix, "Northampton Footwear Industry Business Community 1840-1914" p. 159 et seq.
67 Of the 76 wholesale manufacturing firms trading in 1914, 13 were infant firms, who have been left of this introduction as by this date it was still unsure what their future role in the industry would be.
68 See Appendix, p. 166-68.

and that difference becomes particularly marked at each end of the spectrum. And at one end were the small elite. These oligopolists were the owners of the leading best practice firms of the period. They were men who balanced a high level of practical manufacturing under-standing with keen commercial and retail distribution skills. They demonstrated the business flair of leaders and innovators. They were the people others in the industry followed; who were listened to and took a leadership role both in trade and wider public life and community affairs. Their best practice manufacturing techniques and leading edge distribution and retailing ideas set new standards of enterprise within the industry that other firms followed and adopted. Their verve, ability and energy defined and enabled industry-wide change in this period. All seven firms had achieved a well-developed modern manufacturing, commercial distribution, and retail capability by the Edwardian period. Progressively from 1887 they substantially abandoned what small craft producer approaches to the industry that they had retained. Yet for all of their modernity, most of them used a broad product mix of both dominant volume batch production of standardised lines of footwear, together with smaller volume jobbing production and traditional bespoke hand-sewn lines. This was a market response to their middle range customer base in Britain at this time. They tended to work with medium and higher grades of men's wear, but had ventured into lower grade work where this was profitable, and by the Edwardian period also moved into ladies wear, which had traditionally been made in specific ladies wear centres. And in terms of distribution strategies the use of trade-marks, patents and vigorous advertising were much more universal amongst both them and second rank firms.[69]

Volume producers formed the second of the three wholesale manu-facturer internal groups in the town. It was comprised of fifteen firms who operated as significant producers of standardised product lines.[70] The basic characteristic that binds them is their threshold size of production, which Butnam's 1912 report on the Northampton industry places at a weekly nominal capacity of production of 3,000 pairs. As has

69 For more details on the character and nature of these Northampton wholesale manufacturer internal groups, see Appendix p. 139-45 et seq.
70 Where company order books survive, however, it is clear that volume production at this time was executed in small batches and trouble was taken to meet customers' style and fit requirements. N.R.O. ZA49996, A. & W. Arnold Wholesale Boot & Shoe Manufacturer Order Book for 1907/09 gives such a glimpse of the realities of production and trading at this time. The order book is of one of Arnold's commercial travellers, whose territory covered a wide area in Derbyshire, Lancashire, and Yorkshire. In it the orders for standard lines for anything from 2 to 200 pairs are recorded, and these are punctuated by special orders for single pairs or very small quantities. For example, in August 1907 an order for one pair of boots contains very clear information about materials, stitched eyelets, the exact

already been observed, during the 1890s they had come to concentrate more completely upon wholesale production using similar volume batch production techniques to the industrial elite.[71] Using figures derived from Butnam, a threefold typology of volume producing firms can be identified:

the five top ranking firms had a nominal capacity range of between 5,000 to 6,000 pairs per week – 70 to 100% above the threshold level

the five middle ranking firms had a nominal capacity range of 4,000 pairs per week – 30% above the threshold level

the six bottom ranking firms had a nominal range of 3,000 to 3,500 pairs – at or just above the threshold level.

The top-ranking volume producer firm, G. T. Hawkins & Co,[72] was a third larger than a middle ranking firm like A. & W. Arnold, and twice as big as a bottom ranking firm like J. Robinson & Co.[73] The recorded factory worker population for volume producing firms is, however, much more consistent, being commonly between 300 to 400 workers regardless of the ranking position of the firm. The similarity in the headline employee number can be accounted for by the variation in productivity and the cost efficiencies being achieved by individual firms at the time. But when we look at the capitalisation and profit levels of

fit, size, and the last to be used: "a piece to be added on each last for bunions on both feet." Other special orders are trial and sample pairs for a shop before they commit bigger orders: 13/10/1907 for an Accrington shop, "a trial order for fitting; if satisfactory promised all spring orders. See WA jnr. before giving tickets out to clicking room." 3/10/1908 Stockton on Tees "...three pairs of specials...window display". Some of the special trial pairs are made up imitation of other company's products: 20/10/08 "sample must be crimped to compete with Saxone Shoe"; 12/01/1909 "send two pairs in imitation of AEM (A. E. Marlow & Co.) and C&EL (C. & E. Lewis)". All footwear had a catalogue number and description but also it is very clear that firm would tailor order in terms of colour, leather, fit and so on. Order books for other volume producers in the town and held by N.R.O. reveal similar means of operating their commercial travellers (see, N.R.O, ZA 9651, Messrs J. Branch of Northampton Order Book 1888-1895; ZB 160, G. T. Hawkins Ltd miscellaneous correspondence and agreements with representatives and travellers 1908-1923). By contrast, the small producer Pollard and Son of Northampton maintained separate order books for general and bespoke work (Order Books 1869-1883, Overseas Orders 1898-1900, Bespoke Order Books 1902-1916).

71 As Tables 18, 19 and 20 (Appendix p. 166-68 et seq.) reveal the scale of production was also an important differentiator.

72 See footnote 91, p. 38 for brief details of Hawkin's life.

73 Jonathan Robinson was born at Kislingbury in 1825 and commenced his own business, after serving an apprentice as a shoe maker, in 1850, at Bath Street Northampton. In addition to running this business until his death in 1891, he enjoyed a full public life. He was a prominent dissenter and philanthropist and his organisational skills were widely used by many societies and committees. He was Sunday School Superintendent for over fifty years and Deacon from 1854 at the Doddridge Congregational Church. He died at

these firms there is more difficulty in arriving at a straightforward picture. In terms of operating capital levels, we have sufficient available evidence to form some view. Top ranking firms were commonly operating in a capital range £38,000 to £44,000. However, the operating capital level of Hawkins, the leading firm, was twice this level at £80,000. This might be partly explained by the greater use made by this firm of show and warehouse accommodation in several large cities.[74]

By contrast, the information we have for middle rank volume producer firms is slender but suggestive. It can be tentatively argued that capital stood at around the £25,000 level. J. Dawson was higher at £42,000, but this had reduced to £25,000 by 1920: it could be argued that this firm was over capitalised at the earlier date, derived from its former greater volume of activities. Amongst bottom ranking firms there is some variation in the capital levels of the different firms. Amongst these firms, S. Collier & Co Ltd recorded operating capital of £33,000 appears high and may be explained by this company's declining trading position in the period and its continued ownership of freehold showrooms and warehouses elsewhere in Britain.[75] W. Barratt & Co's £39,000 capital in 1914 appears to be similarly high. But, unlike Collier, Barratt's was a rising company in the years leading up to the Great War, when Barratt was busily adding new productive capacity, he was also developing a retail property portfolio throughout the country upon which its inter-war retail chain was to be founded.[76] The remaining three companies, A. Lee & Co, H. Sharman & Co, and J. Robinson & Co, recorded capital levels that reflect the smaller size of their operations at the margin of

home, Spencer Parade, from stomach cancer. His personal estate was valued at £11,167. At the time of his death he was, with M. P. Manfield and Henry Marshall, the oldest manufacturer in the town. However, he had maintained an up to date business, which his son, J. P. Robinson, took over and run successfully until 1935. He extended the Bath Street factory and finally took a new factory at Countess Road in 1901. The firm made a speciality of sports and tennis shoes and high grade wear, and enjoyed royal patronage. The firm had both a London and Paris office and a full complement of commercial travellers.

74 E.g. *B.S.J.* 23/5/89 p. 289 and *S.L.T. Supplement* p. xxiii.

75 Simon Collier (1838-1928) inherited the firm from his father, William, who was prominent business and political figure in the mid-century town. He was a councillor for thirty years and mayor in 1861/62. Under Simon's forty years of ownership the firm was a leading maker of cheaper grades of footwear. Late in the century the factory was moved to Dallington and housing built for the workforce: a branch factory at Kislingbury was also opened: 500 were employed at the former and 150 at latter by 1897. A tannery also operated from the Dallington site. From his date a decline in business occurred due to loss of key overseas markets; the firm went into voluntary liquidation in 1932. Six of his sons entered the business from 1897, when it was incorporated: Charles and later Simon jnr. were resident salesmen in their key southern Africa markets. Simon was an aggressive employer and trader. He paid high wages for those prepared to operate machinery and dispensed with those not prepared to accept new working practices, which led to disputes with the local union and his workforce. Like his father, he played a prominent part in local affairs. At death his effects were valued at £9,293.

76 William Barratt in the early stages of his company's career was already amassing a property portfolio of retail properties for use as retail outlets for his factory production.

this second group. In terms of profit levels, information is lacking. These were private concerns and records do not survive in sufficient quantity to be of use.

Moving away from numbers, characterisation can be further explored by looking at several identifiable group traits: the mode of production that they adopted, their approach to distribution and merchandising, and the role that the family played in their businesses.

It is clear that the internal group business persona of volume producers differed from that of the elite. Their business world was framed by an approach and attitude to enterprise that relied on steady endeavour and the accretion of success based on established manufacturing practices, wholesale trading practices and business tactics initially pioneered and developed by the industrial elite from the eighteen eighties: few of them had been in the vanguard of change[77] in the years before the date of this listing. The sum of the group's business models marked them substantially as followers rather than innovators: William Arnold's record as a manufacturer is certainly of this character. In both their approach to business and their influence and reach in public and associational life they differed from the elite. As we have seen, the elite had flair matched by an ability to continually address patterns of change behaviour that kept them and their firms in the forefront of the industry. This restless energy assured on-going growth and innovation in business, and sustained their presence at the forefront of the industry and social and political life in local and national life.[78]

In the language of the business analyst, the volume producers listed in 1914 were average practice firms. That is to say, whilst change and even radical innovation had figured in the life of some of these firms in the

77 As Tables 18, 19, and 20 reveal the scale of production was also an important differentiator. It should also be noted that the exception to this point was the leading part that John Marlow & Co made as firms who helped to instigate integrated machine production in the 1880s. William Barratt was one of the leading proponents of mail order business. Simon Collier was heavily involved in the establishment of warehouse showrooms in UK cities and a retail chain of 24 shops in Scotland.

78 On the social character of manufacturers, see below. A. E. Marlow well encapsulates this type of behaviour. The son of a manufacturer, he was the managing director of his father's firm before starting on his own account. Within a few years his business was secure and profitable. With a team of managers to oversee the firm, he was free to pursue trade and public affairs. Heavily committed to local and regional affairs, he became the youngest mayor in 1904. He became a county magistrate in 1912; a county alderman in 1918, and the chairman of several committees. In the early 1920s he was a parliamentary candidate on two occasions (Wellingborough and Leicester East). He held numerous company directorships. At the time of his death in 1922, he was a leading member of the British Empire Exhibition Committee, and widely regarded as a future recipient of a knighthood (on A. E. Marlow see K. B. Brooker "The First Northamptonshire County Council Revisited" *N.P.P.* (2013) No. 68, 70-86.

past, their general character in this period was that of owners who espoused established manufacturing ideals and methods of transacting a wholesale trading business. At the heart of this group identity was their presence as wholesale manufacturers, first and foremost. Unlike the elite they do not extend their business activities significantly through vertical integration developments into direct retailing initiatives and retail chain business.[79] They predominately remained with the recognised wholesale distribution methods of a previous generation: use of trade marking, merchandising and commercial travelling; yet some new distribution practices were embraced.

Two features about footwear firms stand out: the dominance of family ties in the running of the business, and the extent to which professional managers were being used by the turn of the century. This heavy reliance upon the family was complemented in some firms by taking close, trusted friends as partners.[80] The family firm dominated the footwear industry throughout this period. Its presence had an important impact upon the business thinking and decision making of many owners. From the industry of the period there is an accumulation of evidence that demonstrates that family employment, income and financial considerations were part and parcel of business strategy.[81] The family firm over time was there to furnish both income and capital growth for both the nuclear and sometimes the extended family.[82] Balanced alongside this was a continued and significant reliance on family business skills, confidence, discretion, confidentiality, and tireless work and commitment that lay at the heart of the business. The point made by Joel Moyr about the business need during the industrial revolution period for trusted allies as managers was equally relevant in the late nineteenth century.[83] But most practically and immediate was

79 There were exceptions to this: Padmore & Barnes, Simon Collier & Co, and William Barratt & Co.

80 For example, Oakeshott & Finnemore: Henry Oakeshott and Walter Finnemore were managers at Turner Bros. before starting their business in 1902 at Talbot Road. Their successful export business was decimated by the Great War and in 1922 they entered an association with the Norvic Co., and merged with this company in 1935. Both played a role in the town's public affairs. Henry was born in London in 1863 and died at Northampton in 1936: his effects were valued at £35,180. Walter was born in Northamptonshire in 1875 and died at Hemel Hampstead in 1961: his effects were valued at £163,378.

81 An example of family financial changes driving changes in the A. & W. Arnold and Arnold Bros. structures, see impact of Harriet Arnold's death below.

82 There were occasions when the balance to be struck between the financial needs of the family firm and the financial well-being of members of the family came into conflict. *In extremis* there lurked the danger of the insolvency of the firm if this balance moved too far in the favour of members of the family to the detriment of the firm. On this see the example of W. Hickson & Co. at footnote 52, p. 24.

83 In his recent book *The Enlightened Economy* (2009) chapter 16, Joel Moyr writes convincingly about the need for businessmen to have trusted people working with them in the company.

the presence of members of the family as principals controlling the daily life of the family firm that was there to provide for the family.

In a majority of leading elite firms, principals were second generation family owners with an intimate understanding of the trade and the ways of business: they were business inheritors.[84] Most had had a high level of practical shoemaking training with a leaning towards the distribution and capital/accounting activities within the trade. Principals were supported by a team of professional managers, who gave additional strategic impetus to firms' activities. Managers also freed principals to follow other business interests and interests outside of the business.[85] Many of these managers in turn became principals and took a leadership role when the second generation died in the inter war period.[86] By contrast, volume producers were as a group less expansive in matters of business, more reliant upon their own and their family's trade and business skills for success, and less likely to have a full and prominent public life. And yet here too we see the family owners of leading volume production firms supported by the use of professional managers. Unlike elite firms, the use of the professional manager class is present amongst volume producers too, but this becomes less usual amongst the bottom members of this group.[87] This may simply be a question of job titles. Amongst bottom ranking firms it is possible that the more workshop-focused style of these firms led to work supervisors and foremen being used as confidants and lieutenants by owners, although the evidence for this is scant. Also account should be taken of the smaller size of the firms and greater likelihood of direct workroom supervision by the owner.[88]

Inevitably, this question of trusted allies was resolved by looking within the family and friendship circles for business colleagues. Of course, William Arnold's use of Alfred Flint may be an instance that suggests this was never an infallible rule; that it was wise to enquire into the skill base of relatives and friends invited to join the firm.

84 Where a founder has no family to inherit, managers often became heirs: **A. E. Marlow** died in 1922, his children were young and his manager George Webb became managing director until 1927, when he formed his own business. **William Barratt** died in 1939 and had no children. He had used a team of managers and non-executive directors, who took control. **H. E. Randall Ltd**, used a board heavily represented by non-executive directors drawn from outside of the industry: for a short discussion on this, see K. B. Brooker (2013) *op. cit.* The same issue can be seen occurring in volume producer firms too: **G. T. Hawkins** (managers Herbert Edwards and Henry George White succeed to the business on Hawkins' death in 1937 and their families ran the business into the late twentieth century.

85 See K. B. Brooker (2013) *op. cit. Passim.*

86 This happened in Manfield & Sons following the deaths of second generation owners Harry Manfield (1923) and James Manfield (1925). James' daughter Ellen Louise Pigott-Lawrence followed him as Chairman. Amongst the senior managers and directors, A. S. Garrard and J. B. Cartwright were prominent.

87 For example, G. T. Hawkins uses professional managers in the absence of members of the family wishing to be involved. They were Herbert Edwards and Henry George White.

88 Two examples of this type of smaller firm were W. J. Marks & Co. and W. P. Dalton & Co. In both companies, at the death of the founders, their widows took over relying on the

Despite the growing complexity of running a business, volume producers had a preference for direct management based on close personal control of both strategic planning and operational production functions; underscored by a strong and growing focus upon distribution matters. Added to this, the radical re-structuring of workplace organisation, that characterised the modernisation of the industry, added the need for the direct supervision of employees.[89] This preference represents their clear identity with the risks attached to the use of family money in a family enterprise. Nevertheless, this complexity inevitably led to an increasing use of professional managers, who became significant figures in the management of the firms: this also reflected a greater role that some owners were playing in wider trade organisations, other business interests, and wider public life outside of the firm. Another point of contrast is that, as a group, smaller owners were less expansive in matters of business, more reliant upon their own and their family's trade skills for success and less likely to have a full and prominent public life than the elite. Nevertheless, where volume producers used managers they were often present to provide an important element of managerial strengthening; to make up for the deficiencies of family owners. Certainly, William Arnold introduces two strong managers who provided important managerial underpinning in the years after the re-launch of the company in late 1892, and again at the start-up of Arnold Brothers.[90] It is clear from the sub-text of the *Autobiography* that these two men provided the skills and business qualities that William Arnold lacked.

senior employees to aid them. **William Marks** began business in 1886. A practical shoemaker, he did a "small, secure trade", with a nominal weekly output of about 300 pairs. He died in 1907; his effects valued at £2,582. From 1902, his wife ran the business, first with the works foreman, and from 1907 with a manager, J. J. B. Croall. The business was radically re-organised and the factory re-equipped. **William P. Dalton** began manufacturing in 1895. He was an "old school hand-stitch man" and specialised in high grade footwear, with a nominal weekly output of about 400 pairs. He died in 1901; effects valued at £3,575. His widow Jane took charge. The factory was managed by J. Dalton (son) and G. E. Barbey (a senior employee), who had known the business from the start.

89 Close work supervision had been largely introduced from 1895 into the main centres of the footwear industry following at least a decade of conflict between employees and owners. The traditional outwork structure of the industry had enabled shoe workers to retain an effective control over work structure and pace. This was symbolised by the tradition of St Monday; of the keeping of traditional holidays that interrupted production; and worker control of the work process (see p. 10-12, above). From 1887, footwear manufacturers wrestled with their work forces and the footwear unions to gain control of their work places. The termination of the national 1895 strike in the employers' favour assured employer ascendency. In the years that followed, employers progressively took control of the work process and work flow: the era of factory-based, machine production had arrived in Northampton. In the development of employer based, work-flow processes can be seen echoes of the work study techniques of Taylor and others in U.S.A. that were beginning to be explored in Britain during this period.

90 J. H. C. Newton, company secretary, joined A. & W. Arnold in the post-failure to assure that the administration of the company was secure. He and other senior employees were

However, it should also be appreciated that the nature and business behaviour of some volume producers, and thus the mix of the internal group, changed over time. William Arnold's development as a businessman over time shown in this introduction can, in turn, be detected in others. Indeed, several variations of business strategy and behaviour can be isolated amongst them. In the period, the newer firms experienced a step change in the business by the adoption of integrated small batch production using machinery. A. & W. Arnold was amongst this number. And as his *Autobiography* makes clear they had to take brave capital decisions when embarking on installing new plants of machinery; a change that was to assure the firm's future success. One short term outcome for the family was an acceptance of restrictions on the amount of money that could be taken out of the company for family use. Others were established and retained their position of eminence in the group.[91] By contrast, there were those men, once in the forefront of industrial change, whose energy was focused on sustaining an established mode and scale of operation.[92] And lastly, there were the

important figures in the management training of William Arnold's sons. At the time of the start-up of Arnold Brothers, Newton is drafted into that company and plays an important role in its success. The other was F. Mortimer, who later joins Arnold Bros.

91 In terms of their manner of conducting business, available evidence reveals an adherence to update production methods, supporting by sound distribution techniques: the use of branding, standard pricing, advertising, and distribution channels based on warehousing and commercial travelling. In these firms can also be seen the use of managers and the entry of sons but the founders lacked the public flair and authority of members of the elite: they are more focused as steady, manufacturers. They do play a role in the trade, but this is not universally the case. And certainly they do not have a wider profile in public affairs that is one of the hall marks of the elite. Elite careers make their contemporaries' blood race. This difference can be illustrated by briefly contrasting the career of G. T. Hawkins & Co. and John Marlow & Co. **John Marlow:** he ran an established firm, founded in the 1866 that was an important initiator of welted machine methods and new factory industrial discipline: he ran the first full system of machine welting. But he does not develop the new retailing methods and gradually his scale of operation becomes that of a leading volume producer. He was prominent in trade association and arbitration affairs, but played no role in public and social affairs; he was, though, a leading Congregationalist in the town. At his death in 1909, his effects were valued at £33,967. His son J. H. Marlow succeeded as the head of the firm. **G. T. Hawkins:** he, similarly, was a prominent manufacturer and the leading volume producer, who founded his firm in 1882 from small premises in Oakley Street; he moved to Overstone Road in 1886. But his focus was on manufacturing and he initiated none of the retailing developments put forward by others. He laid down the first full set of finishing machinery in the town. He was born at Higham Ferrers in 1857, the son of James, a currier. He worked from seven, first as a stitching boy and later an apprentice clicker. Prior to entering business he was a foreman pattern-cutter for Manfield's. Although a freemason and member of the Conservative party locally, he played no prominent role in either public or social affairs. He was an Anglican and gave freely to hospital funds. He married Lillie Nunn and had three children. The family lived in Abingdon Park Crescent. At his death in 1929, his effects were valued at £115,980. Part ownership of the firm and control of management was taken by managers, following the family's disinclination to control it.

92 An example of this type of firm was H. Sharman & Co. Founded in east London in 1872 by Henry Sharman, subsequently he took his son Henry Brand Sharman into partnership.

transitional members of the group: ambitious owners whose growth and success was to propel them to greater prominence within the industry in the future. Their presence in this internal group was based on their current size of operation, not their business frame of mind. William Barratt is an excellent example of this striving new man. Some contemporary commentators characterised the membership as being of the old school in terms of their approach to manufacturing, and conservative in approach towards distribution[93] this is not really a sustainable summary.

Thus the 1914 volume producers group contains both efficient manufacturers, those who were once in their turn innovators and strategic leaders in the industry, whilst others were in transition towards a more prominent future. In general terms, volume producers sustained patterns of manufacturing and distribution that, not only assured individual profitability, but provided a significant core of economic activity within the British footwear industry, enabling the industry to effectively meet competitive pressures both in home and overseas markets.[94]

Many of the early struggles of A. & W. Arnold eased following the period of rationalisation after the suspension of trading and adoption of factory working. And as these early struggles passed, the firm entered into a period of successful trading. The firm was reputed to be the second largest maker of men's machine welted boots in the town, with a capacity of 5/6,000 pairs weekly, according to one contemporary trade press report, in these goods alone. Production overall had shifted away from the lower grade lines initially made and was now concentrated on high grade men's and youth's footwear; the quality and style of which was recognised in home and overseas markets. Full use was made of branding and distinctive ranges of footwear were quickly established. A contemporary attributed this change of fortune to William Arnold's ability:

...The sturdy independence and hard work of Mr Arnold have had

They traded from various factories in Northampton from 1885 and retained a level pattern of trading into the inter-war period. Neither played a prominent role in trade or town affairs. Henry Sharman was born in London in 1845 and died in Northampton in 1918; probate was granted for £44,050. Herbert Brand Sharman was born in Northampton in 1887 and died there in 1965: his effects were valued at £5,295. Other members of the family, Joseph and John Lewis Sharman, were also involved in the trade.

93 Although they tended to eschew modern patterns of retail distribution and to concentrate on the more traditional patterns of wholesale distribution, they were ready to use emerging in-stock distribution that came into favour in the new century.

94 For further consideration of the role of businessmen in the industry, see Appendix "The footwear industry and the role of entrepreneurship" (p. 179 et seq.).

their reward, for today the firm have a fine up-to-date factory with all the latest and best machinery and appliances for producing high-grade footwear. From the smallest beginnings [he] has built up a business of great importance and has every reason to be proud of his achievement. The grit and persistence he has brought to bear have borne good fruit and placed [business] amongst those to be reckoned with in the production of footwear in this country…[95]

A continuing theme running through the account of his business years was the ever present financial needs of his family. As his family of eleven children grew it is reasonable to accept that domestic costs grew too. Little information has come down to us about his domestic affairs, but biographic evidence shows that increasing amounts of money were being spent on education, more comfortable surroundings, and his children were beginning to make some advantageous marriages.[96] As discussed above, the family laid at the heart of the business, they at once formed a large part of the reason for the firm's existence and that existence relied upon members of the family and trusted friends to sustain it. Like other successful businessmen, William Arnold's sons followed him into business. But here we do see a difference of approach. Of his six sons, three followed their father into A. & W. Arnold, whilst his two eldest sons chose to set up a company of their own.

William jnr.[97] and Matthew[98] founded the firm of Arnold Brothers &

95 *B.S.T.J.* 25/6/09 p. 545.

96 Thus, Thomas went to Elmfield College, York; the family broke with residence in the footwear area to the north of the town to reside in a property opposite Abington Park. Matthew married into a manufacturing family; William into a well-known local musical family; and Thomas into a notable Primitive Methodist clerical family.

97 **William Arnold** junior was the eldest son. He was born in Hunter Street in 1886 and later lived in the family's homes at 80 Turner Street and 49 Colwyn Street Northampton. He was educated at Kettering Road Board School and at twelve years of age entered the industry as an operative; a rounder (Census Enumerators' Return Northampton 1901). After a thorough practical training in his father's firm that laid emphasis on clicking and pattern cutting, William became proficient at leather buying. Amongst this generation of manufacturers' sons this type of training in key skilled operations was the norm. To this was often added experience in the practical management of workers on the shop floor and in the outwork department. Within a matter of a few years the increased financial and business complexity of the industry during the last phase of industrialisation led to their training focusing much more on finance, marketing and so forth, rather than the practical skills of manufacture. Public life held few attractions for him, although he was vice-president of the local Manufacturers' Association in 1929 and a non-conformist lay preacher. He was a life-long abstainer and a Liberal. In 1907, he married Annie, the youngest daughter of William Hawes, the noted local musician, teacher and maker of violins (William's forebear may have been of the London musician William Hawes (1785-1846). He was a chorister of the Chapel Royal and after held a number of musical posts He subsequently held various musical posts in the royal household and was also a music publisher. He was for many years opera musical director at the Lyceum Theatre then noted for its opera productions, and also choral master at St Paul's Cathedral until his death.

Company in 1909 at premises in Henry Street, Northampton. The youngest son, James, elected to join his elder brothers' firm and he probably stayed there through his working life.[99] The initial funding was provided by their father.

...I had just started my sons in business, which was a drain on my

Here he wrote numerous pieces of music). Early in their marriage William and Annie lived at 49 Stimpson Avenue Northampton with their first two children, Aubrey (born 1908) and Ruth (born 1910), and one female servant. Towards the end of the Great War they made their home at "Fairview", Cliftonville, Northampton. They had issue four sons and one daughter: a son, Malcolm, was the noted composer (there are many details of Malcolm's life. See, for example, the short summary in Who's Who (1982) p. 97). His eldest son and two nephews went into the firm of Arnold Brothers (N.I 29/1/54 p .5). Annie, his wife, was born at Northampton in late 1883 to William E. Hawes (born at Abingdon Berks in 1851) and Ellen (born 1861 at Northampton). The family home was at 13 Castilian Street Northampton and later at 17 Balmoral Road Kingsthorpe. Annie was a self-employed music teacher like her father. She had one younger sibling, William, born at Northampton in 1882; he was a commercial traveller: there were also three elder female siblings. She died at Northampton in January 1954 aged 71.William continued to live on in retirement at his home 5 Homestead Way, Northampton. He died at home on 13/12/1978 after suffering from bronchopneumonia.

98 **Matthew Arnold** junior was the second son and born at Hunter Street Northampton in 1887, and lived in the family homes until his first marriage in 1909. He was educated locally and then became a shoe operative as a feeder of a heeling machine (Census Enumerators' Return Northampton 1901). Like his elder brother he subsequently trained as a clicker and pattern cutter prior to entering his father's firm to assisting in its management. In 1909 he entered partnership with his elder brother, William, to form Arnold Brothers Ltd, which had the success enjoyed by their father's firm, prior to its closure in the early 1960s (N.C.E 8/3/1963 p. 1). Matthew married twice. His first wife was Minnie Frisby. She came from a footwear manufacturing family that came out of the same worker-turned-manufacturer background as the Arnold family. There first family home was at 29 Lutterworth Road Northampton, which they shared with their first children, including Ronald (born in 1910). There were to be two sons and two daughters. Minnie Frisby was born at Northampton in early 1887, the daughter of Thomas William Frisby (born at Northampton in 1855) and his wife Emma Elizabeth, formerly a machinist (born at Northampton in 1858). She lived in the family homes at 56 Kettering Road and 25 Stockley Street in childhood. Her grandfather was a printer compositor in Abington Street. Her father worked as a clicker before establishing himself as footwear manufacturer in the 1890s. Minnie was the second child of the marriage and worked as a boot and shoe needle hand before her marriage. There were thirteen children of the marriage, nine of whom survived. The eldest son was Harry Frisby (born 1877) a finisher in his early adult years; Arthur (born 1881), and Frederick (born 1883), both formerly riveters, worked as shoe manufacturers in the family firm. Minnie's father died at 36 Alfred Street Northampton in 1910 aged 54: there was no probate or published will (the family firm at this time was insolvent, see footnote 108, p. 44). Minnie died at 36 East Park Parade, Northampton on 3/9/1951 aged 64: probate was granted to her sons, Ronald Matthew and Thomas Edwin, both shoe manufacturers: her effects were valued at £5,425. Sometime after the death of Minnie, Matthew married, secondly, Patricia, who outlived him. Matthew died on 7/3/1963; he had retired from business in 1951, at the time of Minnie's death, due to ill health. Probate was granted to his widow, Patricia Arnold: his effects were valued at £11,076. He had taken some part in the religious affairs of Methodism locally, but was remembered as a keen sportsman. He played competitive cricket locally, and was a prominent member of both the Kingsthorpe Golf Club and the Abington Bowls Club (*N.C.E, ibid.*).

99 **James Arnold** junior was born at Northampton in 1896 and lived in the family home into

resources, but because of that, I was extra careful and had taken more than ordinary precautions against falling into debt…[100]

Their father's injection of start-up funding gave them much needed assistance. As a result within two years, a large factory at the rear of these premises was taken; an early indication of the future success that this firm was to enjoy. The two premises were linked, improved and rationalised to provide a frontage in both Henry Street and Talbot Road (See Figures 8, 9 and 10). It had originally been intended to specialise in machine-sewn goods, but a rising demand in the market for cheap and medium class welted goods caused the firm to switch to this more profitable class of production. Two branded ranges of men's wear – Master and Cathedral – retailing at standard prices between 8/11d and 12/6d resulted.[101] As was common by this period, the firm adopted an in-stock system to ensure a regular flow of goods into the retail market.

The firm enjoyed an immediate success.[102] From the scant evidence available it appears not to have faced the teething problems so common to most new firms in this period. The reasons for this were probably threefold. First, their father's capital together with the training they received in the family firm, which clearly stood them in good stead: "… Schooled in their father's business, they have his assistance and practical knowledge to draw on…"[103] Secondly, their associate, Mr F. Mortimer, a man of some years standing in the industry was a senior employee of A. & W. Arnold and his long and valuable experience was a prudent influence. Thirdly, from the outset, a close collaboration existed between the two firms of the father and the sons. His sons' experience of starting a new concern stands in stark contrast to their father. This was a mirror of the experience of other manufacturer's sons. William Arnold has written of the joint achievement of the two firms in the following way:

> …After twenty-six years of business experience, our name stands second to none in the trade for honest dealing and good work-manship. It is an untarnished name, honourable and clean. I, with

his adult years. He had joined Arnold Brothers several years before the Great War and assisted there in the management of the firm. At the time of the conversion he became a director of Arnold Brothers (Northampton) Ltd. (C.R.O. 172951, Directors List dated 12 November 1923). He married and continued to be involved in the firm until it closed and then became involved in another Northampton firm. As a retired shoe manufacturer he lived at 15 Abington Grove, Northampton. He died from heart disease on 24/9/1969 at St Crispin Hospital Duston, Northamptonshire.

100 Autobiography p. 127.
101 *B.S.T.J.* 25/6/09 p. 545 and *S.L.T. Supplement* 1916 p. Xvi.
102 *B.S.T.J. loc. cit.* "The firm went at once to the fore and is exceedingly busy". *S.L.T. Supplement loc. cit.*, "[the firm] has made rapid progress from the commencement"
103 *B.S.T.J. loc. cit.*

my sons, have now three factories and together we employ 800 people; we pay £1,000 in wages every week and we produce considerably over half-a-million pairs of boots and shoes per annum. We trade practically all over the world…[104]

This assessment suggests that the relationship between the two firms was close, but quite how close that collaboration was is a matter of conjecture. Two strands of evidence enable the position to be more clearly understood. A surviving order book reveals that A. & W. Arnold fed orders from their commercial travellers into the new firm. William Arnold gave particular instructions about the terms of this business and the way the orders should be handled.[105] This closeness of operation was most clearly shown when both firms converted to limited company status in February 1921. The partners of each firm became directors in the other.[106] The sale agreement valued A. & W. Arnold at £46,533, which price was satisfied by the allotment of 24,998 shares; the balance being in cash. William was the first chairman and Thomas, Alfred, and William the first directors: Alfred retired late in 1921.[107] Thomas was allotted 5,000 shares and Alfred W. 2,750 shares. Arnold Brothers had a nominal capital of £25,000. It can be inferred from background information that both companies shared business plans, order books and some production facilities. Under the registrations, the principals of each firm became directors in the other firm. Each firm, however, retained a separate legal entity, so they were never one concern. If that had been the case then the combined activity of the two firms, plus

104 *Autobiography* p. 131: at this time – 1915 – whilst William had been trading twenty-six years, his sons had worked on their own account for six.

105 N.R.O. ZA49996, A. & W. Arnold Wholesale Boot & Shoe Manufacturer Order Book for 1907/09: for example, 12/01/1909 order for 34 pairs of boots for a Lancashire shop, "…to be sent together but invoice the MS from Henry Street (i.e. Arnold Bros factory). Send when ready as March 1st); 18/01/1909, 101 pairs boots marked Arnold Bros invoice from Henry Street"; 25/01/1909 order for 55 pairs for Lincolnshire shop "…half order Arnold Bros and send all together).

106 Sale Agreements of A. & W. Arnold (C.R.O. Company File 172949) and Arnold Brothers (C.R.O. Company File 172951): C.f. A. W. Arnold Director's List for 1923.

107 Details of the company conversions come from Companies Registration Office, files C.R.O. 172949 [dissolved] and 172951 (dissolved). The two companies undertook conversion to limited company status in 1921. Early that year, Harriet Arnold had died and it is entirely possible that the conversion was required in order to carry out the financial provisions of her will, whilst maintaining the stability of the companies. This tying of family and company finance is another example of the close relationship that inevitably existed between a family firm and members of the owning family. Company conversion at the death of a member of the family was not uncommon at this time. Most Northampton footwear firms were family partnerships. Only 7.8% (31 firms) registered as limited companies. These were by no means the largest, nor were they exclusively elite firms. Those that do register do so significantly "for family reasons." This appears to be the case here, when Harriett Arnold died in 1921. To meet the needs of her will and assure business stability, limited company status was sought. On Harriett's death see p. 74 and 76 below.

Frisby & Co,[108] which had been acquired some time before, would have made the resultant whole the largest volume producer in the town.

William Arnold remained very much in control of A. & W. Arnold, but at the time when Arnold Bros. was begun in 1909 William Arnold took three other of his sons into partnership: Thomas,[109] Harry,[110] and Alfred

108 Frisby & Co had been founded by Thomas W. Frisby, who died in 1910. The business was carried on by his widow and a son Pickering Frisby. Her two sons Frederick and Arthur started their own business, and it was reported begun to take the business of the family firm. As a result, the business remained small and duly failed in 1912: assets £108 and liabilities £414. Few books of account had been kept and the firm had been insolvent by 1910 to the sum of £350: it was reported that close friends and family had provided credit (*B.S.T.J.* 7/6/1912 p. 420-21). Clearly at this stage, Arnold's had stepped in and purchased the concern. Matthew's first wife was Minnie Frisby, the daughter of Thomas; this close family tie was an important consideration in this purchase.

109 **Thomas Arnold** was born in 1889. He lived in the family homes in the centre of the town, and at 445 Wellingborough Road, Northampton until his marriage in 1913. He was educated at Elmfield College in York (Elmfield College was a Primitive Methodist boarding school founded in 1864 to celebrate the denomination's silver jubilee four years earlier. A contemporary report noted: "The College was the outcome of the strong conviction that if the [Primitive Methodist] Connexion did not provide thorough and liberal education for the sons of our ministers and prosperous laymen, we should not retain them in communion with us. The blessing of God upon the industry and economy of our people has raised many of them into comfortable circumstances, and enabled them to provide somewhat liberally for the education of their sons." [*Primitive Methodist World* 17/05/1883, quoted in K. Lyson, *A Little Primitive* (2001). Elmfield was also used as a college for training of Primitive Methodist priests). The choice of this form of religious boarding education reflects both the rising affluence of the family at this time and their involvement with the Primitive Methodist Connexion. At sixteen he went into the family firm. He spent his working life there, except for 1914-18 war service in the Inns of Court OTC. He became a partner, and from 1921 joint managing director with J. H. C. Newton, the company secretary. Thomas died in post in 1940. An obituary noted: …his association with the management of the business in conjunction with his father and J. H. C. Newton had led to the firm becoming one of the best known in the trade of Northampton…" (*S.L.N.* 7/3/40 p. 23) For many years he was the firm's principal commercial traveller. He held directorships in two associated companies: Arnold Bros., and Frisby & Co., of which he was managing director. This company had been acquired by Arnold's to provide further breadth in the class and style of footwear they produced. He took no part in political life, but was at some time a committee member of the local Manufacturers' Association, and was active in the Park Avenue Methodist Church, where he was a trustee and treasurer. He was a freemason. A friendly, charitable man, he was particularly generous to the local Methodist aged rest home, the founding of which had been in the hands of his father. He married Evelyn, the daughter of Rev J. H. Saxton (q.v.), the minister of the Kettering Road Methodist Church. There were four children of the marriage: two sons and two daughters. Later in life the family home was at "The Sheiling", Billing Road East, Northampton. He died on 3 March 1940, aged 51, at Ilkley, Yorkshire. He was survived by his widow and children. Probate was granted to James William Arnold, shoe manufacturer, and Ralph Austin Smith company director: his effects were valued at £22,100.

110 **Harry Arnold** was born in 1892 and lived at home until his marriage which took place in the Great War. He was educated locally and entered the family firm when was this was completed. He was no longer a partner at the time of the conversion of the business in 1921. Little evidence of his later life and interests outside of business are extant. However, like all of his family he retained an active interest in Methodism throughout his life.

Walker.[111] It was said of Thomas, who acted as works manager, that he "…is invaluable to the business and in the commercial department particularly displays that energy so necessary for the firm's welfare…"[112]

A clear difference between the elite and the wholesale volume producers is at one level the scale, character and approach towards their business; at another level it resolves itself around their differing social and political position in the community. For the elite were the leaders of trade and town; they were both influential and authoritative in a way that was not given to volume producers. This introduction now needs to address these matters.

William Arnold's Social and Cultural Character

If this was William Arnold's achievement in business, what do we know of him as a man and of his position in his community? His personal and social life reveals someone whose confidence and sense of self-worth grew as his position as a manufacturer defined the man. Confronted with a drink problem in early adulthood, made worse by a readiness to fight when in drink, he emerges, with the help of his wife and friends, as a man of honour and of religious conviction. This is exemplified by his doggedness in paying the creditors of his business failure; a process that took him over twenty years to accomplish. These are the elements of the human story behind the man of business.

William Arnold, like many in the industry, continued to hold to the abiding values of the footwear industry of their early years that was eclipsed by the industrial change they embraced; values centred upon the workshop, Nonconformity and liberal politics. These traditions and values broke down initially amongst elite manufacturers as second generation principals and professional managers, whose upbringing had not been bounded by these traditions, gradually took control and sought to move in different industrial, social and political circles. But,

---

111 **Alfred Walker Arnold** was the fifth son and was also associated with the industry. He was born at Northampton in 1894 and lived in the Northampton family homes until his marriage in 1912. He joined the family firm of A. & W. Arnold and assisted in the management of the business. By 1914 he had been made a partner, but resigned shortly after the firm's conversion to limited company status in 1921, and ran a boot and shoe repairing business at Harrow, Middlesex for a number of years (*N.I.* 25/3/55 p. 4).He died at his home in North Harrow on 21/3/1955. Administration of his will was granted to his widow, Florence Mabel. He left effects to the value of £2,121.

112 *S.L.T. Supplement* [1916] p. xiv. It is interesting to note that whereas practical shoemaking skills were important to a manufacturer, a generation later principals were very much more often skilled in some aspect of commercial operations. Similarly, the focus of manufacturers' son's training moved away from manufacturing towards commercial aspects.

for William Arnold his social background also set him apart at many points with the experience and character of many of Northampton's successful manufacturers in the tumultuous years of change and development between 1887 and 1914. For his success grew out of a disadvantaged childhood and a working life spent not as an artisan shoemaker but one of the new generation shoe workers. And so he embarked on his business life with few of the business skills and social advantages enjoyed by many of his fellow manufacturers. His building of success was further handicapped by an early business failure; a position from which most shoe workers turned manufacturers seldom recovered.

Many accounts of Victorian and Edwardian businessmen delight in portraying a climb to success from social inequality and obscurity; in William's case, this is a true portrayal. The important social criteria commonly used by historians can be utilised here to give a sharper perspective and deeper understanding of this portrayal. These criteria can inform us about his social origins; his education; his training for work; his personal wealth; his religious affiliation; and the role he played in politics and public affairs. Each will be discussed in turn.

Table 2: Father's occupation of a sample of wholesale Northampton footwear manufacturers

Occupation	Number	%	Number	%
Artisan worker (other)	8	9.6		
Artisan worker (footwear)	4	4.8	12	14.4
Master retail shoemaker	5	6.0		
Manufacturer (footwear)	40	48.2	45	54.2
Manufacturer (other)	4	4.8		
Professional	7	8.4	11	13.2
Unknown	15	18.2	15	18.2
Unknown			83	100.0

Source: K. B. Brooker (1986).

Turning first to his social origins, as noted earlier in this introduction, William Arnold's *Autobiography* portrays him as the son of "a poor working man, a typical old fashioned English village shoemaker."[113] His social origins and childhood was humble, when compared to that of many of his fellow manufacturers of the period. When the time came to look back on their life and provide information to the press for biographical accounts and for future obituaries, it was common for any number of successful manufacturers to attest to their origins.[114] It is

113 *Autobiography* p. 90.
114 See page x, above.

commonplace to see obituaries telling of shoe manufacturers rising from "the seat", having spent their formative years in the straitened circumstances of a humble home of a working family. In reality, as is the case with Arnold, it is much rarer for this actually to be the case. When his social origin is compared with that of the occupations of the fathers of a sample of manufacturers in the Northampton industry it is clear that only 14.4% of manufacturers had fathers with manual occupations and of these only 4.8% were shoe workers (Table 2). The fathers of 67.4% of the sample enjoyed a socially more advantageous social background. The majority of these men were in their turn footwear manufacturers (48.2%) and a further 19.2% of the sample had fathers who ran companies. Note also that 53% of the sample came from families where the breadwinner was employed in the footwear industry.

But not only was his father a working man; an examination of his family background suggests that their circumstances were poor. The headline here is that hunger was a feature of life;[115] that children were required to work from a young age; and that most of them left home at around the age of 13 to fend for themselves, so that room could be made for the newly arrived. His grandmother was living in Everdon during his childhood there and she was in receipt of outdoor poor relief.

His immediate forebears hailed from Everdon, a small village in west Northamptonshire, two miles south of Daventry.[116] The village remained a focus for the Arnold family certainly during his lifetime. His father, Matthew (senior) was the first born in 1838 to William (senior) and his wife Ann.[117] Matthew was the eldest of four boys: there was also a girl of the marriage named Mary, born in 1862.[118] The family lived in a succession of small four roomed cottages in the Church Road area of the village. The Everdon Enumerators' Return for three successive censuses from 1841 names Ann as the head of the household, married

---

115 The autobiography records the extent to which food preoccupied the young William Arnold; see particularly p. 91-95.

116 *The Imperial Gazetteer of England and Wales (1870-71)* describes the village as being on a head-stream of the river Nene, 3 miles of Weedon railway station, and 4 miles from Daventry. It consisted of Great Everdon, Little Everdon, and the hamlet of Snorscomb. The manor was given, in the time of Henry VI., to Eton College, which remains patron of the church living. There was also an Independent Chapel in the village. At this time the population was 740, with inhabited 179 houses. Population had risen through the century: 1801, 111 houses and 585 inhabitants; 1811, 116/578; 1821, 122/640] and peaked later in nineteenth century at around 900 probably causing some levels of overcrowding. Farm mechanisation in the twentieth century and the decline of outwork has led to population falling to around pre-nineteenth century levels of 350.

117 William senior was born in 1803 and Ann in 1809, both at Everdon.

118 All the children were born at Everdon; Mary in 1851, two middle boys in 1842 and 1845, and Anthony in 1849: the 1841 census return also lists a daughter born in 1835. By the 1871 census, Mary is the only sibling at home and is described as "servant out of place".

to a drover's wife.[119] It is to be presumed that William's job as a drover took him from the home, leaving his wife for periods of time with the complete care and supervision of the home and their children. By the 1871 census he is named as the head. Now too old to undertake long droving journeys on foot at 68 years old, he is recorded as being a farm labourer. He died at some point within the next ten years.[120]

Matthew (senior) commenced his working life as an agricultural labourer, and then too spent time as a drover. At some time in the 1850s he became an outworking shoemaker; a job he was to keep almost until his death in 1911.[121] He married Ellen in 1860 (formerly Isham, born at Greatworth near Banbury in 1839). They lived for the rest of their lives in the village. Their first child, James William, the subject of this autobiography, was born in December 1860, the first of twelve children.[122] William Arnold notes in the *Autobiography* that he came from a large family of 14 children. The *Autobiography* attests to both crowded and straitened circumstances of home life. The family occupied at least two small four-roomed cottages that we can identify: 2 Watson's Yard, off Church Road, and a dwelling in Church Road itself. His mother played a pivotal role, not just as a homemaker, but as breadwinner and as head of the family when Matthew was absent as a drover. Clearly, his father's earnings as an outworking shoemaker were not high. The *Autobiography* suggests 16/- per week, and prevailing trade union rates suggest this was broadly accurate. Once seasonal short working and lay-offs are taken into account, despite earnings from harvest and other by-employments, money was tight. At different points in the marriage Ellen was also employed to help bolster the domestic purse as lace maker, nurse and shoe stitcher.[123] One can see several instances below in the families of William Arnold's siblings and relatives where the wife

119 1851 and the 1861 Census Enumerators' Return for Everdon. The 1841 and 1881 Return gives her occupation as a lace maker, whilst the 1871 Census Enumerators' Return for Everdon states that she was a nurse.

120 1881 Census Enumerators' Return for Everdon: Ann is still in the family home sharing it with an agricultural labourer as lodger. At 72 she gives her occupation as a lace maker.

121 Census Enumerators' Returns for Everdon 1851 to 1901: From 1861 his occupation is given as shoemaker and in 1901 as a boot maker. Tom's birth certificate of 1875 described his father as a cordwainer. At the time of his death an obituary noted that he was a director of A. & W. Arnold, but there is little to corroborate this: it is probably either inaccurate or a means of providing a written "tribute" to him. He died at his home, The Bungalow, Everdon following an illness of two years standing. He was 74 years old. He was buried in the village parish church. His brothers William and Anthony and his daughters, in addition to William Arnold's family were in attendance (N.M. 10/3/1911 p 8). It would have been unusual for an outwork shoemaker to warrant a detailed obituary save for the interest William Arnold would have generated amongst the readership.

122 Register of Births for Daventry District Oct-Dec 1860 volume 3b p. 92.

123 Both lacemaking and shoemaking gave employment opportunities. The 1841 and 1881 Census Enumerators' Return gives her occupation as a lace maker, whilst the 1871 return as a nurse. In 1861 she was recorded as a shoe stitcher.

similarly helped to boost family incomes. In contrast, it should be noted that in his own household, his wife and daughters were, significantly, not called upon to fulfil this collective role: for them there was the middle class role of community work as illustrated by Harriett Arnold's commitment to social and religious activities.

William's childhood was not spent in a nuclear family; there were several other of his extended family living in the area. Both in his family life and that of his siblings can be seen the presence of relatives residing for periods of time, maybe as a result of bereavement or of hardship.[124] In his turn, he came to rely on his grandmother as a source of affection and food as a child. As a result, William Arnold appears not to have become detached from his wider kin as his business success widened his social horizon, although some social distance inevitably arose. Throughout his life there are a number of references to his abiding attachment both to his immediate family and his relatives alike.

William Arnold informs us that the family of fourteen children made his childhood poor and their cottage home very crowded. But this assertion requires some qualification. First, his mother's entry in the 1911 Census Enumerators' Return confirms that she gave birth to twelve children, of whom ten survived infancy and one died as a young adult in 1890.[125] She had these children over a period of twenty five years, from 1860 to 1886. And secondly, it is clear that William never lived in the family home with all of his siblings in residence. By the time he left home in 1874 he had shared the cottage with four of them: the last (Matthew Anthony) having been born in 1871. His other siblings were to be born after his leaving in the years between 1874 and 1886. At various points in his early life shelter was given to child relatives, but again this was during a period when there were just two other siblings at home. In his family, there is a pattern that emerges of the children leaving the family home at around the age of thirteen in order to earn a living and make space for younger members of the family. Yet despite William Arnold's exaggeration of family living conditions, there are nevertheless clear indications of restrained circumstances. Later in life he recalled his childhood, by turns, with dismay at having to stand on his own feet at such a young age, and with pride of his ability to be able

---

124 William Arnold's mother provided a home for a nephew in the mid-century; Jane Humphries makes reference to this in her recent book. The 1851 Census Return records him as Charles Isham, her maternal nephew, who is listed as attending Matthew's funeral 1911 with his wife. At that date, the 1911 Census Enumerators' Return for Everdon finds Ellen, William Arnold's mother, residing in a six room dwelling, with a grandson Thomas, born in Everdon four years previously. Other relatives can be found as residents in other Arnold households in various Census Enumerators' Returns, which does suggest that this extended family living was not uncommon within the family.

125 This record is supported by birth and death certificate evidence.

to do so. Family ties were not broken and William Arnold recounts how for a time he comes and goes as work dictates before making the final break. But clearly a limited income and a growing family precluded Matthew (senior) from helping them materially once they were able to work. It should, of course, be remembered that this experience was a common pattern in large rural families of the time. Children leaving home to find work often migrated to local towns where they found resident members of their extended family were able to provide lodging and help with finding employment. In William Arnold's case, he was able to seek the help of his uncles Anthony and William at various points in his early years in Northampton. Nevertheless, he was asked at an early age to deal with the realities of adult life and of his position in the social world of the town.

From what we know about his siblings and past generations of his family, William was to break the family mould. And whilst he found himself moving in very different social circles and enjoying a higher level of well-being, they remained in the more restrictive world of working people: a world that was rapidly changing for many of them through migration and lives spent in employment largely in Northampton's new footwear factories. It is instructive, therefore, to lay out a short biographical sketch of his siblings that can be used as a reflective aide memoire when later dealing with his adult world:

Ann was the second born, in late 1862,[126] and left home in the late 1870s[127] probably for a life of domestic service: there is no record of a marriage. She registers her brother Signor's death in 1881 and this may suggest that she still lived locally.

Henry, born two years later in 1864,[128] lived at home and, like Ann, left in the late 1870s to make his own way in the world.[129] He did not marry. He remained in the Everdon area and worked variously as a general and bricklayer's labourer: at the time of his death as an agricultural labourer. He died on 25th November 1890 aged 26.[130] The cause of death was phthisis haemoptysis. Henry, in effect, was suffering from pulmonary phthisis and this gave rise to haemo-ptysis[131], a common symptom of the disease. Many haemoptysis symptoms were treatable at this time using a prescription of rest, ice,

126 Birth Register Daventry District volume 3b page 89.
127 Census Enumerators' Return for Everdon 1871 and 1881.
128 Birth Register Daventry District volume 3b page 93.
129 Census Enumerators' Return for Everdon 1871 and 1881.
130 Death Register for Daventry District 1890 volume 3b page 70, and Death Certificate.
131 The expectoration of blood from the respiratory tract due usually to a haemorrhage of the mucous membrane of the lungs.

and good diet. Given Henry's social position, the application of such treatment would have been remote. However, the underlying phthisis, though treatable today, was often fatal in the Victorian period. And so if he had survived the haemoptysis his prognosis was not good. The disease came in two forms: phthisis miliaris and phthisis pulmonalis (better known as TB or consumption). This is commonly regarded as disease of poverty.

Albert was born in early 1867[132] and lived in the family home until the mid-1880s.[133] Initially a farm labourer at Everdon,[134] he spent the greater part of his life in the footwear industry, first as a shoemaker and later a boot machinist at Kettering and Northampton. He married at Kettering and raised a large family of eleven.[135] He died early in 1950 at Northampton aged 83.[136] Effects £260/16/9d.

Matthew Anthony was born four years after Albert in 1871.[137] He lived at home until the late 1880s[138] when, like so many of the family he made his way to Northampton, where he spent his working life. He married Amelia Jeanetta Thomason there in 1890.[139] They raised a family, who joined him in the footwear industry. Like Albert and so many other men, he made the transition from being an outwork

132 Birth Register for Daventry District 1867 volume 3b page 646.
133 Census Enumerators' Return for Everdon 1871 and 1881.
134 *Ibid*.
135 **Albert Arnold** married Eliza James in 1887 (Marriage Register for Kettering District volume 3b page 302). She was born in 1866 at Stow Longa Huntingdonshire. In 1891 they were living at 11 Cobden Street Kettering: his occupation is given as a shoemaker. They had two daughters, aged 2 and 1, and a son aged 2 months (1891 Census Enumerators' Return for Kettering 1891). In about 1894, they had moved to a terraced house in the shoe worker residential area north of the Northampton town centre at 29 Henry Street. Change in the industry is reflected in his occupation as a boot machinist. The family in the care of Eliza had grown to eight children: three were born in Kettering, now aged 12 (a half time domestic servant), 11 and 10; two in Everdon, aged 6 and 5; and the remaining three in Northampton, aged 7, 2, and 10 months (Census Enumerators' Return for Northampton 1901). Ten years later again, finds them still at Northampton. Now in early middle age, Albert was a welt sewer; a shoe operative position, producing some welcome additional income for his wife and their surviving 11 children – two infant deaths had occurred – to crowd their six roomed house at 20 Perry Street. The two eldest girls had left (one was a shoe worker, the other a dressmaker). Of the eldest children at home, a daughter was a dressmaker, the eldest son a boot stitcher, and the other two shoe machinists (Census Enumerators' Return for Northampton 1911). Later in life the family home was at 85 Stimpson Avenue Northampton, where he died on 23/3/1950. Probate was granted to Jessie Brown and his effects were valued at £260/16/9d.
136 Death Register Northampton District Volume 3b p. 646.
137 Birth Register Daventry District volume 3b p. 95.
138 Census Enumerators' Return for Everdon 1881 and 1891.
139 Marriage Register Northampton District 1890 volume 3b p. 137.

boot maker to a factory welt sewer.[140] He died in the town in late 1942.[141] Effects £72/8/8d.

Mary Rebecca was born in January 1873.[142] She died in infancy.

Abigail was also born in 1873/4. It is feasible that she was Mary's twin but the Birth Register recording Mary's birth does not contain Abigail's entry of birth.[143] But she does appear in the family's 1881 census return, but not after; so again it is to be presumed that she leaves home, probably in the late 1880s to make her way in life.

Tom Austin was born in 1875 and lived in the family home until around 1890. Initially a shoe riveter at Everdon, he spent the greater part of his life as a factory boot machine operator living in Kingsthorpe. In 1899 he married Annie, born in 1878 at Melton Mowbray, and had one child.[144] He died at Northampton aged 72 in December 1947. No probate was granted.

Signor Austin was born in 1877 and died on 9/3/1881 following what the death certificate describes as a "rubelola collapse." Rubeola is viral illness, a form of measles, characterised by a rash. Signor would probably have been ill for eight to ten days before his death.

Flora born in 1880, lived at home until the mid-1890s.[145] We are

---

140 **Matthew Anthony** was born in Everdon in 1871 (Birth Register Daventry District 1871 vol. 3b p. 107). By the late 1880s he had migrated to Northampton to become a shoemaker. He married Amelia Elizabeth (born 1871 at Everdon) in 1891. In the early 1890s they lived in Northampton at 18 Grove Road: there were two boarders from their home village (Census Enumerators' Return Northampton 1891). Like Albert, he was a shoemaker and in the late 1890s moved back to Everdon, where he worked as a boot maker "on his own account"; they lived at Long Row Everdon (Census Enumerators' Return 1901). But within a few years, in the face of declining work for shoemakers, he went back to Northampton where he worked as a welting machine operator. There they lived at Whitworth Road – a six roomed house – with their three children: one girl and two boys (Census Enumerators' Return 1911). Later they were to live at 73 Ashburnham Road Northampton. He died at Northampton General Hospital on 18/12/1942. Probate was granted to his widow on 11/09/1943 to his widow. His effects were £72/8/8d.

141 Death Register Northampton District 1942 volume 5b p. 85.

142 Birth Certificate.

143 Birth Register Daventry District volume 3b p. 108.

144 **Tom Austin Arnold** was born at Everdon in 1875, where he was initially employed as a riveter (Census Enumerators' Return for Everdon for 1881 and for Kettering 1891). Later he migrated to Northampton, where he was employed as a footwear factory worker throughout his life; he lived at Hill Top Boughton Road Kingsthorpe Northampton (Census Enumerators' Return Kingsthorpe 1911). He married in 1899 (Marriage Register Northampton District 1899 Vol. 5c p. 67). There was one child, Alexander L., born in 1905 (Birth Register Northampton District 1905 vol. 5c, p. 171). He died at Northampton in 1947 (Death Register Northampton District 1947 vol. 3b p. 532).

145 Census Enumerators' Return Everdon 1891 and 1901.

unsure of her movements at this stage, but she probably migrated to Northampton, where she may have entered domestic service. She married Thomas Frederick Kemp in late 1906 at Northampton. Thomas was a G.P.O. Electrician and was born in 1881. In the early years of their marriage they lived at East Dulwich, London.[146]

Sarah was born in 1883, two years after Flora and like her left home in her mid-teenage years.[147] She probably joined her sister, Flora, in Northampton, where she is recorded as being her brother's, William Arnold, in-door domestic servant in 1911.[148] She married later that year.

James, the last child of Matthew and Sarah, was born like the rest of the family at Everdon in 1886 and he left home sometime in the 1900s. Initially a boot riveter at Everdon, and later a machine operator at Northampton. He married Annie Birt in 1907 and there was at least one child of the marriage. Early in the marriage they lived at 53 Palmerston Road, Northampton.[149] No probate will has been located.

The second social criterion that helps to give a fuller portrait of William Arnold is education. And it is here that the social position of his childhood family is thrown in to strong relief when compared against the social study of the sample of Northampton footwear manufacturers. William Arnold's educational experience stands squarely at variance with that sample. 26.2% of the sample received an education beyond that of elementary schooling, which reflects the social advantageous position of their family. Most manufacturers in sample, 59.1%, received elementary schooling, reflecting the working–lower middle class origins of their families (Table 3). William Arnold's opportunity for education was more fractured and inferior than this. From what he reveals about his formal attendance at school this was minimal and spasmodic. Any education he received would have been of a rudimentary sort common to rural schools of the period, with instruction being punctuated by periods of absence to work in the fields at harvest and other times. Indeed, his schooling can be regarded as negligible. This places him in

146 Census Enumerators' Return Dulwich 1911.
147 Census Enumerators' Return Everdon 1891 and 1901.
148 Census Enumerators' Return Northampton 1911.
149 **James Arnold** (senior) was born in Main Street Everdon, where he initially worked as a riveter (Census Enumerators' Returns Everdon 1901). He migrated to Northampton before his marriage in 1907 (Marriage Register Northampton District 1907 vol. 3b p 90). He married Annie Birt, a milliner, born in 1887 at Northampton, Her father was Cornelius Birt (born 1860 at Northampton) a boot laster and her mother Sarah (born 1863 at Northampton) a laundress. Besides Annie, there was William Frost, Cornelius's stepson and two female servants in residence: both the servants gave laundress as their occupation, which suggests that Sarah run her on laundry business.

that category with only 8.4% of the sample whose schooling was on a par with this. Added to this, there was no structured Sunday school provision in the village at this time and so that opportunity for him to gain some literacy and numeracy skills was also closed off. It is only as an adult when he sorely needs these skills in order to function as a manufacturer does he turn to his uncle Anthony for help. At this time, he mentions in the *Autobiography* of his difficulties thus:

> ...Once, I remember, it was decided that I should do a little travelling. I did very well on several journeys. I was no writer, and while I had my book and pencil in hand, and pretended to write down the orders as my customers gave them, as a matter of fact, I was writing the order in the book of my memory only. I was careful not to let the customer see that I was only pretending to write...[150]

Table 3: Education of a sample of Northampton footwear manufacturers

Form of Education	Number	%	Number	%
"Negligible"	7	8.4	7	8.4
Elementary	49	59.1	49	59.1
Technical College Grammar School	2 9	2.4 10.8	11	13.2
Private Boarding/Tutor Public	3 1 5	3.6 1.2 6.0	9	10.8
University	2	2.4	2	2.4
Unknown	5	6.1	5	6.1
Totals			83	100.0

Source: K. B. Brooker (1986)

There are only very sparse records available to us that reveal William Arnold's adult writing skills and these show a legible though rather ungainly hand, together with rather stilted writing style.[151] It will be remembered that his *Autobiography* was ghost-written from his oral testimony and as such reinforces the view of his abiding poor writing skills throughout life. Certainly at several points in the *Autobiography* reference is made, with touching pride, to his having found employment rather than attending school, and of his ability as a child to, not just earn money, but receive high levels of earnings. The other view that surviving records gives is of the limited literacy skill of others in his family. His mother and sister, Ann, sign birth and death

150 *Autobiography* p. 115.
151 N.R.O. ZA49996, A. & W. Arnold Wholesale Boot & Shoe Manufacturer Order Book for 1907/09: hand written comments by him; Birth and Death Certificates; Census Enumerators' Return Northampton 1911.

certificates with their "X" mark during their lifetime.[152]

Rather than education, the family gave a necessary priority to the short term goal of providing income over the long term benefit of education. His *Autobiography* is certainly more voluble about his work experiences as a child than memories of the class room. Clearly the need to work was not only important to the family purse, but also provided him with real and relevant preparation for his later working life. Although lacking in education, these life experiences provided many of the insights and skills he was to bring to company management.

The third social criterion relates to the pattern of work training received by William Arnold. His time as an outwork shoe worker was spent as a riveter. Riveters were one of the new grades of process worker that emerged between 1857 and 1887, as production in the industry begun to be sub-divided. Unlike shoemakers, most of whom could make a complete shoe from cut materials, the new grades of shoe worker merely concentrated upon one process. Process working became divided as machine making in factories begun to become the norm after 1887. Shoe workers who worked with machines often received instruction from a representative from a shoe machinery company but outwork shoe workers like William Arnold would have simply learnt on the job. Apprenticeship was never used with this class of worker, and even amongst shoemakers where it had once been commonplace had by this date fallen into disuse.[153] Often where shoe workers came to the trade at an early age, as William Arnold did, they were put to work by doing ancillary tasks for an adult worker. He worked for George Osborne, a small sub-contractor who had a shoe riveting shop in Daventry: he was a sprigging boy. Once they had learnt the set of manual tasks required, it was then a case of being able to work quickly and neatly, as most were on some form of piecework payment. William Arnold makes a number of references to his dexterity and speed – the key attributes for a successful shoe worker. Later in life when he became a manufacturer, like the majority making the transition from worker to employer, he and his partners simply had to fathom out the best way to proceed: thoughtful men brought with them ideas and observations from past employments. As noted above, in William Arnold's case he also had to catch up on some basic education.

---

152 Certificates signed thus by Ellen were (i) Henry's birth in December 1864; (ii) Tom's birth in July 1875; (iii) Signor's birth in November 1877; (iv) Henry's death in November 1890; Certificate signed thus by Ann was Signor's death in March 1881.

153 Northampton Census Enumerators' Returns 1851 and 1861: There are references to apprentice shoemakers in the town living in with their master. Possibly the most prominent shoemakers still conducting this traditional form of training were Richard Turner, father of Richard and George of Turner Brothers & Hyde, and George Gibbs, father of Joseph Gibbs, who played a significant role in the Kettering Road Methodist Church (see below at page 9, above).

Table 4: Training patterns of a sample of Northampton footwear manufacturers

Mode of training	Number	%	Number	%
Operative, on the job	3	3.6		
Apprenticeship	13	15.7	16	19.3
Pupilage	42	50.7		
Apprentice Pupilage	3	3.6	45	54.3
Clerical	9	10.8		
Professional	7	8.4	16	19.2
Unknown	6	7.2	6	7.2
Totals			83	100.0

Source: K. B. Brooker (1986)

Arnold's industrial training is an experience that is at variance with that of many of his contemporaries. His acquisition of practical skills learnt from an early age at the bench stands in strong contrast, for in fact only three (3.6%) of the sample shared this experience. The majority gained formative training through either apprenticeship or pupillage (70%). This reflects the simple fact that the increasing numbers of successful manufacturers of the period were drawn from the ranks of manu- facturers' families. Those men who tried their hand at manufacturing were amongst the large proportion of infant firm owners whose ambitions ended rapidly in failure.

The fourth social criterion takes the discussion into the area of personal wealth creation. One of the bench marks of wealth which historians use to understand the life and influence of individuals is that of personal wealth left at death. Individual wills in this country are subject to a legal scrutiny process known as probate. These records help in two ways. First, they can locate levels of wealth at death for William Arnold, his partners and his family, and secondly they can provide a comparative picture of William's position in relation to his fellow manufacturers.

First, the family's wealth at death needs to be discussed. By 1915 Arnold certainly regarded himself as a man of some affluence and wealth; and like so many working men made good he could not quite believe it: "... yes, our business is prosperous. When I think of it I am astounded that the poor little village boy should reach where I am today..."[154] Some examples of the wealth at death of members of his immediate and wider family help compare his affluence (Table 5). Many of his relatives died without leaving sufficient wealth to require the seeking of a grant of probate. When those that did are viewed it will be noted that his wealth at death was greater than those who were manufacturers, and very considerably greater than those whose lives were lived as working men.

154 *Autobiography* p. 125.

Table 5: Wealth left at death by James William Arnold and select members of his family

Founder and father: • William £27,980 (£961,800)
Founder and son: • William jnr., founder and son – died 1978   • Matthew, founder and son £11,076 (£183,600)
Second generation and son: • Thomas £22,100 (£990,200)   • Alfred Walker £2,121 (£45,660)   • James junior – died 1969   • Harry no will traced
Siblings and partners: • Anthony £977 (£36,840)   • Alfred – no traceable will: as a pauper inmate in an asylum he presumably died without means   • Albert £260 (£7,310)   • Matthew Anthony £72 (£2,754)

Source: Appropriate probate registers.
Note: [1] All values are given at current value.
[2] In order to give an approximation of present day relative value, see corresponding figure in parenthesis. This has been calculated using a purchase power calculator at:
http://www.measuringworth.com/ukcompare/relativevalue.php
The outcome figure is obtained by multiplying the value by the percentage increase in the RPI from the year of probate to 2011.

Coming back to William Arnold's personal wealth, there is the interesting issue of the way he used his income in life. This can help to contextualise his wealth at death, and this can be understood in part by reflecting on the way he used disposable income for other than business purposes. There are several pointers in this direction that reveal something more about his personality. A main call on his funds would have been for the living expenses of his large family. Less has come down to us about his daughters, but they remained in the family home until marriage. Thomas, his third son, was sent to boarding school at York. Training was provided for all of his sons to enable them to take their place in business. And when William and Matthew wished to start their own business, he readily funded the project.

It is apparent that he did not forget his extended family. Nevertheless, as the firm began to prosper there was a material and social distance that would have opened between them. Both his childhood family and that of his first wife, Harriet, continued to live and remain in the social sphere of their birth.[155] There was to be no sudden social translation for parents or siblings due to William Arnold's rise as a businessman; indeed it would have been pragmatically beyond his means to help if he had wished to act in this way. What small acts of kindness he and

155 On the Arnold family see p. 47 et seq., and on the Walker family see p. 69 et seq.

Harriet showed towards them is not known. Yet there are a number of recorded instances to be found that demonstrates they offered practical assistance to relatives. It is probable that he provided the home at Everdon for his mother and father in old age,[156] as well as an annuity for his mother.[157] Likewise, he had also arranged for his uncle Anthony to retire from the firm in the late 1890s: possibly a mechanism to help move the firm forward? However, as noted elsewhere in this introduction, Harriet's parents continued to work and reside in Hunter Street, where Alfred Walker remained as an outworker in old age, presumably without funds to retire. William Arnold also provided employment for members of his family where he practically could. On two occasions, it is recorded that the family indoor domestic servant in his household was, firstly, his sister-in-law Charlotte Walker,[158] and some years later his sister Sarah Arnold.[159] Another recorded example relates to his wish to purchase land in his native village. This arose at a time of financial pressure when his sons' new firm was being established. So, using his wife's savings he purchased two orchards, a thirty-two acre farm, and, later, two adjacent cottages with attached land.[160] Of this investment he comments:

> …when we were struggling our hardest, I was conscious of an intense desire to own land in my native village. I purchased these and felt I should like to build a home and come and live out here some time or other…[161]

At the time of the publication of his life's story, he had not felt able to make a complete move to the countryside, although a country residence had been built for his wife, who was already in poor health.

156 *N.M.* 10/03/1911 p. 8, "The Bungalow" Everdon.
157 Census Enumerators' Return Daventry 1911.
158 Census Enumerators' Return Northampton 1901. But it should be noted that there is no record of such provision having been made for his wife's family, beyond this instance. His wife's parents remained in the family she left to marry, and her father worked until very close to death. His move from a mainstream job to repairing late in life suggests the need to work remained as his strength declined.
159 Census Enumerators' Return Northampton 1911.
160 He records that as he was not resident in Everdon, two of his brothers-in-law were given employment managing these lands.
161 *Autobiography* p. 113 et seq. Arnold's aspiration mirrors a pattern of social assimilation that has been common amongst men of business and commerce since at least Elizabethan times. Many historians have carefully catalogued this behaviour, though modern historical thinking places strictures on landed gentrification as part of the social evidencing of business success, part of the process that permitted their political transition – their acquiring of power. Here Arnold's aspiration is of modest proportions, amounting to the amenity value of such ownership; whereas amongst some of his contemporaries this aspiration took on a more grandiose form (see K. B. Brooker (2013) op. cit. *passim*).

Nevertheless, continued business commitments ensured the retention of a Northampton residence: at that time 56 York Road. And so he entrusted the management of his country affairs to two brothers-in-law: evidence of his desire to help all members of his family rather than a necessity.[162]

Beyond family cares and responsibilities, it is clear that William and Harriett Arnold's philanthropy and charitable giving was extensive. Something more will be said about the range and extent of their gifts made, particularly to religious causes. Additionally, they adopted her decision to give 10% of income to religious and philanthropic purposes. Contemporary references and obituaries suggest that much of these funds were directed towards the running of Kettering Road Church and the relief of poverty.

Table 6: Wealth left at death by prominent Northampton footwear manufacturers

1 Analysis of wealth left by all prominent manufacturers

Wealth categories	Number	Elite producers		Volume producers		Total wealth (£)
		No.	%	No.	%	
Wealth over £100,000	16	11	69	5	31	4,146,194
Wealth over £50,000	10	6	60	4	40	745,372
Wealth over £25,000	9	2	22	7	78	335,797
Wealth under £25,000	19	4	16	16	84	228,902
Totals	54	23	–	32	–	5,456,265

2 Analysis of wealth left at death by producer group

Category	Elite producers				Volume producers			
	1	2	3	4	1	2	3	4
Founding owners	8	37%	1,343,567	167,946	16	71%	1,303,362	81,460
Family owners	10	47%	1,698,991	169,899	13	23%	420,504	32,346
Professional Manager/Directors	5	16%	570,753	114,151	3	6%	109,093	36,364
Totals	23	100%	3,613,311		32	100%	1,832,959	

Source: Probate registry records 1880-1970.
Notes: Wealth values expressed at original value.
       [1] Sample size
       [2] Size as % of total sample
       [3] Total probate wealth for each sample (£)
       [4] Average probate wealth

162 *Autobiography* p. 124. He comments: "I don't get anything out of the farm, I can assure you, but it interests me and it gives, besides others, a living to these two men."

Secondly, we can set William's wealth at death in the context of the wealth left by his fellow prominent footwear manufacturers in Northampton. As noted above, there were 22 prominent firms in the town's industry at 1914. These firms are categorised as 7 elite firms and 15 volume production firms. The cross-generation probate records of a total of 55 leading owners of these firms have been accessed. These 55 leaders can be split into three types of owner (an owner in this context is a person who has a financial and an on-going strategic and senior operational management role within the company. Those people who hold shares or are sleeping partners have been ignored for the purpose of this exercise):

Founding owners – those who are directly identifiable as starting the company.

Family owners – those from the second and third generation owners predominate, as do men: only one woman owner is present.

Professional manager/directors – these are people who have more than a managerial role within the company. These are men who are critical "right hand" men to the current principal owner. Many become close friends and not a few inherit the firm on the death of the principal owner, where there is a lack of an immediate next generation principal from amongst the family.

Most of these concerns were privately owned family firms, but do show a tendency to migrate towards the use of professional managers, who provided increasing levels of support to both business and the interests of the family. Only a minority, however, made use of professional business directors objectively appointed as people whose broad financial and business skills could bring material advantage to the firm's future. Similarly, only a minority of these firms register as limited companies. Where this does happen, it is primarily to enable future family control and wealth holding. Very few move to a position of having a wider shareholding basis, with the attendant shareholder dividend behaviour.

Table 6 (1) and (2) reveals a concentration of wealth in the hands of 22 manufacturing, and 8 professional manager and director families – 30 families, representing 55 individuals in total – drawn from the local footwear business community in the period. A closer view of the pattern of wealth holding levels between members of elite firms and volume production firms, the following points of comparison emerge. First, 76% of all wealth at death in this sample was vested in those leaving over £100,000 and so the concentration within this small number of 30 families is actually much smaller. Just 16 individuals drawn from 8 manufacturing and 2 professional and director families are of this stature. And secondly, it will be noted that in overall terms, elite producers consistently left more wealth than the volume producers. 66.6% of all wealth at death in this sample was vested in the elite wealth holders in the sample as a group: 23 individuals in total. This leaves 33.4% of all wealth at death in this sample vested in 32 individual volume producers.

Looking more closely, it can be observed that amongst the elite, wealth was more concentrated amongst family owners than founding owners: second generation owners figuring particularly strongly. Whilst amongst volume producers, founding owners were richer at death than other family owners. The sample of professional managers and directors is small and must be treated with some caution. When it comes to William Arnold and those of his family involved in the industry, they appear amongst the less wealthy, when measured against all prominent manufacturers. Based on the wealth left by founding owners of volume production firms, William Arnold's wealth ranks considerably below that of the average amount left.

As has already been noted, not only wealth at death but patterns of income spending during a person's life can reveal something about their affluence and perception of their social position. And part of this mix, was their place of residence. From the time of his arrival right up until very near the end of century, William Arnold can be found residing in the shoe manufacturing district to the north of the town centre. This was a mixed industrial and working class residential area, where factories, workshops and terraced housing had been built cheek by jowl[163] (For illustrations of some of his homes, see Figures 11 to 17). In the early eighteen eighties, on his arrival in the town he lodged at 41 Victoria Road, with George Baker, a commercial traveller and his family, and thereafter spent time with both his uncle William and uncle Anthony at 47 Lorne Road and 109 Hunter Street. At marriage in late 1885, he initially lived with his in-laws at 78 Hunter Street, and then in quick succession moved to a house in Shakespeare Road and then to 29 Hunter Street. The early eighteen nineties, just prior to his suspension of trading, finds him and his growing family at 80 Turner Street, a slightly less cramped street, but one that was in close proximity to industrial premises. His years of business recovery after the suspension

---

163 Such mixed function urban areas were common in East Midland towns at this time: See T. H. Mawson, *County Borough of Northampton: Proposals for its Development & Reconstruction* (1925) on the mixed residential and industrial development of the Victorian town. See also, H. E. Bates' account of his childhood at Rushden and Kettering in the early chapters of his autobiography, *The Vanished World* (1969).

witnessed the beginnings of success, and this marks a social rise in the status of the family's residence. At first this is modest: in the last years of the eighteen nineties came the move to 49 Colwyn Road. Although still in the shoe workers' residential area, the house was more substantial and afforded both more room, still a priority for the continued growth in family size, and gave a residence that socially proclaimed his growing business position. Up to this point in their married life, the Arnold's homes had been within a few hundred yards of each other. Now there was a more significant move that sent a stronger statement of having arrived and of affluence. This was the acquisition of a property adjacent to Abington Park. 445 Wellingborough Road was a fourteen-room house that gave the family greater levels of middle-class comfort and social prestige. In the last years of Harriet's life, a move was made back to the town centre; to a main middle-class residential thoroughfare near to the factory; at 56 York Road. Meanwhile, a move had been made for the family to make use of Everdon. Land and a house in the country were purchased, but rather underutilised if William Arnold's comment in the *Autobiography* are to be believed. In his last years, probably after his second marriage, a move was made to Queen's Park, to 26 Kingsley Road.[164] The family's use of domestic servants dates from the time of taking up residence in Colwyn Road, and continues from that point.

Table 7: Religious affiliation of a sample of prominent Northampton manufacturers.

Religious affiliation	Number	%	Number	%
Anglican	22	26.5	22	26.5
Congregationalist	13	15.7		
Methodist	4	4.8		
Primitive Methodist	5	6.0		
Baptist	1	1.2		
Unspecified Non-Conformist	14	16.9	37	44.6
Unknown	24	28.9	24	28.9
Totals			83	100.0

Source: K. B. Brooker (1986)

From matters of personal wealth, the next and fifth social criterion shifts to questions about religious affiliation. Like 44.6% of the sample in Table 7, William Arnold publicly affirmed his affiliation to a Nonconformist denomination.[165] This compares sharply with the 26.5% of the sample

164 In William Arnold's day, Kingsley Road was a middle class suburban road in The Kingsthorpe area of the town. It was adjacent to Kingsthorpe Golf Club. The Bethany Homestead Homes that he helped to found were built in this road.
165 There was a strong membership of Nonconformist churches and chapels within the town at this period amongst both local manufacturers and workers alike.

with an Anglican affiliation. William Arnold was a Primitive Methodist, of whom there are relatively few in the sample, when compared with the Congregationalists amongst manufacturers at this time.[166] Of course declaring an affiliation and being a regular worshipper and committed Christian are quite different matters. And in the case of William we have very clear evidence of both his faith and active religious work in Northampton, both at the time when he was a manufacturer and later in his life, became a mainstay of his pattern of living.

Religious observance, however, appears to have formed little part of Arnold's childhood in other than a socially conventional way. He recalls:

> …There was no Sunday School, and no one in the whole village seemed to care a halfpenny whether the children received any religious instruction or not…The clergyman, the Vicar of Everdon, the Rev. H. Luxmoore, was also an old man, a good simple gentleman, with no aspirations except to live at peace…[167]

Nevertheless, once he had moved to Northampton as a youth, he tells us that his attendance at church became regular:

> …And then, I suppose, because it was Sunday morning, my thoughts took me to All Saints' Church, and to the earnest sermons of Canon Hull, which had so often appealed to me. I had always gone to church from my first going to Northampton, chiefly to All Saints…[168]

At this point he turned to religion to provide meaning to his life; a life that had already became centred upon his drinking habit. In Canon Robert Hull, the vicar of All Saints', William Arnold found a strong and compelling preacher who strengthened his resolve to stop drinking,

---

166 By the eighteenth century the town was a stronghold of 'respectable' Dissent, notably during the ministry of Philip Doddridge. By the mid-century, the county was visited by several prominent dissenters of the day: James Hervey; George Whitfield; and John Wesley. The first Methodist group was founded in the town in 1767 and the first chapel in 1793 at King's Head Lane. Later chapels were erected as the congregation grew and the Burland Circuit begun in 1834. In 1840 the Horsemarket Chapel followed, with another in 1880 at Kettering Road with the active support of Joseph Gibbs, boot and shoe manufacturer: the circuit was divided into two in 1886. A further chapel was built in Park Avenue in 1925.

167 *Autobiography* p. 94: Rev. Henry Luxmoore was born in 1794 and graduated B.A. from St John's College Cambridge in 1817 (M.A. 1820). He became a deacon in 1819 and priest in 1820. Vicar of Barnstaple, Devon 1820-60, and Rector of Everdon 1860-76. He died on 15 June 1876, aged 82. He married and had two sons: the youngest was Henry Elford Luxmoore, Pembroke College Oxford M.A. 1867 (H. I. Longden, *Northamptonshire & Rutland Clergy* (1940) Vol. XX p. 691.

168 *Autobiography* p. 109.

Figure 11: 41 Victoria Road, Northampton

Figure 12: 109 Hunter Street, Northampton

Figure 13: Shakespeare Road, Northampton

Figure 14: 29 Hunter Street, Northampton

Figure 15: 80 Turner Street, Northampton

Figure 16: Turner Street from Perry Street, Northampton, showing mixed housing and industrial development

Figure 17: 49 Colwyn Road

Figure 18: 445 Wellingborough Road, Northampton

Figure 19: 56 York Road, Northampton

only to find that that resolve vanished when he met drinking companions. Hull had arrived in Northampton in 1877, a young Evangelical priest, who quickly made his mark in slum missions of the town. His ardent devotion to the cause of temperance across the whole town, his keen support of the St Saviour's Refuge at Kingsthorpe, and his work for the Northampton Prison Gate Mission, all claimed his attention.[169] Indeed, William Arnold may, like many other young men of the time, have been attracted by the magnetic energy and earnestness of Hull.[170] He encouraged William Arnold to begin to address his drinking, yet, despite Hull's social conscious and the evangelical character of the parish, William Arnold was uncomfortable in what he perceived to be the distant and unfamiliar social atmosphere of this Anglican parish church. And so, he shied away from making religious commitment. He summarised his thoughts in the following way:

> …The Rev. Canon Hull's preaching made a great impression on me, and if, with the same preacher, it had been a Nonconformist place of worship instead of being a parish church, I should have been converted when I was sixteen. In most Nonconformist chapels they will take an interest in a young man, or in any stranger, but I used to

169 Rev. R. M. Sergeantson, *A History of the Church of All Saints', Northampton* (1901) p. 231-33.
170 Sergeantson *op. cit.* p. 231 "…Young men, attracted by the earnestness and lofty ideals of the new vicar, offered themselves for service in the work of the church…"

go in and out of that place for years, and nobody ever took the slightest notice of me…[171]

He clearly needed the support and fellowship of others in his attempts to lead a more orderly, religious life. Later in life, William Arnold would assert that he owed the influence of Canon Hull to his adopting abstinence. At one point he had failed to embrace the Good Templars[172] because of their ritual. Similarly, he had briefly courted with the Independent Order of Rechabites (IOR)[173], of which his Uncle Anthony was a member: it may have been through the IOR that he first made contact with Primitive Methodism[174], which was to give the moral direction and social steadiness he craved and direct his life both as a shoe manufacturer and a citizen of Northampton.

However, it was to be the support provided by his wife, Harriett, which finally enabled him to change the pattern of his life. Elizabeth Harriett Walker was born at Northampton in 1860 into a shoe workers' family. Her father was Alfred Walker, a boot fitter, who was born in 1833 at Alfred's Place, St Sepulchre's Northampton.[175] Her mother was Elizabeth Harriett, born at Thrapston, Northamptonshire in 1832. She too became a shoe fitter once her children had grown. There were at least seven children of the marriage.[176] The family lived in the shoe district to the north of the town in a number of terraced houses whilst the children were growing: Bailiff Street, 1 Deal Street, and 31 Craven Street. They finally settled at 78 Hunter Street, where both Alfred and his wife died; he in 1918, she in 1904. Her sister Charlotte remained single, staying in the family home to look after the couple as they aged.[177] Alfred probably remained an outworker all of his working life. Later in life he became a shoe repairer working from home.

---

171 *Autobiography* p. 109.
172 The Independent Order of Good Templars was founded in 1851, founded in U.S.A. by Daniel Cady. The organisation had spread to Britain by 1868. It was a fraternal society for teetotallers and its meetings and structure was based on ritual and regalia.
173 The Independent Order of Rechabites was a friendly society founded in 1835. It was a wider British temperance organisation to promote total abstinence for the use of alcoholic drinks. It gradually transformed into a benefit society promoting abstinence. It spread to Australia and the United States, and still exists today.
174 The early temperance movement was strongly associated with religious sects like the Primitive Methodists. Primitive Methodism was particularly strongly associated with Rechabitism.
175 Alfred's mother, Sarah Walker, was born at Spratton Northamptonshire in 1797. She was living with the family at the time of Harriet's birth and is described as "of independent means."
176 A son Alfred (born 1861) who became a carpenter; Sarah Ann (born 1856); Emma (born 1866); Annie (born 1868); Louise (born 1868); and Charlotte born 1872). All of the daughters worked as shoe machinists during their early years.
177 Charlotte is recorded as a domestic servant for her sister Harriet and husband William Arnold at 49 Colwyn Road Northampton: Census Enumerators' Return Northampton 1901.

By the time that she and William Arnold met, Harriett was already a conviction Christian, who gave 10% of her annual income to the church. It is not known if her family were religious or whether Harriett came to faith outside of the home. Her presence in William Arnold's life gave him the stability required to finally commit to abstinence. After a short courtship they married at St Michael's Church in late 1885.[178] Together, they both now searched for a suitable place of worship and fellowship. This search lasted over a period of about ten years and led them to spend time in the congregations of several of Northampton's denominations. In the *Autobiography* he names the Princes' Street Baptist Chapel,[179] the Doddridge Congregational Church,[180] and the new Salvation Army Barracks in Gold Street.

The last named became a place of worship for them for a number of years prior to their final commitment to the Kettering Road Primitive Methodist Church. At the time his firm suspended trading in 1892 he chanced to witness a case of animal cruelty outside this Church and this became the catalyst to exploring the Church itself. From this chance beginning, he and Harriet were to quickly become influential workers for this chapel. The 1927 Jubilee Celebration book described their position in the following words:

> …It was during Mr Parkin's ministry that Mr J. W. Arnold, who was to become one of the future pillars of the Church, joined Kettering Road Church…[181]

The Rev Parkin, together with the two succeeding ministers at the church, Rev Henry J. Pickett and Rev James H. Saxton, provided William Arnold with the religious home that he had been looking for over a number of years. When one takes into account his reaction to the social atmosphere of All Saints' and particularly his choice of the muscular Christianity of the Salvation Army and the working class focus of the Army's missionary work at this time, it is interesting to reflect not only upon their working social backgrounds, but also upon the powerful and direct ministry of these three men, which did so much

---

178 Marriage Register Northampton District vol. 3b p 160: The reason for this choice of church is not known and could have been that they automatically used their parish church, rather than use the chapel they were currently attending.
179 Formerly the Mount Zion Baptist Chapel.
180 Doddridge Congregational Church (now the Castle Hill United Reformed Church) in Doddridge Street, Northampton, was the scene of the ministry of Doddridge from 1729-51. The church was founded in 1662, built in 1695 and enlarged 1842. Of the then incumbent Arnold notes: "The Rev. J. J. Cooper, who was there then, did me a lot of good, but it was such a long way from Hunter Street".
181 T. W. Britten, *Ventures of Faith, the Story of the Kettering Road Primitive Methodist Church Northampton* (1927) p. 13, (Figure 21).

to cement and continue to extent the influence of Nonconformity amongst working people in the town. All three came from working backgrounds and had life experiences that would have resonated strongly with William Arnold; a man who although ambitious was still culturally rooted in his social world of his birth cultural background. For him, his sense of identity was something to embrace rather than conceal.[182] They were in turn not only to become spiritual guides but also friends and men he worked with in the wider interests of Primitive Methodism and the church in Kettering Road. Indeed, one of the Rev Saxton's daughter's was to marry into the Arnold family.

But before passing on to look at his religious work and influence in the Methodist cause, it is interesting to note the possible influence of Joseph Gibbs[183] (see Figure 21). Earlier in this introduction it was noted that Gibbs was one of the manufacturers that William Arnold worked for when he first came to Northampton in the late 1870s. He was a committed Primitive Methodist and one the key influencers behind the early development of the Kettering Road church. Whether Gibbs acted as a spur and role model to William Arnold in his early search for religion is not known. But certainly for him to find Gibbs active in the church, and indeed in company of other footwear manufacturers,[184] would have surely only served to encourage the Arnolds' commitment to this church? Gibbs' family were committed Primitive Methodists from the early days of the denomination's presence in the town. His father George was greatly influenced by the Primitive Methodists first visit there in 1839.

He quickly became a class leader and a local preacher and his children attended the first Primitive Methodist Sunday School in Northampton. It has been noted that George's "...house was a hospitable home for both itinerant and local preachers..."[185] Indeed, the 1851 Northampton Census Return records that the family home at 3 Mount Street was being shared by three lodgers: John Davey, aged 51, a Primitive Methodist minister and two shoemakers. As an adult, Gibbs emulated his father's role in the denomination. He acted as the circuit steward of the Northampton second circuit. He was the chairman of the Metropolitan Missionary Meeting in 1884, and also joint district treasurer, with Sir William Hartley, for the Connexional Orphanage. Towards the end of

---

182 For brief biographies of Rev. G. Parkin, Rev. Henry J. Pickett and Rev. James H. Saxton, see below, p. 132-33.

183 For his life and manufacturing activities, see p. 9.

184 It should also not be lost to sight that several other footwear manufacturers were heavily committed to the work of the Kettering Road Church, including Thomas Singlehurst. Thomas Britten, his brother in law, was the author of the book is Gibbs successor in his firm.

185 Geoff Dickinson, http://www.myprimitivemethodists.org.uk/page_id_1295_path.aspx

Figure 20: Kettering Road Primitive Methodist Church *c.* 1900

Figure 21: Joseph Gibbs

Figure 22: Park Avenue Church 2013

Figure 23: Rev. H. J. Pickett   **Figure 24:** Rev. J. H. Saxton

Figure 25: Elizabeth Harriett Arnold (*c.* 1915)

his life Joseph travelled to the United States as a Primitive Methodist delegate to the Methodist Ecumenical Conference in Washington in 1891.[186] But above all his lasting contribution was as the benefactor and driving force behind the development of the Kettering Road Church from the 1860s up to the time of his death: the jubilee book of the church fulsomely outlines that contribution.[187]

Following Gibb's death in 1893, William Arnold's involvement and influence in the church begun to flourish. It has already been noted that he was not a publicly prominent figure, but rather used his business organisation skills to render service behind the scenes. Also, he and his wife used their purse to ease the financial affairs of the church. An assessment of Harriett made after her death catches the essence of their quiet, thoughtful work for her fellow man and woman:

> …Mrs Harriett Arnold…was a mother of Israel. She encouraged her husband in all those admirable works that have characterised [their lives]. Like Dorcas she was full of good works and alms deeds. Given to hospitality, the prophets of the Lord found shelter and comfort

186 Dickinson *op. cit.*
187 Britten *op. cit.* p. 11. He was a trustee for the acquisition of land and development of the church. Over a period of twenty years he was provide much needed financial underpinning for this and other religious activities.

beneath her roof. [At her death] the Church lost a devout and ardent worker and the poor a friend...[188]

This sense of helping others and their religious feeling developed within them a belief in systematic charitable giving and philanthropy. What can also be detected in his life away from business is the development of voluntary public service in local chapel circles:

> ...They soon made use of me at Grove Road chapel.[189] I have been honoured by the church as a trustee, society steward, and class leader. But I am no public speaker; my efforts are not in that direction. We help in other ways. My dear wife, since she was twenty-one years old, has had a system of giving one-tenth away. I have done the same regarding my income, but frequently overstep the mark. I believe that our giving has been as important as anything that has gone to make up our lives. I firmly believe in the grace of giving...[190]

Probably the most prominent of his activities was the founding of a private trust, the local Bethany Homestead in 1925-29. This was a local scheme involving Baptists and Congregationalists and is today seen as a forerunner of palliative care for the elderly.[191] William Arnold and another local businessman, Charles J. Pearce, provided ten of the twenty seven cottages for elderly Methodists within the wider scheme. This sheltered home development anticipated the work of the national Methodist Homes Association of the 1940s. The essence of the Northampton scheme was to provide a complex of twenty seven individual sheltered homes, together with a nursing home and social facilities. The initial capital cost was £30,000, with an annual maintenance cost of £4,000. The nursing home was never self-funding and required annual donations. The 30-40 residents paid affordable fees for their upkeep.[192]

An earlier example of his giving was in 1917, when William Arnold acted as one of the trustees for "...arrangements for the (Northampton) Sunday School Union to have a country house as a rest, holiday or convalescent home for the teachers and scholars..."[193] This was an inter-denominational venture and amongst the ten trustees were six footwear

---

188 Britten *op. cit.* p. 24, see Figure 27.
189 The Kettering Road Church stands at the junction of Kettering Road and Grove Road. William Arnold is probably using the local vernacular name for the church.
190 *Autobiography* p. 121.
191 *N.P.L. NPTN362.61, 75th Annual Report of the Bethany Homestead Northampton* (2001).
192 This paragraph draws on R. L. Thompson "Bethany Homestead Northampton" *Congregational Quarterly* XXIV No 2, April 1946.
193 N.R.O ZA9999, Agreement between the Trustees and Mary Beattie for the purchase of Shuthanger, Bruerine, Northamptonshire.

manufacturers, including William Arnold jnr. The cost of the purchase price and conversion exceeded £6,000, and the trustees continued to oversee the management of the venture.

T. W. Britten summed up his many contributions in the following way:

> …J. W. Arnold is deeply conscious of his debt to Primitive Methodism. He acknowledged that next to the Grace of God he owed most to the Kettering Road Church. From humble beginnings he has become one of the leading boot manufacturers at Northampton. Holding this as a stewardship he has been princely in his generosity. Since he joined the church he has been Society Steward, Class Leader, and one of the Circuit Stewards. A fitting reward of his magnificent service to the Church was his election to Vice Presidency of Conference…[194]

And that munificence was most clearly seen in his practical and above all his financial support in the building of the Park Avenue Methodist Church, Northampton. This was intended by him and his family as a memorial to Harriett, who had died in March 1921[195] (see Figure 22). The Arnold family met about a half of the £18,000 building and commissioning costs. In recognition, the Church and Schools were opened in September 1925 by William Arnold. Some years earlier he and C. J. Pearce had paid off the debt owing for the building of the Kettering Road Church, which had weighed heavily on the congregation for some years. A local reporter witnessed the scene and wrote: "…there was a dramatic climax when Mr Arnold applied a match to the mortgage deeds from the platform followed by the congregation singing *Praise God from who all blessings flow*…"[196] Shortly after he gave £1,500 for a new organ.[197]

But Arnold's influence within the denomination went beyond his activities in Northampton. He became active in Primitive Methodist

194 T.W. Britten *op. cit.* p. 23-4.
195 **Elizabeth Harriett Arnold** died on 11/3/1921 at the family home, 56 York Road Northampton, following a protracted illness: she had suffered from arteriosclerosis for some years, but the immediate cause of death was a stroke. Probate was granted at London on 23/2/1922 to her executors, George Francis Sharpen and Frederick William Sharpen licensed victuallers. Effects £3,075/8/0d: N.I. 19/3/1921 "…After an illness lasting several years Mrs W. Arnold passed away on Friday aged 60. The deceased like other members of the family was a devoted worker of the Kettering Road Primitive Methodist Church, where the funeral service took place…amid signs of sorrow…[the service was] conducted by Rev H. J. Pickett…"
196 *N.I.* 10/8/1945 p. 6. The building cost £4,000 and was built between 1878 and 1880, when it was opened. Payment of the interest part of the loan had been met, but this left much of the capital to be paid off.
197 *Ibid.*

affairs nationally. He attended the Annual Conference and in 1927[198] he was elected Vice-President of Conference for that year: the senior post for the laity within the denomination.[199] He had already been involved for some years in some of the many schemes initiated by Sir William Hartley to promote and extend the well-being of Primitive Methodism. For example, in 1917 the Preachers Friendly Society ran into financial problems and at the instigation of Sir William it was resolved to appoint a committee to provide an improvement fund.

> …The Conference decided that a committee of laymen should be appointed to raise a fund of £60,000. Some of the leading laymen in the denomination – Sir Thomas Robinson, Mr William Arnold, Mr Moses Bourne, Mr Joseph Longsta – gave themselves without stint to the task of advocating the claims of the Fund…[200]

His Vice-Presidency of the Conference in 1927 was marked by his launching a fund to supplement the then scanty stipends of superannuated ministers.

Thus, his religious belief informed both his business behaviour and wider social life. In business life this belief gave him great resilience and focus in his conduct of business matters and high levels of honesty and probity. Socially, he grew more aware of the needs of the community, and the many acts of philanthropy of both him and his wife attracted wide public esteem.

The sixth and final social criterion in this social portrait is his role he played in politics and public affairs. Historically dissent and Liberal and radical politics, with its ideals of personal freedom and independence of action, had been closely linked. This can be clearly seen in North-ampton's history. Indeed, amongst nineteenth-century contemporaries the town's shoemakers enjoyed a reputation for their extreme radicalism. Biographical evidence of prominent manufacturers clearly demonstrates that many played important leadership roles in both the town's dissenting chapels and in liberal politics in the council

198 See *N.I. op. cit.* p. 2 "…(he) shed a lasting lustre upon his name by being elected to the highest national honour that the Primitive Methodist Connexion can confer…"

199 The other Northampton manufacturer to hold the Vice Presidency in this period was Charles Lewis, of C. & E. Lewis, a member of the elite. He was connected with the Horsemarket Chapel, which operated in the No. 1 Circuit. He held the post in 1918.

200 A. S. Peake, *Life of Sir William Hartley* (1926) p. 86-7. It should be noted that three successive ministers from Kettering Road Chapel between 1898 and 1916 became principals of Hartley College: Rev. G. Parkin, Rev. H. J. Pickett, and Rev. J. H. Saxton. It is probable that this played some part in William Arnold's increasing prominence in the denomination's national deliberations.

chamber.[201] Clearly William Arnold's religious belief and work was very centrally located within dissent. The public esteem he attracted was in no small way related to this religious work and unselfish philanthropy and charitable giving that sprung from it. This in no small part was the measure of the man. However, at first sight he was not a man of public affairs and political intrigue.

Table 8: Public life: political and social association activities of prominent Northampton manfacturers

Name	Industry activities	Political activities	Wider roles	Community organisations	Religious activities	Cultural & Sporting
34 Elite producers	24: 70%	19: 56%	7: 21%	14: 41%	10: 29%	17: 50%
29 Volume producers	21: 72%	5: 17%	1: 3%	6: 20%	10: 35%	10: 35%
63 Elite producers	45: 71%	24: 38%	8: 13%	20: 32%	20: 32%	27: 43%

Source: K. B. Brooker (1986: modified. This analysis of political and social association activities of prominent Northampton manufacturers has been specifically prepared for this introduction.)

Notes:
- **Industry activities:** directorships in other industrial or commercial concerns; trade bodies
- **Political activities:** District Councillor; Mayor; Borough JP; School Board; PL Guardian; participation in local political organisations
- **Wider roles:** MP; County Councillor; County JP; Deputy Lieutenant; High Sheriff
- **Community organisations:** leading role in philanthropic; Friendly Society; Building Society; Temperance; Hospital Charity; Volunteer/TA; and other organisations
- **Religious activities:** identified attendance at services and a role in a local church or chapel, and wider religious affairs
- **Cultural & Sporting:** prominent memberships of and/or leading role in cultural societies and clubs; sporting organisations; and Rotarian or Freemason

From the prominence of business success and wealth many Victorian and early twentieth century businessmen took a leading role in trade, political and social association activities within their town or city. The narrative of this activity suggests there were a number of reasons why they became "pillars within their own communities." Some of these reasons sprung from a sense of public duty and service of voluntary activity. There was a public expectation that those with wealth and position should give both of their time and money in the interest of their community. As such, participation in local public affairs and activities became a logical extension of their position as businessmen. And as

201 Sir Moses Philip Manfield, a Liberal, and Sir Henry E. Randall, a conservative, were leading figures and have been mentioned elsewhere in this introduction. Another important Liberal figure was George Minards Tebbutt who established his business in 1872. He was born in the town in 1839, the son of Thomas, a manufacturer and prominent in local affairs. George was prominent in local affairs for many years, serving as a councillor, J.P., a member of the School Board and of many other committees. As a young man he was an early member of the Northampton Radical Association, but later came to be regarded as a Nonconformist and Liberal of the old school. He challenged the boisterous radicalism of those later years. He was also senior deacon of the College Street Baptist Chapel and an influential member of the local Manufacturers' Association. At his death in 1923, his effects were valued at £40,309.

leaders of economic importance within their community, businessmen were sought as providers, supporters and patrons of local social and cultural activities. They not only lent weight and prestige to these activities, but also provided much needed finance and organisation, thus bringing their business skills to bear upon community activities and affairs. But, in addition to these motivations, there was self-interest; for participation in local community activities served also to legitimise their business success. Additionally, for some, their participation was enlivened by a personal interest and ability to act.

Turning to the political and social association activities of the sample of prominent Northampton manufacturers, it can be demonstrated that both elite producers and volume producers took an interest in industry activities. These activities were most strongly in their immediate economic interest and thus prominent manufacturers generally were seen to be active in the local Manufacturers' Association and the range of other trade bodies of the period. The highest community participation rates are seen in this category: a role in managing the interests of the industry, both locally and nationally, inevitably fell to these men (Table 8). But when the focus is shifted to participation in local, county and national political and other ceremonial roles the elite manufacturers are more heavily represented. Similarly, when roles within community organisations are examined it is again found that elite manufacturers are more heavily represented. It is only when manufacturers' participation in religious activities are viewed that volume producers are seen to have a slightly more prominent involvement.

William Arnold's apparent shunning of public speaking and of being in the limelight, together with the efforts required by him to turn the company around after the 1892 suspension of trading, were probably sufficient reasons why he did not seek public political office before he was an older man. There is little in the written record of him involving himself formally and openly in the political life of the town until late in his life, although he had interested himself in political matters generally and been a member of the Liberal cause for a number of years. At the age of 66 he was first elected to the town council and served two terms in office before retiring from the council aged 75. No other public preferment came his way – whether this was due to age, personal inclination, the judgment of others about his public skills is not readily understood. His obituary merely notes:

> …A liberal of the old school in politics, Mr Arnold represented the Abington Ward…from 1926 to 1930 and was later returned for St George's Ward. He retired from the Council in 1935…[202]

202 *N.I.* 10/8/1945 p. 6.

The late political blossoming of William Arnold may have been linked to the declining fortunes of the Liberal Party in the town in the face of the rise of Labour Party interests in the inter-war period.[203] Was he asked to take a more active role by the Liberal Party locally because of the public regard and respect for him as a working man turned successful manufacturer?

The inter-war years were an important turning point in the history of Northampton's local governance. For many years previously local Liberal and Conservative interests had been to the fore. In the late nineteenth century the town had become noted politically as a staunch radical liberal place. Local support for Bradlaugh's fight to represent the town in Parliament has become too well known to require detailed mention here.[204] At this time Liberals dominated the council chamber, and drew councillors from the ranks of footwear manufacturers, as well as local trades and professions. The party's founding of the North-ampton Freehold Land Association in the late eighteen sixties had helped to cement this Liberal ascendancy by giving local people an opportunity to own their own homes. The prominent late nineteenth figure was, of course, M. P. Manfield, who played an influential political role in both town and county Liberal affairs and electoral success. He represented the town in Parliament and served in the local council chamber and magistrate's bench. But he was conscious of the working class nature of the town, although held in high regard in his last years "…his brand of unevenly radical Liberalism was being undercut by the growth of a local socialist movement which was critical of the role of local employers as a class…"[205]

And, as happened in so many other towns and cities in the country, it was the political interests of working communities, together with the rise of organised working people in local and later national politics, that was to bring about a steady Liberal decline in the first half of the twentieth century: the last Northampton Liberal M.P. lost his seat in 1923. Locally, the rise of Labour from 1880 was driven by shoemakers and other organised labour interests, and by the continued inability of the moderate and radical wings of the local Liberal Party to find an accommodation, which compromised their success. This resulted in the formation of a progressive party which gained ascendancy. This was made up of radical liberals, and the emergence of a very active, though

203 See M. Dickie "Town Patriotism and the Rise of Labour: Northampton 1918-1939" (unpublished PhD thesis, Warwick University (1987)) chapter 4.
204 On Bradlaugh and Northampton see E. Royle, "Charles Bradlaugh, Freethought and Northampton" *N.P.P.* Vol. VI. 3 (1980) p 141-50; W.W. Hadley "Bradlaugh & Labouchere" *N.P.P.* Vol. II, No. 6, (1959).
205 M. Haynes "Sir Philip Moses Manfield (1819-1899)" O.D.N.B. (2004) Vol. 36, p. 409.

numerically small, local branch of the Social Democratic Federation under the dynamic leadership of James Gribble.[206] Through these agencies, numbers of working people were voted onto elected bodies: the local Poor Law Guardians and the Northampton School Board, as well as the Town Council.[207] Much of this success had been driven by the increase of popular support for the SDF in the wake of the changes in workplace place conditions, the result of the changes brought about by N.U.B.S.O.'s failure in the 1895 dispute and the effect of worsening trading conditions on take home pay. The inter-war period saw a gradual emergence of the Labour Party at the expense of Liberal power. In the early 1930s local Liberals and Conservatives formed a pact to stop the advance of Labour interests but by the eve of the Second World War this had proved to be more a delaying rather than preventative strategy.[208] Another prominent footwear manufacturer who served on the town council at the same time as William Arnold was William Barratt. Barratt sat as a Labour Party member. He had been a pre-war member of the local SDF and strong supporter of James Gribble and the local Pioneer Cooperative Boot Society Ltd. The society espoused Barratt's concept of boot by post. He served as a Town Councillor, at the same time as William Arnold, but resigned in protest against the unbusinesslike character of local government.[209]

Beyond these activities, William Arnold took no recorded role in the wider range of cultural and social organisations in the town, beyond what has been discussed above of his considerable role in local Nonconformity. It is tempting to speculate that here was a businessman too focused on his business activities to spend his leisure time in this manner.

206 James Gribble (1868-1934) was a committed trade unionist and socialist and remained a tireless worker in working people's interests for over thirty years. He helped launch the local SDF paper, The Northampton Pioneer, and managed one of two cooperative production societies in Northampton early in the twentieth century. On Gribble see K. B. Brooker (i) "James Gribble, 1868-1934" *Dictionary of Labour Biography* (1982) Vol. 7 p. 99-103; (ii) "James Gribble & the Raunds Strike of 1905" *N.P.P.* (1982) Vol. VI No. 5. An outline of the formation of socialist support in the town through the small SDF branch there, see M. Dickie, "Liberals, Radicals and Socialists in Northampton before the Great War" *N.P.P.* VII:1 (1983-84) p. 51-4; and P. A. Watmough, "The Membership of the Social Democratic Federation, 1885-1902", *Bulletin of the Society for the Study of Labour History*, No. 34 (1977), p. 35-40.

207 E. L. Poulton helped to found the local Trades Council and became the first working man to become the town's mayor in 1906. Poulton was a trade union moderate and pragmatic Liberal. On him, see Standish Meacham, *A Life Apart* (1977) p. 147 and 212, & D. Howell, *British Workers and the Independent Labour Party* (1983) p. 101, 418.

208 On the rise of the Labour Party to power in the local council chamber from the Great War see M. Dickie (1987) *op. cit. passim*.

209 K. B. Brooker, "Arthur William Barratt", *D.B.B.* (1985) Vol. 1 p 184 -188: see also M Haynes "(Arthur) William Barratt (1877-1939)", *D.N.B.* (2004) Vol. 4 p 33-4.

Conclusion

James William Arnold, boot manufacturer, died 2 August 1945 at his home 26 Kingsley Road, Northampton; his wife Mrs S. B. Arnold was at his bedside. A diagnosis of cancer of the liver and stomach had been given only a short while before. Aged 84, he died as he had lived from the age of six, scaring crows, focused on his work. His obituary noted:

> "…his constitution was as sturdy as his character, for, up to a month ago he went every day to his factory as usual…"[210]

Thus, although he became well known in the town for his religious activity, he was esteemed at large in the town as a working man made good, and probably less so for his political activities in later life. His background and mercurial personality did not lend itself to a sustained prominence in the world of public debating and diplomacy. As we have seen, his active public life was carried out behind the cloak of religious service and charitable giving. A self-made man, he was equally driven by a degree of material aspiration; the need to insulate his family and himself from the fear of poverty.[211] Arnold's working class roots give him a different set of goals and horizon from someone whose entry to business is from a business family like so many prominent shoe manufacturers at this time.

At the beginning of this introduction a series of questions were asked about the typicality of William Arnold's experiences when set against Northampton footwear manufacturers generally. To what extent are his recollections merely a fascinating insight into the life of an individual late Victorian wholesale manufacturer, and to what extent can it be regarded as an accurate portrait of this class of manufacturer? Of course, to provide a fully documented comparison has been outside the scope and length of an introduction of this kind, but it has been possible to place William Arnold in the context of his time. In terms of his business activities, he must rank as one of the new breed of successful volume producers, who used modern factory production techniques to help place Northampton as one of the leading centres for the wholesale manufacture of footwear. His success at the level of his firm was the more remarkable because he started business life as a shoe worker with few business advantages, and he was able to recover from an early suspension of trading.

Shifting the perspective away from business, it has been argued here

---

210 *N.I.* 10/8/1945 p. 2.

211 See p. 47 et seq., where his provision for relatives is discussed. However, Harriett's parents do not appear to have been assisted in the same way.

that the portrayal of his life as a successful emergence from social inequality and obscurity is accurate when measured against a set of standard social criteria. His social origins clearly demonstrate the humble and restrained character of his childhood and early adult years. A sample of contemporary manufacturers reveals that only 14.4% came from a humble background. In terms of the extent of his schooling, again witnesses William Arnold as being at the lower end of the social scale when compared with the sample. Only 8.4% of the group received education of a character similar to his. When the focus is moved to the industry training he received yet again the disadvantage of his social background is evident. Only 3.6% of the sample received the kind of operative, on the job, training he received. This same echo of lowly social origins resounds when his personal wealth at death is considered. He left only 34% of the average wealth left by a founding owner of a volume production firm. In part this may be considered to relate to the way he used his resources in life but the relatively modest wealth at death again can be argued to echo his lowly start in life. There was not for him the boost of inherited wealth or the guidance of an established firm founded by an earlier generation. But lastly when religious affiliation and the role he played in politics and public affairs are studied, we see that William Arnold did make a visible and positive impact in the wider life of the town. Like 44.6% of the sample he too espoused dissent. But this was not merely for political gain or out of a sense of public duty. For him, religion was a personal revelation that tempered the way he lived his life, dealt with hardship and disappointment, and helped his community. It is here that his significant contribution outside of business was made. In terms of his role in public affairs he does play a leadership role in politics and in religious life, but like many in the sample, no role in cultural and social matters. The surprising matter is that he plays no leadership role in trade or industry affairs. Possibly this part of the profile reflects the close attention he had to pay to business in order for his firm to survive and prosper.[212]

And finally, what of William Arnold's life after the publication of this book in 1915? He was then 54 years old and the next thirty years before his death in 1945 were not devoid of incident: this was not a period of quietude and relaxation for him. The two main forces in his life outside of his family continued to influence the pattern of his later years. Business remained a constant focus for him as the obituary in the *Northampton Independent* quoted above shows: he went to the factory daily until his last illness a month before his death. Equally, religion continued to influence his life and provide a driving force. The

---

212 For some observations about the insights into William Arnold's relationship with the wider social and cultural world of the town and the wider historical debate about the role of entrepreneurial failure in Britain's economic decline, see p. 179 et seq.

culmination of his religious activities was only to come in the years after his *Autobiography* was published. The other area of prominent public service in later life was his more active engagement in local politics, where his role as Councillor was to span a decade. Lastly, Harriett, his first wife, had in many ways been central to his success. She died in 1921, following a long illness. Within a few years, he was to marry for a second time.

RECOLLECTIONS OF

WILLIAM ARNOLD

PRIVATELY PRINTED

NORTHAMPTON
1915

From a photograph by W. ILLINGWORTH

Figure 26: William Arnold in 1915

Preface

THE story told in the following pages is truly "a romance of reality." It is composed of just such material as Samuel Smiles would have coveted for his "Self-help," and is an equally striking example of struggle and triumph. By industry, tact, perseverance, and, beyond all, character, similar to that shining through this narrative, some of the greatest and most honoured business reputations of this country have been lowly built up. The land is not poor of which such honest records as this are true. Nor will its commercial supremacy be seriously challenged, so long as it rests on manhood as unimpeachable.

In these days of swift movement, and with the patience hardly able to brook delay, a quick and easy success is often desired, even at the risk of descending to compromises, such as an earlier day, and a high ethical standard, would have scorned. While no one desires that our young people shall pass through such a fight with poverty, and such a struggle with untoward conditions, one does covet for them this dogged determination to conquer difficulty, and this same quality of sterling manhood and true independence. Add to this, the fine tribute paid in this book, to the value of personal religion, the power of prayer, the intimate association between "true godliness and the life that now is" – all this gives the story an intrinsic value as a testimony to the Christian Faith, and as a guide and inspiration to all young people.

It is a pleasure to write this foreword, out of an intimate knowledge, alike of the struggle and its issue. It has been a greater joy still, to mark the steady growth from "more to more," not only in material prosperity, but in what matters much more, proportion and strength of manhood. The book is a fresh piece of evidence of the faith by which man truly lives; because, undaunted by adversity, our friend remains unspoiled by success, and is, with growing opportunity, the helper of the poor, the thorough believer in goodness, the earnest Christian, whose religion, as the good Shaftesbury wrote in his diary of his own, "enters into everything he does."

He has come through his winter to his summer. May it tarry long to throw its light and bear its fruit for others, until for him and his readers, the land of unsullied light and perennial fruitfulness is reached.

Henry Pickett[i]

HARTLEY COLLEGE
MANCHESTER[ii]
AUGUST 1915

Introductory Note

The "Recollections" of this little book were in the first instance jotted down in short-hand by a friend for private purposes, and the names of persons and places were suppressed. But to prevent any misunderstanding of the purpose, and to guard against any suggestion of parade, I wish to say that, after being permitted to read the pages in manuscript, I urged that names should be given and the story frankly told. It is due to Mr Arnold to say that he never dreamed of it being "made into a book," but now that he has given reluctant consent, it will be agreed that the recognition of the personality gives added interest and force to the record.

James H. Saxton [signature][iii]
STIMPSON AVENUE,
NORTHAMPTON

I Early Life

The Great War – The Village of Everdon – The Old-time shoemaker – A Strong Woman – Hungry Days – Partridges and Swedes – Village Life – A Hunting Walk.

It was during the Great War, when many Territorials in training were stationed at Northampton, that I was introduced to two London schoolteachers, who had joined the Army in order to assist their country in the fight against German oppression and wrong. These two young men were billeted at the house of one of Mr Arnold's sons, where there was a charming little family of father, mother, and children. Grandfather Arnold came in sometimes, and once he had an interesting talk with the soldiers. They thought him a wonderful man; and as he told them, in simple, unadorned language, some of the hardships and trials of his early life, they listened with breathless amazement.

"You should write a history of your life!" said one. "It would be such an encouragement to many of our poor London lads."

"I couldn't write a book, Mister!" was the honest response; "I never went to school, only a week or two at a time; and not as much as three months all through my life."

"But it is wonderful!" said the teacher.

And talking it over it was arranged that Mr Arnold should tell me his story; and that I should write it down as nearly as possible in his own words. Everyone will see that it is indeed a wonderful life. I asked a friend who knew something of his life what he thought of him. "He's a miracle!" was the answer. As I heard the following story I felt how true it is. There is only one way to describe him: Mr Arnold is "a wonder unto many."

Mr William Arnold is one of the best known among the shoe manufacturers of Northampton. He is just over fifty-four years of age, in the prime of life, a well-built, strong, pleasant-looking man, with a face you feel you can trust, and a manner that at once puts you at your ease. He was born at Everdon, a village about twelve miles South-West of Northampton. You will not find it on the map of England, it is too small. Once it was larger, and had many more people living in it than it has to-day. Farming then employed a larger number of men and boys than now, and every village supported its own tradesmen and local industries, brickmaking, shoemaking, weaving, and so on. Everdon had begun to decline when Mr William Arnold first saw the light of day, December 30th, 1860. His father, Matthew Arnold, was a poor working man, a typical old-fashioned English village shoemaker, who was employed by Mr C. Rodhouse in the neighbouring town of Daventry, and did the work at home. He made boots in the old way of sewing the soles to the uppers with waxed thread, his employer supplying him with the uppers already made up, and with the leather for the soles. By working hard he could make six pairs in a week: a very quick workman, by putting in an extra half-hour a day, might manage seven, but a pair a day was always considered a good day's work. Seldom, however, did a shoemaker make seven pairs, or even six, in a week, because the employers frequently had not enough trade to keep their men fully at work; and so he many times had not enough to do, and probably never in his life earned more than sixteen shillings in any one week, except at harvest time. Boots were laid aside when harvest was on, for Arnold went reaping for a month or five weeks, and his wife went with him. She was a woman of quite exceptional strength, often spoken of as the strongest in the village, which was something; and with the sickle in her hand she could always reap as well, and do as much work, or more, than most men. (See portrait on page 96.) And so, in August and September, by husband and wife working in the corn field from early dawn until late at night, they were able to earn sufficient money to pay-off the few debts they had incurred, and to spend a little, a very little, on some necessary clothing for the year.

In talking with Mr William Arnold I was impressed by one indication of the hard times of his childhood. He seems hardly ever to have had sufficient food, nor can we wonder, when we bear in mind that he was one of a family of fourteen children. Boys are always ready to eat, but few boys nowadays are really hungry for long at a time. Fifty years ago, however, in the country villages, when work was at all slack, whole families for weeks together never had sufficient: they were always hungry. Many of the recollections of his childhood centre round some good meal. His father was a hard worker, but frequently there were no boots to make; and his allotment, which he kept as well as any man, did not provide much, so he was tempted on occasion by the thin and pinched faces of his wife and children, to go out at night with one or two others to snare the squire's rabbits, or, it may be, capture a partridge, and if a hare should happen to come in the way, well, so much the better. He remembers several times being aroused in the middle of the night, brought downstairs with the other children, and feasted on partridge and potatoes. One can imagine the little brick-floored kitchen, the eager faces and bright hungry eyes of the youngsters, the delicious odour, and the glorious repast.

The meal was always announced as partridge, but hare and pheasants sometimes appeared on the board. Hunger, "the best sauce," was there in abundance, and they were always equal to the great occasion. Nor were the elements of care and caution absent. As soon as the game had disappeared, all the feathers and fur were carefully collected and cremated, so that if the gamekeeper, or the policeman, should come in the morning, he would find no trace of the midnight revelry, not so much as a tell-tale feather, as an outward sign of inward satisfaction. Sometimes, Mr Arnold is grieved to say, things in the little cottage were so bad that his father, unable any longer to see his children hungry for days together, would come home in the night with a bushel of meal, or a sack of swedes, that he had "found" in a neighbouring barn or adjacent field.

Mr Arnold's recital of those early days is almost wholly a story of poverty and struggle. Even the youthful escapades, the childish sports, and the buoyancy of health, were shadowed by grim spectres, or haunted by the thought of the wolf that was always at the door. Fortunately, the Arnold family was a very healthy one, and the free air and bright sunshine were their very own; but in other respects the life was grey in the extreme, and nothing ever occurred to change the grey into gold.

The next meal, the coming winter, sufficient clothing, a fire to warm and a roof to cover the children, these were the supreme questions of life. The battle of life was the struggle to exist, and there was no respite. The questions of comfort and advancement, of education and refinement, of the wider outlook upon life and society, did not exist. The story of voteless, penniless, and almost friendless father, and of ever-hungry

THE OLD-WORLD VILLAGE OF EVERDON

Where earth is quiet and her face unchanged
Save by the simplest toil of human hands
Or season's difference.
                    —WORDSWORTH

Figure 27: "Olde World Village of Everdon"

children crowding together in the labourer's cottage, and all doomed to the dullness and drudgery of unromantic village life, provides us with a very sad picture of the conditions of life among the destitute in the last century.

"Many a time," said Mr Arnold to me one day when we were

strolling over the uplands around his native village, "Many a time I have been on these hills at Christmas and later in the winter, and I have picked up and eaten pieces of Swedes where the sheep had been feeding, and had a big meal off them: you can hardly say a good meal, but a big one. I have done it hundreds of times."

"Then, in the winter, if I had no work to do, I, with other lads, would frequently go and see the foxhounds."

"You know Northamptonshire is considered one of the best hunting counties in England, and the hounds were often here, or in the neighbourhood. Two or three of us would follow the hunt to see as much as we could, and in the afternoon or evening there would often be a long trudging journey home. If we came across a turnip field or a sheep fold I always picked up a swede or two to eat. I remember once I was coming back with a companion. His family was better off than ours, his father being in a decent position. I picked up a turnip and was eating it on our way back. He was by my side, but he did not want any."

"No," he said "when I get home I shall have a nice dinner! My mother will have it in the oven nice and hot for me! Well do I remember the longing feeling that came over me when he said that it was not envy, but from the bottom of my heart I wished that I was that lad so that I might have 'a nice hot dinner' on a cold winter's day."

II Childhood

Slipping into Church – Afternoon Breakfast – Grand-father's Supper – My Good Mother – The Converted Sawyer – Out to Work – The Lost Dinner – Despair and Loneliness – Sheep and Pig Minding – Plough Boy and Weariness

[In] Mr Arnold's early years the necessity for every child to help in the earning of the family bread prevented all possibility of school education, and so Mr Arnold, as a lad, had none; and, further, he never went to church or any place of worship. At Everdon there was a large parish church as well as a little village school. Mr Arnold senior, like many other weary toilers in rural England seemed to think that the church of the Squire and the landlord was no place for him. The mother found her large and growing family more than sufficient to occupy her time and care. The children did not go to church because their clothes were so shockingly poor that it was thought sacrilege for them to be in the House of God. They themselves felt that somehow they were not smart enough to enter, though young Arnold often thought how much he would like to be at a service. In the summertime, when the church was open on Sunday evenings, young men on the farms used to attend. These young labourers in their working clothes (for few had any others, and all did some Sunday labour) used to sit together at the back of the church. Young Arnold would sometimes slip in with them and fancy that, surrounded by labouring men, he was not noticed. He used to enjoy the service immensely, little as he understood it; and he never lost his desire to attend some place of worship on Sundays. There was no Sunday School, and no one in the whole village seemed to care a halfpenny whether the children received any religious instruction or not. As for the day school, it was a charity school, and the children could go if they liked, but they were not sent. If they played truant, none seemed to mind, least of all, the poor old feeble schoolmaster, whose name was Carter.

The clergyman, the Vicar of Everdon, the Rev H. Luxmoore, was also an old man, a good simple gentleman, with no aspirations except to live at peace. Sometimes, however, he would be energetic, and on one of these occasions young Arnold was an undeserving victim. This was in one of the periods when he had no work and he was sent to school. His mother had gone to Daventry to take some boots and to bring back some food. The family had no breakfast that morning and could have no dinner until the mother was back. She had promised to bring some sausages, and all were awaiting her return with anxious pleasure. Young Arnold was on the little village green trying to play with others, but with a constant eye on the Daventry road. At last he could see his mother in the distance, and at that unlucky moment the bell rang for afternoon school. Young Arnold started off to meet his mother, but it happened that Parson Luxmoore was at hand.

Seeing the lad running away at the sound of the school bell, he concluded that he was off truanting.

"No, no; you don't," said the clergyman, seizing him by the ear. "You come to school!"

And to school he was taken, to spend two more hungry hours, before he was liberated to go home at four o'clock to breakfast!

The Vicarage was a roomy building with a large and fruitful garden. There was a nice bed of strawberries, and all boys are fond of strawberries.

"I have been among the old gentleman's strawberries again and again," said Mr Arnold, "plucking them and eating them; and he has been walking in the garden at the same time; but with care on my part he never once saw me. There was an orchard close by and I have had many an apple out of there. You see, we boys were always hungry."

It was not the boys alone who were always hungry. The labouring classes in English villages seldom had sufficient food. "My old grandmother," Mr Arnold said to me one day, "used to go out monthly nursing. My grandfather was a very old man, so old that it was not considered safe for him to be left entirely alone. As I was his eldest grandson – I was not six years old – I was often sent to his house when his wife was away, and used to sleep in the same room with him in case he should want any assistance. He used to fare pretty hard, I can tell you. He cooked his own meals. He boiled the potatoes with the jackets on so as to avoid waste in peeling. He would frizzle a bit of bacon, and for supper we would have the fat and the potatoes. The bacon he would save to warm up again next morning for his breakfast. I did not get much of the bacon: I did not expect it."

"Rice was a chief article of food because it was the cheapest we could get. Grandfather used to boil rice and a few currants together in a bag. I have had many a feed off that!"

"With sugar and a little milk?"

"Oh, no; no sugar, nor anything like that; just the rice with a few currants. The currants were supposed to sweeten it! That was the way the old gentleman fared when grandmother was away. When she returned, I was sent home until she went out again."

"I mention these things to show the terrible poverty of the family; and yet, as though their own boys and girls were not enough to keep, the fatherless boy of Mrs Arnold's sister was added generously to the family when a mere babe. "It was only one more mouth to feed," said the kindly mother. Mrs Arnold was an extremely generous woman, poor as she was she knew that "It never was loving that emptied the heart nor giving that emptied the purse."

She was always ready to help any of her neighbours who came to her, no matter what the trouble might be. (See portrait on page 98.) This good woman was a native of Greatworth, near Banbury.

"Her father, my grandfather Isham," said Mr Arnold "was one of the old-fashioned sawyers who used to earn a living by sawing timber for different masters. His family were all good people, but he turned out just the opposite. Most sawyers in those days were terrible drinkers and

WILLIAM ARNOLD'S MOTHER

WITH TWO OF HER GRANDCHILDREN AND THE OLD HOME AT EVERDON

Figure 28: William Arnold's mother

he was one of the worst. He was a wicked man. But I have heard him say that he heard someone preaching somewhere, and he was convicted of sin. And then he was in great trouble, uneasy about everything; and one night when going home – I do not know whether he was drunk or not – he saw the wood on fire. All the trees and bushes were flaming, and he thought it was Hell, and that there was no escape for him. How he got home he did not know, and it so worked on him that he was converted. He became a good man. As a Christian he had to endure unusual persecution, but he held on the good way, and I have no doubt at all that he is in heaven to-day."

Mr Arnold's grandfather on his father's side was a drover of the old type. (See portrait on page 98). He used to collect beasts round about Everdon and drive them, for the farmers, to Smithfield market in London. His wife was named Morgan, she was of Welsh origin, as the name implies. "What," I asked, "are your earliest recollections?" "I think the first thing I remember was having my finger crushed in a gate. I was only about two years old then. I can recollect later being taken into the harvest field and having to look after the other children while father and mother were harvesting. When I was six years and two months old I was sent off to work. Fancy that, only just over six years of age! This was at the end of February, or early in March, and I do not think I shall ever forget those long and hungry days in the fields scaring crows. I will show you one day where that was. My work was about a mile from home, and I had for wages eighteen pence a week and my dinner on Sundays. The dinner they gave me made the Sunday the greatest and happiest day of the week. I used to have as much as I could eat, and that never happened at home I can tell you, and the servant girl at the farmhouse, who came from Everdon, and the servant chap, knowing how poor I was, used to pack me up some food on the Sunday to take away with me for a weekday meal.

"I remember, the first Sunday that they did that, I took the food to the little hut I had in the field, a shelter made of hurdles stuffed with straw, or furze, and I hid the parcel among the straw. When I went home that night I was full of the thoughts of the good meal I should have next day. But alas! When I went on the Monday morning the food was gone: whether a fox, or rats, had got it, or a tramp had stolen it, I do not know. All I know is that I was terribly disappointed, and had to go without. I took more care with next Sunday's packet: I did not part with it until I had eaten all it contained."

"When the barley was up, and the scaring of crows was unnecessary, I had to mind a flock of a hundred sheep in Westcombe Lane. You can imagine the fearsome loneliness of a little lad of six, having this number of sheep in his charge, and seeing that they kept in the grass-lined lane, grazing along a distance of one and a half miles. It was a twisting lane, full of "doubles, that you could not see very far ahead or behind. There

WILLIAM AND ANNIE ARNOLD

THE GRANDPARENTS OF WILLIAM ARNOLD

Figure 29: William and Annie Arnold

was little or no traffic, hours and hours passed without a living creature coming near. The sense of loneliness and responsibility frequently overcame me, and in my despair I cried most of the time and in desperation would shout as loud as I could 'Mother! Mother! Mother!' But mother could not hear: she was at that time working in the hayfield two miles away."

"Thus the weary hours passed, and the time to drive the sheep home came as a great relief; and then I could walk on the two miles where mother was at work. Of course this meant a long trudge for a tiny chap, but it was grand to be with mother again."

"This weary, arduous life went on until the corn harvest arrived, about August; and I left the sheep, to go with my father and mother into the fields, and mind the baby while they were reaping with the sickle. After the cutting, there was the carrying to be done. I was found work, leading the first horse of the wagon team. I recollect how I was instructed always to shout, 'Holdjer' ('Hold you!') as soon as the horses were ready to start with the load. This was a warning to those on and about the waggon that we were going to move. Of course I had to walk amongst the stubble, and I remember how my little bare legs were scratched and made to bleed. My parents were so poor that money could not be spared for stockings."

"When harvest was finished, I had the job of minding about forty pigs on their feeding ground. They were driven to oak trees so that they could feed on the fallen acorns, of which pigs are passionately fond. They knew quickly enough where the oak trees were, and as soon as they were liberated off they would scamper, some this way, some that. Pigs are very different animals to mind from sheep. Sheep will keep together: every pig will go its own way careless of the others. The worry, the trouble, the running to and fro, the constant exertion of trying to keep those forty pigs together, I shall always remember. I was not seven years of age, and it was pitiful work for a child."

"After the mast harvest[iv] I went driving a plough at Westcombe [near Fawlsey]; that is, I led the horses up and down the field, while the ploughman held and guided the plough. For that I had two shillings a week – a rise of sixpence. I was at this work on my seventh birthday. I remember I wore a smock frock, with frills in front. It made me look smart and workmanlike, and it did not matter about my coat and trousers being ragged, as they were hidden and could not be seen. Such a smock, covering everything, was a perfect godsend, and it was because of this that I remember it so well."

"Westcombe is about a mile-and-a-half from Everdon, and it was the rule that any repairs to plough or harness had to be taken to tradesmen at Everdon overnight and brought back completed in the morning. Young as I was, I was made to carry the different articles to Everdon after my work was done. I remember once, after working all day long, that I had to carry to Everdon a plough horse collar that required whittling[v], and a plough coulter that needed repairs at the blacksmith's.

These two heavy things made a burden far too much for me; but I had to trudge with them, as best I could, the mile-and-a-half across the fields to Everdon. I had to get over eight stiles in the journey, and the only way I could manage it was first to throw the coulter and the horse collar over the stile, and then to climb over myself. You can picture me, a mere child of seven, struggling with these heavy burdens. It is an experience that stands out as one of the very worst in all those long and hungry years. I often wonder that any little fellow could bear the physical strain, and struggle through. "Soon after this I had another sixpence put on my wages, making half-a-crown a week, which was the regular wage, in those days, for ploughboys."

III Getting on

Long Journeys – "The Country Kid" – The Franco-German War – Droving by Lantern Light – Northampton Market – Back at the Shoe Trade – Big Wages – A Large Family – My New Suit

EVERDON is in a hilly district, and the country roads at the best of times are exceedingly lonely. "Surely," I said, "you did not walk to Daventry and back every day all alone; and you a mere child? Why the eight miles a day was as much as you ought to do, without hours and hours of work on the top of it!"

Mr Arnold responded:-

"Yes, they were hard times for the poor, and I think especially for the children. In those days, for the country working people, there was no childhood. It was always work, work, work, earning money for food; no matter if it were only a few pence. Bread was dear, and every half-penny was needed by the family at home."

"It was a long and tiring journey for my young legs, both ways; but though I always started out alone, I had company part of the way. At this time about twenty-five young men and women of Newnham worked at Daventry. As my way from Everdon was through Newnham, I had company for two miles each journey. I can assure you that those lonely walks on winter mornings, before it was light, and in the evenings after it was dark, pitch dark, and raining, and blowing, and snowing sometimes, were terrible trials to me. Many a time my heart seemed to stand still with fright. For I was then not nine years of age; as you say, a mere child."

"Though I was so young, and had this terribly tiring journey every morning and night, and often felt that I had not had enough to eat, I was remarkably quick at my work. Osborne was then working in a little shop in the Waggon yard, Sheep Street, Daventry. Our work was mostly sprigged Bluchers, that is, riveted boots. It was soon talked about the town that there was a little nipper from Everdon working wonderfully fast up this yard, and people used to come to the window and door to watch the 'country kid,' as they called me. I loved the work: I put my whole heart and soul into it."

"I worked for Mr Osborne quite a number of times. I would keep with him until trade fell off, and go back when it picked up again. When I was not working for him I did anything I could, but frequently I could find nothing to do, and that made things terribly hard at home, because when my work was short father's was short too."

"When the great war between France and Germany broke out suddenly, in 1870, there was immediately plenty of work in making boots for the French Army. The four young men I have already mentioned as having started riveting at Everdon got together again. They started working in the same little shop, and they had large quantities of Army boots to make. The pay, too, was good: money was easily earned, and they boozed worse than ever. I do not know how many days a week we worked while the War was on, but not many. The War ended about Christmas, the Army trade collapsed, and again I had nothing to do."

"It was soon after this, when I was between ten and eleven that I took to droving. There was an old man named Rodgers, of Flore, who used to come to Everdon on Tuesday mornings, and gather up the cattle from the farmers for Wednesday's market at Northampton. He drove the Everdon cattle on the way to Northampton, putting them up in a field, belonging to the Half-way House in Heyford, for the Tuesday night. On the Wednesday morning he would be up very early, collect the cattle from Flore, and drive them with the others to Northampton. At that time the Cattle Market was held in the Market Square. I went with this man Rodgers, helping him with the cattle on Tuesday and Wednesday, and standing in the market minding them until they were sold. When they were sold, we drovers had checks from the auctioneers, authorising us to go somewhere and have bread and cheese and beer. We were hungry after our long journey and long wait, and as we could have all the bread and cheese we liked, I can assure you that I obtained much satisfaction out of going to market at Northampton. Then we walked the thirteen miles back to Everdon, and thought ourselves fortunate if anyone wanted us to drive any beast in that direction, for that meant a little more money. But it was a long and weary day for a little one of my age, notwithstanding the rattling meal of bread and cheese and beer."

"I had to give this up because, with winter coming on, I was unable to stand the long journeys and longer hours. The mornings being dark we collected the cattle with the aid of a lantern, and in the cold and rain it was too much for me. Besides that, Rodgers was not only a drunken rascal, he was a cruel old man. When he was sober he was all right, but when he was drunk it was just the other way. I cannot say that he was cruel to the animals, but he was to me, and so I left him."

"Again I went to work for Mr Osborne, who had returned to live at Newnham, but who was still working at Daventry. As soon as he obtained shoe work he would have me, because I was reckoned to be very quick and very ready. When winter came, I stayed with him at Newnham, instead of coming home to Everdon. I used to go out to sleep at some place or other in the village, and Mrs Osborne used to cook me a bit of food to take with me to Daventry, and she looked after me a little. At this time, and I was not eleven years of age, I received twelve shillings a week wages, an extraordinary amount for a boy of that age. It was almost as much as my father earned with his big family to keep."

"I used to live very economically, and bring home every copper I possibly could to my mother. I knew the position we were in, always poor, and at that time there were five or six little ones to be kept. My money was a wonderful help to mother, I knew."

"There was a boy at Everdon named Fred Carvell. He and I were companions, though he was the elder by two or three years. Some relations of his in London sent for him to go and live with them; and he had to have a complete rig-out, new clothes, and so on. He left his old ones behind; and whether my father and mother begged them, or bought them, I do not know, but I had Fred Carvell's old clothes. There was a fustian jacket with corduroy trousers. I forget the waistcoat. I felt rarely grand in these clothes; they were fine clothes to me, because I had never had anything so smart to wear in my life; I had always to have what other people had pretty well worn out. I may have put on a bit of a swagger when I went to Daventry for the first time in those decent clothes: I thought I should be admired or envied. But to my surprise, when I got to Daventry the boys ran after me, chaffing me and laughing at me. I suppose the clothes were too big. I think I could have stood that without much trouble, though I was grievously disappointed; but they also teased me for a misfortune which had been mine from birth. I only had one eye. I was very sensitive about that, and they knew it, and of course that made them all the worse. It was terrible, what I had to put up with sometimes, it almost drove me mad. The men too, in the workshop, for mere devilry, would bother and plague me about it."

IV On My Own

At Work in Northampton – An Awful Christmas – George Osborne Drunk – A Man at Last – A Great Day – Northampton Again – A Long Tramp – At Work a Laycock's - Easy Come, Easy Go

"SO things went on until I was about twelve years of age, when another break came, and I went home and learned from my father how to stitch and to sew and I did my best to assist him. He was a splendid craftsman, as he took the greatest possible pride in his work, and he was extremely particular over every little point. There were very few who did well enough for him, it was difficult and trying to help him at all; not many came up to his ideas as a boot maker. He was a hasty man, and although I loved him, and helped him, I was thankful when I could get away and work somewhere else."

"I went back to Osborne and worked again with him at Daventry; but trade was not good and I wanted to earn more money than I did with him. I had an uncle in Northampton, Anthony Arnold. He had been in the Marines, and he had learned shoemaking, by which he kept himself after he left the Service. Once, when he was over at Everdon, I told him I should like to go to Northampton. It was arranged that I should, and I got work at Mr Joseph Gibbs', in Cyril Street, making youths' and boys' boots and shoes. I went there in September, but, as usual, the trade got bad before Christmas, and after about two months I went back home. In this short stay in Northampton I lodged with my uncle William in St. Giles' Street."

"If trade was bad at Northampton, it was bad also at Everdon, and I could earn nothing at home. Although I ought to have been keeping myself at that age, I was nearly thirteen, I earned scarcely anything. I shared the food in the house at Everdon with the others as we could get it, but that was a very rough time. I think we were more pinched then than at any time in my life. For one thing the family was larger. I had many brothers and sisters then, all younger than myself. I hardly know how we got through that Christmas: the winter was, for us, the worst I ever remember. In the spring I went back to Osborne and worked again for him until I got his employer, a Mr Dickens, to give me work direct."

"It happened in this way. George Osborne was far too fond of drink, and one Sunday night when he had been boozing he fell out with another man and they had a fight. Osborne got the worst of it and was laid up. I went on working for him as usual for the first fortnight, just as if he had been there. His son took the work to Mr Dickens and drew the money, and paid me my portion, fifteen shillings. The rest that he had for my work he took home to his father who had been in bed all the time. I thought that if I could do as well as that for him, I might just as well do it for myself."

"I was always a shy nervous boy, and it took all my courage to go to the governor, Mr William Dickens, and ask him if I could not work for him direct. He said 'Yes, you can go on for yourself.' So, on the Monday, I started. I know that I was anxious to be very careful, so that he should not find fault with my work. I tried to do it extra well, and therefore was not so quick as usual. When Saturday came I was a proud lad. I drew something over a sovereign, more than my father had ever earned at the trade in a week during his whole life. Elated, I went and bought a little pork pie, which I enjoyed very much, and a pint of beer at the Rifleman public house, which suited also. I was a man now, taking man's wages, though I was not fifteen! I remember I brought something nice home from Daventry for the others, and then gave my mother all the rest, every penny. Pleased as I was, I think my dear old mother was more overjoyed than I was. She felt then that there was to be an end to the terrible pinch of poverty from which we had all so long suffered. It was a great day for mother."

"Well, I earned more than that some weeks, sometimes less; and all I earned I took home. Mother gave me a few coppers if I wanted them, but I knew how things were at home, and I did not often want anything for myself. I was pleased to give all I could to her. I worked like this until May, 1875. At Whitsuntide my uncle Anthony came over to Everdon, and asked me when I thought about going to Northampton again."

"I said I should like to work in Northampton, but my previous experience of only getting two months' work made me cautious. He said I would have no difficulty now, and advised me to go. After thinking It over I made up my mind to have another try."

"On the Thursday, the Thursday in Whit-week, I went over to Northampton, 'casioning as it was called in the trade, that is, seeking work. The very first factory I went to promised to take me on. This was Laycock's, in St. Edmund's Road, then known as Bird's Piece. When I got to Northampton I went to my uncle William's in St. Giles' Street. When I left his house I went along the only road I knew that side of the Market Square, that was, along St. Giles' Street into Bird's Piece. Laycock's was the first factory I came to, and they said I could start on the Monday morning. I arranged also that I should again lodge with uncle William."

"Mr Dickens' shop at Daventry was closed all Whitweek, and my kit[vi] was there. I could not get it until Monday. So once more, early in the morning, I started off for Daventry, thinking a great deal, I can tell you, of my many lonely walks along the familiar road, and wondering whether this was to be the very last time I should make the journey. I reached Daventry before seven. The shop in Staverton Road was not open, so I had some difficulty in getting in to secure my kit. But I got it and hurried back along the main road to Weedon, the nearest railway station, as at that time there was no railway to Daventry as is the case now. I caught the first train from Weedon, reached Northampton about ten, went straight up to Bird's Piece, got some work out, and so started at half-past ten after a walk of ten miles. The Whitsuntide holiday had exhausted all my money, and to pay the railway fare from Weedon, and to keep me at Northampton, until I could draw some wages, I had to borrow three shillings and sixpence from my grandmother, and the good old soul was then on the parish. (See portrait on page 98). Of course no one knew that she lent it to me, and I can assure you she did not hurt for her kindness to me and her confidence in me."

"The first week I was in Northampton at Laycock's I drew just over twenty-seven shillings, remarkably good money. I know that I surprised the foreman, George Gardiner, and many others, by earning so much; they were astonished that a lad of fifteen could do the riveting so quickly. As I got used to the place and the work, I worked myself up to such a pitch that in a little while I could earn anything I liked within reason. The old hands there made a great deal of me, for it was a case with me, I am sorry to say, of 'easy come, easy go.' Not that I forgot my family at home – far from it, but the money I earned was so much more than any of us had been used to, that after fooling a lot of it away, there was always a tidy bit for the old folks at home. I used to go over to Everdon most week-ends, or once a fortnight, and I used to give part of my money to my mother and the rest used to go. I got hanked in with a few pals at Laycock's where the old hands were the most wicked and drunken lot of shoemakers I ever came across. I got to love skittles and card playing, but not gambling. I never would gamble for money: I used to play for a pint of beer or a quart, not more. But I used to fool away a lot."

V Shoemaking in Northampton

Shoemakers' Saint Monday – Drinking Bouts – Smart Day's Work – A Contest and a Dead Heat – A Rapid Workman – Good Templary – Drink at Everdon Feast – Boughton Green Fair – A Saturday Night Ill Spent

I COULD scarcely credit that a young man with no expensive tastes, earning as much as Mr Arnold did in his youth, could really spend so much money on "beer and skittles." He explained that sometimes there was not work for them, and then of course nothing was earned. But when there was plenty of work the shoemakers would often take it into their heads to have a holiday. Mr Arnold went on to say:-

"We used to have St. Monday always and perhaps St. Tuesday as well.[vii] In those days footings were the regular things. If a fresh man came to work he was expected to pay for a gallon of beer. The others would put three pence each to it, and that was only the commencement. When that beer was gone we had more; it was a regular beano, and lasted a day or two or more. There was something of this sort nearly every week. We used to turn out of the factory and go in Sam Simon's public house in Bird's Piece and drink. I should think Laycock's men alone spent enough in that house to keep the landlord. This went on for one or two years, and I was always in the thick of it, for I was very young and dearly loved the fun."

"I remember on one occasion we had played the game rather thick and the men did not commence work until Friday. I dare say I began on the Thursday, but I always had some dead horse. Dead horse meant that one had an advance from the employer before the work was done, and so you had to make so many pairs before the debt was wiped off. On the Friday morning I made up my mind to have a big day. I worked as hard as I could. I was at work on riveted spring sides that is boots with elastic sides, sometimes called jemimas. I made thirty pairs that day at nine pence a pair, which comes to one pound two shillings and sixpence; not at all, I think, a bad day's work for a youth. With a little that I drew in advance on Saturday, my wages that week came out very fair. This, remember, was before I was seventeen years of age."

"To give you an idea of how quick I was at work I can tell you one incident at Laycock's. One Monday morning a fellow workman and myself went up for our work together; and we each got exactly the same, six pairs of precisely the same kind of boots and the same size. He was a fast riveter and there had always been a little bit of feeling, not jealousy, but rivalry on his part, and when we got back to the shop he said:-

"Now Matthew (they always called me Matthew then), I will just have a bet with you over this six pair for a gallon."

"Nothing lo[a]th, I agreed, and having got everything ready, we started." There was a little excitement in the shop over the contest, and we both worked our hardest. We both made the six pairs in two hours that is ten minutes a shoe, and the payment was nine pence per pair, four and sixpence for the two hours. We made them through, ready for finishing. Anyone in the trade will tell you that that was very quick work."

"Well, the result of the contest was that neither of us won, it was absolutely a tie to the tick. I was not eighteen then, and I can assure you that the old hands were astonished. A mature workman, one of the best in the town, certainly the best in the factory, was equalled in quickness of work by a youth of seventeen, not long come from the country! Some people talked a good deal about me. Although neither of us won the wager, it did not prevent our having the gallon, and then we went on to more drink, and we kept on the 'spree' until Thursday morning."

"As I grew older, I became even more ready and quick, and I really believe that there was no one in the trade who could beat me for speed. B. C. Smith, the Northamptonshire cricketer, was a very ready chap, and some people were anxious to get up a contest between us. Some were in favour of him, some favoured me. Some thought that he could do better perhaps for a day, but that I should beat him in a contest spread over a week. But we never tried. I never laid down my tools to any man, and that is not mere boasting. After I became of age, I could earn just what money I liked, if I could get the work. I have drawn five pounds a week single-handed, and I have even got up to as much as six pounds."

"I was about eighteen when I began to think that I was entirely on the wrong track in wasting so much money, and I made up my mind to be a Good Templar. It was not so very difficult after the start, and I kept to it for about two years, and straightened myself a bit, but I never saved any money, although at this time I was earning as much as four pounds or five pounds a week. It would all depend how trade was, of course. If anyone wanted help, it seemed that I must help, and especially if it were my mother or any of my relations. I did not spend much on myself."

"Good Templary did not exactly suit me, I could not fall in with the forms and the ceremonies, but I have lived long enough to see that it is useful, especially to some types of mind, though it did not appeal to me."

"While I was still a Good Templar I went home at Everdon Feast, and started drinking again: and I did not give it up when I went back to Northampton. I did not drink a lot, but I fell back to my old carelessness and indifference, as my large earnings became a source of temptation. I kept on like that until I was between twenty-four and twenty-five. Sometimes I thought of what I had lost, for there is no doubt, if I had not fooled away my money, I should have had about a thousand pounds at that time."

"At this period of my life I was working for Mr Manfield on Campbell Square. It was the practice there to pay us up if we shopped after the dinner hour on Friday. It happened that on the last Friday in June – this was in 1884 – I took in my work just after dinner. They paid me for the week, and I got more work out and took it home. On the way I recollected that Boughton Green Fair was on, and I made up my mind to have a wash and go to the fair."

"I walked to Boughton Green, and I saw people there that I knew and 'made merry with my friends.' I came back at night; it was a very hot day I remember, and I had rather more than I could carry comfortably. I got up on the Saturday morning and started work in the little shop, but I was terribly ill, and felt like famishing for more drink. A friend came in to borrow some lasts. I remember how glad I was to see him, I felt I wanted company."

"'Jack,' I said, 'Will you come and have a wet?'"

"Of course he jumped at the opportunity. So we went out just after seven on the Saturday morning, and I started drinking again, and kept on all that day."

"The same night, when I was on the Market Square, hardly knowing what I was doing, I entered into conversation with a young woman, who was destined to become my wife. (See portrait on page 129.) I knew her by sight, but I do not think I had ever spoken to her before. Her father lived in Hunter Street, just opposite my uncle's, where I lodged. Her sister and my cousin were friendly, and sometimes I and my dog – I always had a dog – would go with those two for a short stroll, generally on the Racecourse close by."

"I do not know exactly what passed between my wife-to-be and myself on the Market Square. She endeavoured to persuade me to go home, I believe, and I suggested that we should have a walk on the racecourse the next morning. I do not suppose I thought anything more about it."

"I picked up with two pals, and we kept on drinking until eleven o'clock, closing time. We took home some more drink, and we drifted down to Scarletwell Street, to the house of one of them, and there I stayed until all the drink was consumed."

"Fearfully muddled I started for home. I remember nothing except this: they were building St. Crispin's Church then. There was a hoarding all-round the place, and I recollect looking over the boards and thinking that I would get over and lie down and sleep. I felt so ill that I wanted to sleep. I can remember nothing at all after that."

VI Reflection and Resolve

Sunday Morning Reflection – Canon Hull and All Saints' Church – Lurking Pals – God the Helper – The Sage Publican – My Resolve – My Last Drinks – A Rechabite

I WAS curious to ask Mr Arnold whether he did climb the hoarding, or whether he went to sleep by the side. He seemed scarcely to notice my interruption, for he continued the narrative of the preceding chapter:-

"I did not get over the boards, because I woke early on Sunday morning in my bed at my uncle's in Hunter Street. How ill I felt when I awoke I could not describe. I suppose the stuff I had had at Boughton Fair was rank poison, if we only knew. I never felt so bad in my life. I got up and went on the Racecourse, and I walked about there alone for two or three hours. I began to think what a fool I was, and the more I thought the less I liked the look of myself. I could see that I was altogether on the wrong road, and that if I did not stop there would soon be an end of me."

"And then, I suppose, because it was Sunday morning, my thoughts took me to All Saints' Church, and to the earnest sermons of Canon Hull, which had so often appealed to me. I had always gone to church from my first going to Northampton, chiefly to All Saints'. The Rev Canon Hull's preaching made a great impression on me, and if, with the same preacher, it had been a Nonconformist place of worship instead of being a parish church, I should have been converted when I was sixteen. In most Nonconformist chapels they will take an interest in a young man, or in any stranger, but I used to go in and out of that place for years, and nobody ever took the slightest notice of me."

"I had come out of All Saints' Church, after a beautiful service, very many times, with the determination to be a better man. And whilst in this state of mind, instead of someone in the church taking me by the hand, one of my old pals waiting for me in the street would come up, my resolution would disappear, and we would go straight into a public-house and start drinking. I was always of a jovial, lively disposition, and as I earned a lot of money I always had plenty of companions. They were not shoemakers; I do not know that I ever had a companion in the same trade as myself; they were tailors, grocers' assistants, shop people, and so on; very 'dressy' in appearance, and very fond of 'Billy' as they called me, fond of me because it was my money that used to be spent."

"I could see all this as I was walking and reflecting on the Racecourse on this Sunday morning. If I had only kept to the resolutions that I had made over and over again in All Saints' Church! Why had I not? I remembered particularly how Canon Hull had once preached on the Power of God: how he had convincingly shown me that no one has ever come to God and been disappointed, no one has ever been turned away by Him. And if no one, then He would help me. Why not take His help? And so I made up my mind on the Racecourse on that Sunday morning that, God helping me, I would never touch the drink again after dinner time that day. Yes, I felt so bad that I said that I must have just one more glass to put me right."

"I used the Cricketers' Arms in Hervey Street. The landlord, William Gubbins, had given me as good fatherly advice as any man possibly could give another. He had talked to me dozens of times and told me seriously what a fool I was to waste my time and money in drink."

"I will take your money, of course, if you come here," he said, "But you are not the same sort as the ordinary drinking man; you are a different kind altogether. I wish you would not come here and spend your money; you should pull yourself together, there is a man in you."

"This was the earnest and repeated advice of a man who was in 'the Trade'."

"Well, this Sunday, as soon as the public-houses opened at dinner-time, I was at William Gubbins' to have a glass or two for the last time, as I thought, for I had made up my mind it was to be the end. But I felt so ill all through the rest of the day that I had to have another drink at night. That was the last; I made up my mind I would never touch it again, and thank God I have not."

"You may think it curious that after seeing how foolish I was, and making up my mind on the Racecourse to give up drinking, that I had another glass at dinnertime, and another the same evening. But that is what I did."

"And I will tell you more: I think I did something more than determine to be a teetotaler on that Sunday morning; I think in my rough ignorant way I put God to the test. He had promised to help, as Canon Hull said, if I would trust Him. I felt I could trust Him, and He has helped. I am certain that He has been my Help and Stay and Guide from that day to this. I am sure of it; I honestly believe that I was also converted that Sunday morning on our Racecourse."

"I need not tell you that I had severe struggles during the next week. My uncle was a Rechabite, and the club night was that week, and I asked him to propose me in the Rechabites, a strict teetotal Society."

"He laughed at me, quite naturally; he could not believe it; but I was in earnest, and he and everybody else were soon supplied with the proof."

VII Courtship and Marriage

Meeting my Wife – Sick of the Old Way – My Wife's Trust – Married at Church – My Next Day's Work – Bad Trade – A Broken Reed – House Furnishing – Our Children

"THE first week of my new life passed, and Sunday morning came. Again I went for a walk on the Racecourse alone. On coming home, my wife-to-be, who was on her doorstep, saw me, and spoke about disappointing her on the previous Sunday. We arranged another meeting, and both turned up at the appointed time and place. It seems to me very wonderful that just when I was breaking with drink and its associations, the companion of my life should appear on the scene. Temperance, religion, and marriage were all closely linked in my life: here was 'the Divinity that shapes our ends'."

"As soon as I became a teetotaler, I felt sick and tired with my old life, and very much regretted that I had been so foolish in wasting so many years. Instead of having a nice little sum of money, as I could have had, and ought to have had, I was in debt, rather heavily for a working man. I had to lay to and clear off my debts first of all. I worked hard, and went home to my lodgings after long and weary days. I became tired of lodgings. I realised how much comfort I had missed, how much I had lost in having no decent companionships, only men whose sole object seemed to be drink, drink, drink! Every way I looked, my past stared me in the face and condemned me."

"The lady who became my wife was a young and earnest Christian; and I was fully determined to be a teetotaler and a good man. We found great delight in one another's company, and a love match was the result. It seems marvellous how we came together, and became so attached to one another."

"Very naturally, some of my companions looked with suspicion on the change in my life. The father and mother of the lady, as well as other friends, were against the match, opposition to which at that time I can well understand. If she married me, they told her, she would find that I would speedily return to my old habits, and she would rue the day. It was evident, they said, that I had turned teetotal and religious only to get her."

"She was very spirited and open, and she told them in return, that if she married, she would marry a man she could trust, and she was certain she could trust William Arnold. In less than six months we were married. It was one Monday morning at St. Michael's Church."

"It was a very humble affair and very quiet. Being self-conscious, I did not want many in the church; and, at the very last, I went to the Minister and arranged for the wedding to be an hour earlier than was originally fixed. I did it on purpose to avoid people being there. My little ruse was quite successful. It was a wet morning, and, besides the vicar and the verger, there was only one other person present, the old landlady where I used to lodge. We had no cab, we felt we could not afford it, and, after the wedding, we walked in the rain to the house of my wife's father in Hunter Street."

"It was arranged that we should live with her parents for a short time. My wife thought she should like to be at home and learn from her mother something of house-keeping, as previous to this her time had been spent in the boot trade, assisting her father. This was fortunate, for we were very poor; we had only about ten pounds to get married on. The next morning I was at work by seven o'clock, and I earned over a sovereign that day."

"There was any amount of work right up to the time of my marriage, but again it fell off before Christmas. After the first fortnight, I did not make a full week for a long time, only earning a pound, or from that to thirty shillings a week, for months and months. Instead of our position improving, as we expected, we seemed to make no headway at all. Then in due time our first baby was born, our eldest boy, and this, of course, did not improve our finances: and naturally, my wife's parents, owing to the new arrival, were tired of our being in their house, and so we decided to remove and make a home for ourselves."

"The difficulty was that we had not the money to buy the furniture we required for another house, having very little of our own, not much besides the things in the bedroom. Suddenly I recollected a conversation with a tradesman on my wedding day. He professed to be a friend, and he was married to a cousin of mine. I went into his shop in the Drapery to buy a piece of ham for the wedding party."

"Unfortunately, though I was willing to work day and night, there was not the work to do. We had taken a house in Shakespeare Road, but we had no means of furnishing it. The one friend I had counted on failed us. It was no use going to anyone for favours – I felt convinced of that – and besides, after the snub I had had, I was far too sensitive to risk another. There was nothing else to do but try to make a business arrangement. I did not know at that time how house furnishers were willing to let you have furniture on the hire system. I went to a furniture dealer in Gold Street and told him my position exactly. The old gentleman met me a great deal better than I expected. I paid him the little money I had, and he sent us a nice lot of furniture, but not a stick more than was necessary. We had as few things as we could possibly do with. I made arrangements to pay all off in a certain time, and as trade picked up a bit, and I earned more money, I was able to do it."

"I was working at my uncle's little shop in Hunter Street when we removed our home to the same street, No. 29, where there was a nice little riveting shop at the back, large enough for five men to work in. We kept struggling on, and our second and third children were born. Of course our expenses were increasing, and there never seemed to be enough trade to enable me to earn the large sums that I did when I was single. I was not satisfied, neither was Uncle Anthony, in the same street, and we talked of starting manufacturing ourselves. Others were doing it, and were getting on, why should not we?"

VIII Starting in Business

A Partnership – Borrowed Money – Discharged from Work – A Struggle – Life on £1 a Week – A Partner who Drank – Removal to Everdon – A Good Customer – Considerate Creditors – A Fresh Start – An Enlarged Factory

I HAVE sufficient acquaintance with the boot and shoe trade of Northampton to know that many of the largest manufacturing businesses have grown from small beginnings. I have known, too, very many attempts that have been complete failures. I remember when there were nearly three hundred boot and shoe manufacturers in Northampton; now, I think, there are not so many as seventy five. Some people have been successful, many more have been unsuccessful. Mr Arnold tells his experience in these words:-

"Three of us got together: my uncle, his brother-in-law, who was an old gentleman named Alfred Flint, and myself. We discussed the thing all round, and decided to make a start under the style of Arnold & Co. Between us we thought we knew a lot, and that the three of us working together could almost beat creation making boots."

"As for capital, the other two had some money; I had little or none; but I was so necessary for the concern, as an expert workman, that I believe they would have taken me in without any. Everything looked so rosy, our prospects we thought were so glowing, that I insisted on finding as much as they did. I mustered up courage and asked a friend to lend me some, and to my surprise, and great delight, he did so. We put the money together, ninety-four pounds in all, and we thought we were going to do well."

"We knew that £94 would not go far, and we knew therefore that it was necessary to proceed in a very small way – as a sort of overtime employment for us. A man we knew, named Smith, who worked at Mr Manfield's was to do the pattern-cutting and clicking for us.[viii] Uncle was to cut the sole leathers, and so on. I was to do the riveting. The finishing we would give out to workpeople. The other partner, Mr Flint, was to do the books, and his wife the closing or stitching of uppers. It all seemed very simple, and we took a little place in Duke Street to start in, one room up some steps."

"We had over-looked one thing, however. As soon as Manfields' found that we had started for ourselves, they refused to let us have any more work. I had been going on very well just then, earning good money, and employing a brother to help me. All this was stopped and we had to rely entirely on the orders we could get for our own little business."

"This was a severe blow to all our prospects. We saw at once how careful and alert we must be. We three partners decided to draw only £1 a week each in wages; the other few workers were paid what they earned. I was by far the worst placed in this arrangement. Out of my £1 a week was paid 8/6 for rent and rates, and there were three children, and my wife and myself, to keep with the remainder. My wife, with her carefulness, managed to pay our way, and we never went into debt a single penny. Slowly, very slowly, business improved. After about two years, and, obtaining more customers, we removed our factory from the one room in Duke Street to a house in Military Road, which had been made into a shoe factory. We raised our wages to 25/- a week, as we thought the business could now stand that."

"Now a fresh trouble arose. Mr Flint was a nervous, cautious man. He feared that although business was gradually increasing, we were not making money. This upset him, and for solace he took to drink. When he started drinking he would go on the booze for a month together, and there never was a man more foolish than he when drunk. Neither my uncle nor myself were book-keepers, so, in regard to accounts, we were entirely in Flint's hands; and when he was drunk we had to get a man to come in at nights and keep our books posted up. He also had to write letters and hunt up money so that we could pay wages on the Saturday."

"This was a fearfully harrassing time. We were always on the precipice, as it were. We were always cogitating as to what we could do to improve. Once, I remember, it was decided that I should do a little travelling. I did very well on several journeys. I was no writer, and while I had my book and pencil in hand, and pretended to write down the orders as my customers gave them, as a matter of fact, I was writing the order in the book of my memory only. I was careful not to let the customer see that I was only pretending to write."

"When I was travelling I was of course very little at home, and my wife and I thought it would be much cheaper to remove to Everdon, and have a little cottage where she and the children could live, and where I could go at week-ends. So we went to Everdon, and lived in a cottage at 1/9 a week rent. As soon as we made this change we found it was a mistake. I only went travelling once after this removal, for the firm found that if I, the chief operative, was away, they might just as well shut up. In three months' time we came back to Northampton: my wife was miserable at Everdon without me; I was miserable without her at Northampton. I decided, hundreds of times, owing to the great worry and drag of the trade, that I would leave the partners and go back to the bench, and never have anything more to do with business as long as I lived. This was the decision I came to night after night, after long and weary days. I worked from seven in the morning until nine, and ten, and eleven o'clock at night. But in the morning I would see things a little differently and decide to make another effort: perhaps things would improve."

"We returned from Everdon to Northampton, into a house in Turner Street, again paying eight-and-sixpence a week rent and rates. There our fourth child was born, our eldest daughter. How we managed to live on the sixteen-and-sixpence that was left out of my twenty five shillings neither of us could say."

"But my wife managed it, and we struggled on a[t] home, and the firm struggled on at the factory. More and more it seemed to fall upon me to keep the business going, for one of the partners was an obstacle rather than a help, and uncle, like myself, entirely lacked all business training. I remember how every night found me harassed and disappointed, but I did not live [give] up the struggle, and slowly the business grew until once more a larger factory was necessary. This time we removed into Louise Road, and, as the growth continued, the partners felt themselves justified in drawing thirty shillings a week each."

"At this time one of our customers was a large London firm, and we did an increasing trade with them until it amounted to £200 a week. This firm had a good reputation, and the Union Bank at Northampton, where we banked, would take thousands of pounds worth of their Bills. Their business was so useful to us that we cultivated it as much as we could, and took their Bills without scruple. We thought that if the Union Bank[ix] was satisfied we need not trouble; and we went on, we thought, rather finely. But in a year or two they failed. They owed us about £1,100, and of course, as soon as they could not pay us, we could not pay what we owed."

"We had to call a meeting of creditors and explain to them the whole position. Well, working in the factory all day, struggling and worrying, was bad enough, but it was nothing to those awful days before the creditors' meeting. The factory was closed because there was no money for wages, and I thought everyone I met was talking about us, calling us thieves, which we were not, and I knew we were not. I was ashamed to be seen, so was my uncle, and we used to get up early in the morning, and go out into the country for the day, returning only at night, when dark. My wife suffered the same: it was a terrible time. It settled me: I decided that I would never have anything to do with business again, but would go back to the bench and be a workman."

"At last the meeting of creditors came, and to my surprise we were not condemned: we had the sympathy of the few that we owed money to. Everything was so clean and straightforward, every penny was accounted for: they could see we had made an honest attempt at success, and that we had not drawn from the business, in wages for ourselves, a single shilling more than was justified. But uncle and I had had enough of it: we were truly sorry that we had not done better, and we were not going through it again. One of the creditors thought we were very unwise in coming to this decision. We had collected some trade, there was the nucleus of a good business, we had tried, but had been unfortunate. That was no reason why we should leave off, indeed, it would be a pity not to continue."

"This was altogether different from what we had expected, and it cheered us up a bit. Why should we not have another try? It's a speculation. That is what we thought business was, even then – merely speculation. And so, with the approval of our creditors, we decided to keep on. They promised to help us, and, as Mr Flint was now out of it, we thought we had a better chance of success than before. So out of the difficulty a new firm came, uncle and myself, under the name of A. & W. Arnold."

"We managed in the first twelve months to make a little headway, and in the second year we still further improved. Then came a crisis. The Shoe Operatives' Union had arranged with the manufacturers that there should be an end to the system of finishers, riveters, and all others, taking work home. It was all to be done in the future in the employer's factory. This required much more factory room, and manufacturers had to make the best arrangements they could. Some built new factories, and smaller firms moved into their places, and other firms into theirs. It was the only way."

"We had to find a larger factory than our place in Louise Road, and so we rented the premises in St. Giles' Terrace. Messrs Allinson & Co. were removing to the top of Earl Street, and though the factory they were leaving was larger than we wanted, it was the only one we could get. It was a big undertaking for us. We had to take over all the fittings, fixtures, and different things; and standing at bigger expense in this way the change did not bring in any more business. This time, like all that had gone before, was one long struggle. All who are in business will understand, when I say that for a long time there was nothing but work and worry, planning and scheming, pinching and saving, forecasting and grinding, to hold our own and make just a little headway. Practically everything depended upon the energy of one pair of hands; and every week brought its crop of difficulty and care. The struggle in the home, with my growing family, was quite as great as our fight to keep the doors of our factory open, and I remember my pleasure, and my wife's relief, when I began to draw two pounds a week from the business instead of thirty shillings."

IX Religious Experience

Honesty in Business – The Preaching Tradesman – Religious Doubts – Salvation Army – The Drayman's Holiness – Led to Chapel – The Rev. George Parkin – Hi, I want you! – Happy Years – The Rev. H. J. Pickett – My Simple Faith – Church Work and Charity

FEW men, I think, realise, as Mr Arnold realises, the great part that personal religion plays in business enterprise and success. He says: "I made up my mind that in my business, come what might, be the result whatever it might be, I would be honest and honorable [sic]. There were many things, however, which pressed heavily on my shoulders. An early rebuff came to me directly after we made our second start in business. Our creditors had said that they would continue to let us have credit up to a certain amount. Among them was a tradesman somewhat prominent in religious circles in the town. I had listened to his addresses indoors and in the streets. To his firm we sent for a three-and-sixpenny tin of polish, and he sent word back that if we sent the money we could have it, but he would not think of trusting us again! There is no denying that this action shook me very much: it came very near to destroying my faith in religious matters altogether. Here was the Christian brother treating a struggling honorable [sic] man like this. And the other creditors, worldly men, so-called worldly men, were willing to assist us, as they all did, at their own risk, but the rich Christian speaker, who professed so much, was not willing to trust us to the extent of three-and-sixpence."

"I passed through a wonderful time of religious anxiety and experience, but I thank God that He gave me strength to hold to Him through it all. You must know that during the long years of struggle to form a business, with a large family and small means, I got into very prudent ways. For years and years I never spent a penny needlessly on myself. I took every copper home, where it was severely needed. Our family came so fast, that five times we had three children under three years of age. Habits of prudence, then formed by the pressure of necessity, have stuck to me all through life. Even now I never spend anything on myself unless it is for a cigar."

"I continued to attend All Saints' Church after I turned teetotaler, but my wife and I, before we were married, went to Mount Zion Baptist Chapel, now called Princes' Street Chapel. Leaving there, we went to Doddridge Congregational Church. The Rev. J. J. Cooper, who was there then, did me a lot of good, but it was such a long way from Hunter Street that we felt it was too far to go. I then picked up with the Salvation Army, and was a member for several years, but I never got any further there. You see I never had any religious training when I was young; I was ignorant of religious things until I was grown up, and I suppose things affected my mind differently from what they would had I been properly trained. I had sampled, as it were, different denominations, and I had compared people's actions with their professions, and I began to get very much jumbled up. At one time I would doubt this and that, and at another time doubt religion altogether; and yet, all the time, there seemed to be something assuring me that religion itself was true, whether other people followed it or not. The Salvation Army seemed to fail me altogether. They seemed to preach one thing and one thing only – Holiness. They had Holiness meetings; it was all Holiness. But I never could understand Holiness; my mind failed to grasp it I they never could explain it sufficiently for me. Besides, I saw this: that certain people in the Barracks used to say one thing there, and, it seemed to me, act very differently outside. I made no professions, but I was sure my life was as good as theirs. I did not get up and speak as they did: I had no inclination to do so. Yet they seemed to feel all they were saying. I was bewildered. I began to get into a terrible state: I did not know where I was."

"One day I was going down Kettering Road, and I saw a railway carman who had a beautiful cart-horse. He belonged to the Salvation Army, and I remembered that the Sunday before he had spoken about this Holiness, and gave a glowing account of his own life. And now, as I was passing – I do not know what made me notice it – I saw this man in a side street, and because his horse did not do just as he wanted, he kicked it two or three times as hard as he could. Seeing this cruelty on the part of this man, I doubted, I could not help it, whether there were really honest religious people in the world at all. Next Sunday morning at the Army this same man was talking again about Holiness! It was all so strange, unreal, untrue. If I had not had a good Christian wife, one of the best I believe that ever walked, and had it not been for her prayers and her pleadings, I have no doubt I should have gone to the Devil again."

"But I had always prayed in my humble way to be led aright, and I know that at this time I prayed many times, and earnestly, that I should be led somewhere where I could get what I desired. While I was pleading like this for guidance, I was walking down Kettering Road one Sunday night, and passing Grove Road Primitive Methodist Chapel I thought I would go in there. I did, and it proved to be a lovely service. The Rev. George Parkin was minister then. That Sunday night I shall never forget, for I found what I had been wanting for years. His idea, and the simple rich way he presented it that night, seemed to fit me like lock and key. I shall never forget it. The Rev. George Parkin played one of the most important parts in my life, and this at the most critical period it was possible for me to pass through." (See illustration and portrait on page 123.)

"I went home after the service and I said to my wife: 'You must go to Grove Road Chapel^x on Sunday morning. I have been and I am not going anywhere else!'"

"I went to the Chapel the next Sunday evening, and felt the same influence and satisfaction. I went the third Sunday night, and still I was delighted. As, I have told you I was always very shy. On this third Sunday evening I could see that Mr Parkin had got his eye on me. I knew very well what he wanted. He wanted to speak to me before I left the building, but I rushed out so as not to give him the opportunity."

"On the following Sunday night, he had his eye on me still. The moment the service was over, I got up to walk out quickly, but he shouted from the rostrum 'Hi, I want you!'"

"I imagine I can hear his voice now. Of course I knew that he meant me, and I thought that everybody else also knew that he meant me. So I had to stop, I was compelled to stop."

"Mr Parkin came and gripped me by the hand. 'I want to know who you are, and where you live. I am coming to see you. Not any more to-night. Pleased to see you here! Are you a stranger to the town?'"

"I told him in a few words. We lived in Adams Avenue then and he was up at the house the next day at one o'clock. We had a chat, he put me right, and he welcomed me to the church."

"My wife was as much struck with his ministry as I was, and from that day to this, which is close upon twenty years now, I have been in but two other places of worship in Northampton. We have been so suited, and so happy, that we have had no desire to leave our church, let who might be in the town, or whatever might be on."

"We had two happy years under Mr Parkin's ministry, and then the Rev. H. J. Pickett came along. (See portrait on page 123). He played another part, and a very important part, in my experience. I became so closely associated with him that our friendship, although we do not meet very often now, grows stronger the longer we know one another. I believe he feels this quite as much as I do."

"These two honoured ministers stand out very prominently in my life, and one prepared the way for the other in a remarkable manner. Mr Parkin was a great teacher, and laid a good foundation, and Mr Pickett in his thirteen years' ministry built well on the good foundation. I am glad, as a busy business man, to bear witness to my need of the House of God, and to the great influence in my life of the ministry of the Church I love."

"I consider that to Grove Road Church and the friends there, to my dear wife, and to God, I owe everything, all that I am, my condition, my hopes, my life. When I look back and see how I have been led through difficulties, and troubles, and trials – and I do not think there are many men living who have had more than I have – it is all very wonderful. I have always known that there has been a Higher Power than my own; no one ever told me, but I have known it, and if I am not able to explain it now, I am still absolutely certain of it, or else I should not be where I am, and what I am. I have been guided, guarded, led: how, I do not know. I am a mystery to myself, a greater mystery to myself than to anybody else."

"Oh yes! They soon made use of me at Grove Road Chapel. I have been honoured by the Church as a Trustee, Society Steward, and Class Leader. But I am no public speaker, my efforts are not in that direction. We help in other ways. My dear wife, since she was twenty one years old, has had a system of giving one-tenth away. I have done the same regarding my income, but frequently overstep the mark. I believe that our giving has been as important as anything that has gone to make up our lives. Many a time both my wife and myself have given our last five shilling to our Church, or wherever we have found it needed. I firmly believe in the grace of giving."

X Prosperity

Benevolence – Old Friends – Belgian Refugees – Buying an Orchard – A Farm at Everdon – The Trade Dispute of 1887 – Change in the Boot Trade – Prayer and Business Enterprise – Our Firms To-day – A Wise Precaution

ONE afternoon I called at the home of Mr Arnold in Northampton for a motor ride. He was just ready, and the car was against the door. On the opposite side of the road was an old grey-headed man, feebly walking with a strong stick. "Ellen," said Mr Arnold to his youngest daughter, "take this to that old gentleman over the way. Tell him I sent it," and he placed some silver in her hand. Away bounded the girl on her pleasant errand.

"One of your pensioners?" I ventured.

"No," returned Mr Arnold. "Poor old chap, he has missed me because I am not going back to the factory this afternoon. One of the finest men I know: a splendid character, but he has lived through hard times. Well, Ellen, what did he say?"

"He said 'Thank Mr Arnold,'" replied the girl, who had quickly returned, and indeed it was easy to see by the old man's demeanour that his very heart said 'God bless you, my friend.'

We were soon on our journey into the country: a swift ride, but the evident carefulness of the chauffeur gave a sense of safety. On we went, through delightful scenes, past flocks and villages; we threaded our way through the military depot of Weedon, skirted an open wood speckled with early primroses, and bounded up a slight hill into Everdon. We dismounted near a small thatched cottage, at the little window of which sat an old dame mending her husband's garments.

"Well, Jane, how are you?" greeted Mr Arnold.

"I am not quite first-class," came the answer through the closed window; "and John, he does complain."

"What is it, his rheumatism?" The old lady nodded her head. "Do you think he would like a little ride in the motor?" asked Mr Arnold. Again the head nodded.

Arrangements were quickly made for the little excursion, the chauffeur was enjoined to drive carefully, and we walked on, through a gate into the small garden of a spic and span little house, wood built, called by the people, a bungalow. On the white front to the street, in large green letters are the words "Rest a Wyle." We accepted the invitation, occupying a sheltered seat under a projecting roof, screened from the wind and in full view of the April sun. (See illustration on page 129.)

"And this is your country residence?" I queried.

"Yes," was the answer; "but, you know, we had to give it up." "Who are here now?" I asked; for it was evidently nicely furnished, and there was a clatter of dinner things from the kitchen.

"Oh, some Belgians. Our Chapel has undertaken to keep some refugees, and I have let them have this. The men are working now in Northampton, they go on their bicycles."

And here I may interpose that when the Germans entered Belgium, scattering ruin right and left, and England opened her arms to tens of thousands of refugees, the first to come into Northampton were the guests of the Primitive Methodist Church, and to Mr W. Arnold belongs the credit of making the first offer of a home. This fine example was soon followed by other individuals and churches.

A little chubby, healthy-looking toddler appeared, with wondering eyes, and then a buxom woman, evidently the mother.

"Good day, Mr Arnold," she said, "Weel you have some tay?" "Tea?"

Rev. H. J. PICKETT   Rev. GEORGE PARKIN, M.A., B.D.
AND
GROVE ROAD PRIMITIVE METHODIST CHURCH

Figure 30: Grove Road Primitive Methodist Church

was the response; "Yes, but not just yet."

"Cuffee?" she asked. But it was a cup of tea we had set our minds on, and a cup of tea we could not persuade her we should like. She could only suggest "cuffee." At last we nodded assent.

"Weeth meelik?" was the next question, and it was some moments before we recognised her endeavour to ask if we would have it "with milk."

Again we nodded, and, by moving the hands of a watch before her eyes, we succeeded in letting her know we should like it at half-past four.

"Ah," said Mr Arnold, "we thought we should like to live here in my old village, at least in the summer time; but it did not suit my wife. Fortunately we got back to Northampton before her health broke down. I laid out this garden; it used to be an orchard. Many a time I have got in here after apples."

"You were fortunate in being able to buy a nice piece of ground like this in the country," I suggested.

He replied:

"Yes, I was. A few years ago, when we were struggling our hardest, I was conscious of an intense desire to own a little bit of land, or some other property, in my native village. These two orchards were for sale, close to the cottage there where my father and mother lived. I had not the money to purchase them, I knew, but I mentioned it to my wife. To my surprise, she had got a little money put aside. I knew nothing whatever about it. With her assistance I bought these two little orchards. In connection with these, there was a little farm to be sold the same day, but at the auction it was not purchased. When I was going out of the village with my wife, in a little trap, a gentleman we met said:

"Why, Billy, did you not buy the farm as well?"

"I had never given that a thought, but driving home we talked about it, and the wife acknowledged that she had some more money. So the next morning I purchased the farm, about thirty-two acres. I have never made any money out of it, but it has satisfied a little longing. A year or two after, there were two old cottages to sell, and a piece of land, where this bungalow stands. I purchased those and felt I should like to build a little home, and come and live out here, some time or another."

"We have tried to live here; we spent several summers here, and two years ago we thought we should come and live here altogether, but, on account of the business in Northampton, we found that it was not practical. Now my dad and my mother are both gone, and the village has not seemed quite the same since."

"Yes, our business is prosperous. When I think of it I am astounded: that the poor little village boy should reach to where I am to-day. You remember the 1887 lock-out, that dreadful Jubilee Year when all the shoe factories in Northampton were closed, and there was fearful distress all over the town. I was absolutely stranded. We had spent all our money within one pound on the day that the dispute was settled that was Christmas Eve, a sorry Christmas for thousands. Since then the Shoe trade has undergone the greatest change it has experienced since it was an industry, and I am sure it can never undergo such a change again. It has been a trying and critical time for manufacturers, and, although dozens have gone under, I have been fortunate enough to keep my head above water."

"It has not been done without constant attention to business, and to my habit of carefully thinking things out, and looking at all sides of a question, as far as I have been able. When machinery was introduced after the dispute of 1895, and began to get a strong foothold in the trade, I could see, that if I did not go in for machinery, I should be quickly left behind, and go under. This was an important time in my life. 'I must make the change,' I thought, 'or lose my business.' I made it a matter of prayer, and, confident that I was doing the right thing, I speculated on thousands of pounds' worth of machinery when I had not got a spare shilling. Although confident, I sometimes wondered what the result would be. It was about this time that my uncle Anthony decided to leave the business, and so I carried it on single-handed."

"Happily I came through it. It was a great plunge, but it was a plunge that enabled me to keep up with the others. And now to-day, after twenty-six years of business experience, our name stands second to none in the trade, for honest dealing and good workmanship. It is an untarnished name, honourable and clean. I, with my sons, have now three factories, and together we employ 800 people; we pay £1,000 in wages every week, and we produce considerably over half-a-million pairs of boots and shoes per annum. We trade practically all over the world; we have customers in almost every civilised country under the sun."

"There is one thing about my business practice which I think important. No one ever suggested it to me, but somehow I saw it was a

Photo by H. COOPER & SON

FOUR GENERATIONS

WILLIAM ARNOLD
(grandson)

WILLIAM ARNOLD   MATTHEW ARNOLD
(son)   (father)

WILLIAM AUBREY ARNOLD
(great-grandson)

Figure 31: Four generations of the Arnold family

good thing to do. I have always had enough money at the bank, or I have always been able to get enough, to pay my biggest creditor instantly, if required, all that was owing to him. For one thing, I always had what I asked for from the Bank: the banker knowing me, and knowing my life, knew that he could depend on my integrity."[xi]

"Well, we were doing business with a big firm who took in another partner, at a time when I owed them a decent bit of money. I had owed them more, prior to the alteration in their business. The new partner, looking through the accounts, thought that mine was too large, and they wrote a letter to me. Now, I had just started my sons in business, which was a drain on my resources, but, because of that, I was extra careful, and had taken more than ordinary precautions. The firm sent me the month's statement with the letter, and I owed them a little more besides, for material that had come in since the statement was rendered. I asked them what extra discount they would give me if I sent a cheque by return for the whole to date. They said they could allow no more than the usual discount, but I posted a cheque for all I owed them, £1,200. Probably they were surprised to receive a cheque for the entire amount, but their letter when sending the receipt was very friendly, and the partner expressed his desire that business relationships would long continue."

XI Retrospect
The Labourer and the Pledge – Reliance on God – Prayer and Temperance – The Help of God – His Goodness – Conclusion

ONE bright spring day, Mr Arnold and myself had a quiet stroll round his little farm at Everdon. It is very well managed by his two brothers-in-law, another instance of Mr Arnold's desire to help all the members of his family.

"No," he said, "I do not get anything out of the farm, I can assure you, but it interests me, and it gives, besides others, a living to these two men."

Just then a labouring man about fifty, rake in hand, came through a gate.

"Well, George!" greeted Mr Arnold, "how are you? Are you still teetotal?"

Mr Arnold calls them all by their Christian names. He knew them as boys, and he knows them, just as intimately as men.

"Yes, sir!" was the reply; "yes, I am; and I don't intend to go back again, if I can avoid it. I don't want to go through what I have been through, if I can possibly help it!"

"But you must help it, George!"

"Yes, yes; that's all right sir," replied George; "I shan't if I can help it!"

"It depends on yourself, George!"

"Yes sir!"

"No one can keep the pledge for you, George you know that! You must keep it!"

"And I intend to, God helping me!" was the response.

"That's it," replied Mr Arnold; "that's the way to stick to it. God and yourself. That I firmly believe!"

It is pleasing to know that George had previously signed the pledge through the instrumentality of Mr Arnold.

And when George had departed Mr Arnold turned to me:

"Yes, I think my success in life, and I think for a poor village lad I have been successful, has been due to several things, but chiefly because I have asked God to help me. It has been Prayer and Temperance. It is true I was not temperate as a young man, I got mixed up with drinking shoemakers, but since I resolved to leave the drink alone, I have never touched it, and never wanted to touch it. Then, of course, being brought up in a very poor home, I got into very frugal habits, and they have never left me. I never have spent money on myself. People talk about holidays. I had very few holidays, not even when we were working day and night trying to make a business. Only once in my life have I been away for as long as ten days. I have also cultivated a habit of trying to look at a question from all sides, thinking things out in all directions, and also looking forward."

"All these have been great helps, but the greatest of all has been Prayer. My dear old granny taught me to say the Lord's Prayer when I was a very little child; and ever since, single and married, happy and despondent, teetotaler or a drinker, I have always knelt down and said the Lord's Prayer, and some little prayer of my own, in my uneducated way, every night and every morning of my life. I believe the influence

PORTRAIT OF MRS. WILLIAM ARNOLD
WITH A PHOTOGRAPH OF THE COUNTRY HOUSE AT EVERDON

Figure 32: Mrs William Arnold and the house in the country at Everdon

Photo by H. COOPER & SON

WILLIAM ARNOLD AND HIS SIX SONS

HARRY ARNOLD MATTHEW ARNOLD JAMES ARNOLD ALFRED W. ARNOLD
WILLIAM ARNOLD, Jun. WILLIAM ARNOLD THOMAS ARNOLD

Figure 33: William Arnold and his six sons

of this has, in every respect, made me what I am."

"I can look back on my life now, and I can see how great a part God has played in my life: a greater part than I have myself, or could have done however I tried. I owe everything to Him, I can see it quite plainly now; and the longer I live the plainer it becomes. When I was thinking nothing about Him, He was taking care of me and protecting me. I am as certain of that as I am that you and I are here talking together; and now, I am thankful to say, nothing will ever take that assurance away from me."

"It is a wonder to me, a mystery, how it was that my wife and I came together, but I honestly believe that God's hand was in that. And I am perfectly sure that if I had not had a careful, loving, sympathetic wife, the load I had to carry would have crushed me. But all this, again, is only the Goodness of God revealed to me through my helpmate."

"I could shed tears of joy, and I have done it, when I look back and see how I have been led, see where I have come from, see how I have been cared for and shielded, and see where I am now placed, and the opportunities I have of helping others."

"There is another thing. Ever since the old firm of Arnold & Co. had the misfortune to call its creditors together, it has been my great desire, my chief ambition, to reach a position so that I could repay all who lost money by us. The failure was owing to no fault of mine, and the creditors were all kind, as I have said, and were quite prepared to put down their losses to the ordinary hazards of business. But I have always felt that it would be my duty – as it would be my pleasure, if I ever could – to repay them every penny. I am thankful to say, that by the goodness of God, I believe I am within sight of the ability to do this, and I have every hope of repaying all claims against the old firm, with interest, at the end of this year. I think I ought to mention this in my narrative, but not because I want any praise. I give God all the glory and all the praise for this, and for all His mercies and all the goodness He has shown to me: I take no praise to myself."

"I am not cleverer than other men; I am not more worthy than other men. I have simply tried in an honest, straightforward way, to play my part manfully each day. That is what I am striving to do now. I believe, in a human sense, that is the secret of my success. I am not a brilliant man, I never can be, but I am a plodding man, and I believe that an honest, humble, plodding man is helped, and strengthened, and led, when he recognises Something higher than himself, a Power greater than his own, a God who cares for him, loves him, and guides him. It is not myself: it is God above, and to Him I give all the praise and all the glory."

"Not more than others I deserve. But God has given me more."

"I often feel that; I always feel it. He has showered His blessings on us, and, after all our struggles, we gratefully thank Him for all His goodness. We are happy and contented: our business is prosperous; we have six sons, as fine and as good as man could possibly have, or wish to have. (See portrait group on page 130.) We have four honest daughters, kind and tender. We are happy, and we are blest."

THE END.

Notes on the text

i **Henry John Pickett** was formerly minister of Kettering Road Church and was a friend of William Arnold during his ministry in the town. Pickett served as the seventh principal of Hartley College since its foundation in 1881. He was in post between 1913 and 1918. The Rev Pickett was born at Wootton Bassett, Wiltshire in 1860. He was the youngest child of Moses Pickett, labourer in a brewery (born in 1824 at Berwick Bassett, Wiltshire) and his wife Sarah (born in 1829 at Monckton, Wiltshire). They had at least five children. In early life Pickett was a working man before training as minister: he began his ministry in 1886. Prior to his time at Northampton, he was a Primitive Methodist minister at Bradford and Aylestone, Blaby in Leicestershire. He married Mary Ann Morris (born in 1866) of Soham, Cambridgeshire in 1888. There were no children of the marriage. He died aged 71 in late 1931 in south Manchester: there was no published probate will.

ii By the time Pickett and Saxton served as principals of the college, Hartley College Manchester had become the main Primitive Methodist theological college: it opened in 1881. Primitive Methodist ministerial training had been provided from 1865 by Elmfield College York as a one-year preparation for circuit work. This was superseded by the Sunderland Theological Institute in 1868. A second college opened thirteen years later in Manchester. Through the generosity of Sir William Hartley, the Primitive Methodist Church was able to support a two-year training programme in an extended building housing over sixty students; the construction of which took place between 1897 and 1906. The college, along with Victoria Park College, were ministerial training colleges. They were largely endowed by Sir William P. Hartley JP, CC; Christina Hartley CBE, MA JP; and Alderman Sir James Duckworth MP. Hartley College is still in existence today as one of four colleges that makes up Hartley Hall, Manchester.

iii **James Saxton** succeeded Pickett as the minister of Kettering Road Church in 1911. James H. Saxton was born at Hucknall Torkard, Nottinghamshire in 1863, the eldest son of James Saxton (born at Hucknall Torkard in1832 and died there in 1911) and his wife Mary (born at Claypool, Nottinghamshire in 1833). They lived at various places in the working class area of the town. In their early married life, James was a framework knitter and Mary a stitcher: later as the local knitting industry declined he became an elastic bandage maker. There were at least six children of the marriage. Arthur (born 1865) became a shoemaker in Watnall Street, Hucknall, and Charles (born 1875) an elementary school teacher in Hucknall. James initially became a coal miner in the late 1870s: mining was expanding rapidly in this area at this time. However, within a few years he had trained as a Primitive Methodist minister and by was 1885 a minister at Nottingham. There then followed a number of years of successive appointments in working class districts of Midlands' towns. Through the years 1891 and 1894 he was resident in the St Mary's area of Leicester. He married Amy Evelyn Nutman (born at Leicester in 1870) there in mid-1892. Shortly after, his ministry took his young family to Sutton in Ashfield, then the St Ann's area of Nottingham, before a move to Birmingham early in the new century. There he lived at Sparkhill in the immediate years prior to his move to Northampton in 1911. His stay in Northampton was cut short in 1918 by his move to Manchester as Principal of the Hartley College in succession to Pickett, where he remained until the early 1920s. His ministry then took him first to Chesterfield, Derbyshire and then Walsall, Staffordshire. There in the summer of 1929 he died: no probate or will was published.

iv Fallen acorns are known as mast in many places.

v To whittle is to pare down, to adjust in size; from whittle, an old name for knife.

vi Kit, the shoemaker's name for his tools.

vii Shoemakers traditionally always made Monday a holiday, and "St. Monday" was a popular term for the weekly merrymaking. When the drinking spread over the next day, it was not infrequently called "St. Tuesday."

viii Clicking is the cutting of the upper leathers to the exact shape and size required. These are cut according to a pattern, usually of paper in small factories, and in the making of the pattern great skill is required. Closing is the sewing or stitching of the upper leathers together to form the top part of the boot. Finishing is trimming, colouring, polishing, &c., the sole, heel and under part of the boot.

ix Northamptonshire Union Bank.

x This is the Kettering Road Primitive Methodist Church. William Arnold, like many of his contemporaries referred to it as Grove Road Chapel.

xi "We do not lend money on balance sheets," said a leading London banker last year, "we advance money on character!"

APPENDIX

THE FOOTWEAR INDUSTRY OF NORTHAMPTON[1]

It has often been noted that Northampton's wholesale footwear industry developed from the 1640s. However, sustained growth only takes place from the late eighteenth century. From this date a number of regional production centres, including Northampton, fed the lucrative Metropolitan markets. A number of large wealthy London footwear manufacturing merchants strongly influenced the development of the Northampton industry from this time. The town developed strong business links with substantial merchants in the capital. An example of this type of collaboration was that between Richard and George Turner and Henry A. K. Hyde begun in 1859. This partnership of the Turner brothers in Northampton and Hyde, a London merchant, built the company into one of the world's biggest by the 1870s. Also a number of London merchants directly operated manufacturing concerns in Northampton, of whom Ebenezer Homan was the most prominent.

By the middle decades, John Foster has noted that in Northampton: "… several firms were operating on a fairly large scale and there was considerable concentration of the two thousand Northampton shoe workers covered by the thirty nine returns of employment made by the 1851 Census…twelve firms employing over one hundred (workers each)…"[2] The total of shoemakers in the town at this time was 7,167. Some firms had already grown to a significant size. At Stafford as early as 1780 William Horton & Co employed circa 1,000, whilst at the new centre of Leicester, the pioneering firm of Thomas Crick & Co found work for a similar number by the early 1860s. Even outside of the main regional centres large employers of labour were to be found; for example, at Cookham, Berkshire, W. J. Burrows & Sons were employing circa 1,200 by the 1850s. But all were overshadowed by Turner Bros & Hyde of Northampton, who by the 1870s were reputed to employ 4,000 outworkers alone in the town and surrounding countryside.

Despite the presence of local retail shoemakers in most Victorian towns and villages, regional wholesale manufacturing centres had an impact. By William Arnold's time wholesale centres had begun to dominate the industry, using radically new methods of production, distribution and retailing. Like other consumer industries, the final modernisation of the

---

1 Information about bibliographical sources and more information relating to issues in this appendix can be found in K. B. Brooker (1985, revised 2010) and (1986).

2 J. Foster, *Class Struggle and the Industrial Revolution* (1974), p. 284.

footwear industry took place in the late nineteenth century. Driven by competitive pressures both from home and foreign competition, this change-process saw a small group of oligopolistic wholesale manufacturers emerge from the industry's small master base. This was not simply a dominance relationship, for these larger manufacturers continued to need the support of their smaller counterparts in order to deliver growth: the role of smaller manufacturers was never completely eclipsed by this transformative process.

Structural and Organisational Change in the Footwear Industry

Secular transformation was characterised by three distinct breaks with past business practice in the industry, and within each there existed a cogent developmental theme, which was crucial in the final shaping of the modern twentieth-century shoe industry.

1. *1857-1887 Development of distribution and retailing capability*: a radical change in retail distribution techniques in the industry together with the initial commercial application of machinery, which, despite the continued emergence of larger manufacturers, gave increased opportunities for small masters to enter the industry.

2. *1887-95 Development of integrated machinery capability*: a machinery revolution, with a growth of intensive production methods by best practice firms, and a commitment made to ending outworking: first indications of declining entrepreneurial entry opportunities.

3. *1895-1905 Development of manufacturer control over production capability*: a period of radical change in production techniques and supervision in the workplace, accompanied by increasing entrepreneurial barriers of entry.

Each of these phases of change are indelibly linked, with elements begun in one period being further developed and refined in the next, that together give a total picture of industrial transformation.

Amongst the range of economic evidence revealing patterns of growth in the Northampton footwear industry, the rate of construction of footwear building is useful. Table 9 is an analysis of the building applications made by the industry from 1860 to 1914 that clearly show the additional building required to facilitate industrial growth. First, there was the use of warehouses important in the transitional industry structure, followed by a growing predominance of factory construction, and lastly of factory extensions after 1895 to meet the demands of full mechanisation. Additionally, as the utility of warehouses faded with the

Table 9: Summary of deposited building plans for new industrial buildings and extensions for the footwear industry 1860-1914

Sub-period	Shoe warehouse	Shoe factory	Additions to footwear mfrs business premises	Total applications	Total applications in sub-period as % all applications	Annual average applications in sub-period
1860-86						
1860-69	21	3	3	27	7.2%	2.7
1870-79	8	43	9	60	16.0%	0.8
1880-86	9	16	17	42 (129)	11.2% (34.4%)	7.0 (10.5)
1887-95	11	21	59	91	24.2%	10.1
1896-1905	–	19	39	58	15.4%	5.8
1906-14	–	7	91	98	26.0%	10.1
1860-1914	49 [13%]	109 [29%]	218 [58%]	376 [100%]	100.0%	7.0

Source: Northampton Borough Council Register of Northampton Building Plans 1860-1914. In three volumes comprising:
1. applications made to [i] Northampton Improvement Commissioners 1860-1872; [ii] Northampton Urban Sanitary Authority 1873-1878
2. applications made to Northampton Urban Sanitary Authority 1888-1901
3. applications made to Northampton County Borough Engineers Department 1902-1914

Notes:
- Although many workshops for component manufacturers were erected, applications for these could not be separated from the generality of workshop applications and so have been omitted. The same applies to the many outworking workshops built in the gardens of domestic houses.
- The totals for "Additions to footwear manufacturers' business premises" exclude all applications submitted to fire sprinkler systems, fire escapes, sanitary facilities, etc. that were required by the Factory & Workshop Acts of 1890 and 1901.
- Applications for shoe warehouses are made between 1860 and 1882. Thereafter two applications are made in 1887, five in 1890 and four in 1891. Thereafter they cease.
- Applications for shoe factories commence in 1868 and run steadily through the period.

decline of outwork, they were turned over to factory production too. Contemporary planning law did not require owners to apply for permission to convert and so little evidence charts such changes. Of course, there was never a smooth shift from one category of building application to another as the table demonstrates. Nor is there a simple correlation between the number of applications and changes in the volume of economic activity in the industry, as the size of footwear factories and factory extensions also increases significantly as factory working becomes the norm after 1895. The single storey factories built in the west of Northampton were significantly larger than the older three storey factories in the shoe district north and east of the town centre. Yet these individual planning applications signify a decision to build, although taking no any account of the size of the building or extension being applied for: more detailed research would be required to access this level of detail.

Another identifiable feature was the speculative building of premises and extensions. Clearly some Northampton builders, notably Martin and Hawtin, built speculatively in the wake of the change that swept the industry: possibly as many as 70% of applications between 1887 and 1900 were of this character. Of course, not all manufacturers built new premises, but rather used and adapted unwanted premises. Both William Arnold and his sons' firm used the existing premises of others; thus, the St Giles' Terrace factory of A. & W. Arnold had been built by Allinson & Co, who had made relocated. The factories taken by Arnold Brothers were merely re-modelled and extended. Another feature of the industry was the makeshift use of outwork workshops and converted houses from which to manufacture. Contemporary planning require-ments did not cover such change of use at this time. Again, in their early years, William Arnold and his partners used both types of buildings: a workshop in Hunter Street and a converted house in Military Road.

1857-1887 Development of distribution and retailing capability
Technical change in the transition period from 1857 to 1887 was dominated by the introduction of sewing machines, which mechanised the process of closing, and machines for lasting and attaching the uppers to the bottom stuff of the shoe by various fastenings. Many of these machines required no external power source and so growth at this stage was achieved by the extension of the existing organisation of outwork and sub-contracting. But change in the British footwear industry prior to 1887 was as much about radical changes in both distribution and retailing as it was about changes in production techniques. This movement was driven partly by growing consumer demand as urban population expanded and real wages rose, and partly by the need to respond to the radical increase in wholesale productive capacity resulting from technical and organisational change. Both required a market response by the wholesale industry if it was to thrive. It was these developments in distribution and retailing linked to the new production techniques and society's development of a culture of consumerism[3] that gave opportunity for a relatively small number of large wholesale manufacturers at the major wholesale centres to dominate the UK footwear industry.

Like any business person, the wholesale manufacturer was concerned to assure their ability to distribute their production to market. Many

3 J. Benson, *The Rise of Consumer Society in Britain 1880-1980* (1994). Recent studies have focused on gender patterns of consumerism; see, M. C. Finn, "Sex & the City…", *Victorian Studies* Vol. 44 no.1 (2001); B. Shannon, *The Cut of His Coat: Dress and Consumerism Culture in Britain 1860-1914* (2006); C. Rose, *Making, Selling & Wearing Boys' Clothes in Late Victorian England* (2010); B. Shannon *op. cit.* and P. Johnson "Conspicuous & Working Class Consumption in Late Victorian & Edwardian Britain", *Transactions of the Royal Historical Society 5th Series* Vol. 38 (1988).

were primarily focused upon the large London market. At an early date distribution and retail channels were developed between the dominant London manufacturer-merchants in the capital and the Northampton trade. Carrier networks were set between the capital and the county for the inward movement of materials to be made up and the return of the finished product. In the capital, merchants were largely responsible for wholesale distribution and some retailing activity. From being a small wholesale sector in 1857, producing for Government contracts, the needs of the large metropolitan market, and export markets, wholesaler manufacturers progressively became dominant figures in the late Victorian domestic and overseas consumer boom. Distribution issues became a central focus for them, with footwear manufacturers leading the retailing and distribution developments that dominated UK domestic markets later in the century. This change generated intense competition between local producer-retailers and the ascendant whole-sale centres.

Manufacturers' forward vertical integration into distribution and retailing took a variety of forms and was based on sound wholesale distribution techniques: the use of multiple trading, trade-marking; marketing; advertising; agency agreements; advertising; mail order activities; standard pricing and price maintenance.[4] All wholesale firms continued to develop these already familiar distribution channels to some degree as the century progressed. Many prominent Northampton manufacturers, like J. Sears & Co., carried on a factoring trade too, though not to the extent it was exercised in Leicester, whilst others took over warehousing and stock control activities from the London merchants both in the capital and at other major provincial centres. As early as the 1830s V. A. Hatley notes that Northampton's leading manufacturers like Hallam & Edens and George Moore were already heavily committed to retailing in Britain's leading industrial towns.[5] Later other firms joined; these included Manfield & Co and H. E. Randall Ltd in London; Simon Collier Ltd in Glasgow and South Africa; John Marlow had extensive showrooms in London at 76 Finsbury Pavement, and at Glasgow and Sydney; and J. Sears & Co Ltd and C. & E. Lewis in Liverpool and Glasgow. John Emmett Ltd likewise operated factories in Northampton and Towcester, together with retail and warehouse premises at Barbican, London which "...considerably improved his trade for he was able to supply numerous customers who require filling-up sizes and small orders which they can get from stock

4 Emerging government competition policy was not as strong in Britain as in the US. In the footwear industry there were significant developments in price maintenance agreements. Footwear manufacturer trade associations gave support to such strategies. The standard pricing of different grades and qualities of footwear was widely adopted.
5 V. A. Hatley *"Some aspects of Northampton's History 1815-51", N.P.P.* 6 (1965/66) p. 247.

without delay..."[6] Such premises not only provided a useful contact point for clients in major markets, but gave the potential to address customer needs and begin to increase levels of service to them. It became common to give over space to develop show room for the display of goods. Other manufacturers operated a single or small number of retail outlets, usually focused on medium and high grade footwear, and run a hand-made and bespoke business in this way. As has already been noted a majority of wholesalers continued to develop their selling to small independent retailers, whilst others again increased their business with the new departmental stores.[7]

The other main wholesale distribution channel was commercial travelling. As more salesmen were used to sell directly to independent retailers, wholesale warehouses again solely became storage facilities, rather than showrooms. Many firms now introduced specialised management roles, with increasing numbers of partners and directors of firms focusing on distribution and sales. Some took up long term residence away from Northampton, to look after company interests. Simon Collier junior's residence in South Africa has already been mentioned. Alfred Walker Arnold resided in London and looked after the company's interests there. Walter Finnemore of Oakeshott and Finnemore lived in Hertfordshire; George Roe of Roe Bros. in Hampshire. London-based firms which moved production to Northampton show similar split residence patterns. James, the founder of James Branch Ltd., remained in London. His sons managed factory production in Northampton. Later, the brothers were divided between Northampton (Charles S. and Ernest E.) and London (Archibald, and Sydney G.). J. Dawson & Co., founded in London in 1780, came to Northampton in 1836. The directors of each successive generation divided themselves between the company's manufacturing interests in Northampton, and their metropolitan merchant interests.

The acquisition of salesmanship skills and knowledge was emphasised in training manufacturers' sons. An increased status was accorded to this function as is shown by the support given by manufacturers to the UK Commercial Travellers Association Northampton branch in the 1890s. The Northampton branch officers and committee was dominated by manufacturers, predominately of founders' sons. The need for active selling in the marketplace emerged, although some still spoke of good quality products selling themselves. Older established firms like Simon Collier continued to rely upon freehold showroom and warehouse facilities in their main trading centres, but newer firms went for cheaper

---

6 *B.S.T.J.*, 24/1/1891 p. 105.

7 For a recent survey of department store development see the essays in G. Crossick (ed.), *Cathedrals of Consumption: The Department Store in European Society 1850-1940* (1999).

options like rented premises, or simply the use of travellers and a reliance on carriage facilities of railway companies for distribution between the factory and retailer.[8]

In many ways, the commercial traveller role was a passive, reactive process: the retailer demands and the traveller responds. One of A. & W. Arnold's order books survives and reveals how production was directly linked to orders secured at each shop visited.[9] Orders were passed back to the factory, where the order was passed into the making process. This had clear ramifications for both the production process and the sales function too. Thus, if orders were required swiftly or required particular detailing, size or fit, then this meant factory operations being constantly re-arranged at the margin. And late orders meant a potential loss of future business. However, other firms used various methods of express delivery service for independent retailers, which avoided constant changes to the production schedule. This technique saved retailers the cost of holding extensive stocks, which fell to the manufacturer. He now stocked the majority of his current catalogue range across all sizes, fits and styles to meet both small and large orders. Some used factory warehouse space, whilst others retained regional storage. Known as the "in-stock" system this was adopted by many wholesale manufacturers from the 1890s. Padmore & Barnes developed the system, which they operated through their warehouses and express train services. This and their shop displays to some degree anticipated aspects of the later radical Norvic Concentration Plan.[10] It was a warehousing solution that sought to provide items within the firm's current catalogue of stock lines with a minimum of delay. The in-stock system provided a means to regulate seasonal fluctuations in factory production. Although the manufacturer had the cost of holding stock, he was able to supply retailers from stock at minimum notice. Where it operated efficiently it meant that factory production was not continually distorted by the vagaries of order requirements, and for the retailers it delivered the widest stock range to his customers quickly and without the need for the retailer to hold unduly heavy stocks. In

8 V. A. Hatley on mid-century Northampton railway connections, 'Northampton Re-Vindicated', *N.P.P.* Vol. II No.6 (1959).

9 N.R.O. ZA 4996, A. & W. Arnold Wholesale Boot & Shoe Manufacturer Order Book for 1907/09: the order book is punctuated with delivery-time information by the traveller: for example 'when ready'; "now, most urgent"; "deliver in ten days sure to keep well up, a large shop"; "deliver on the 1st certain". These entries suggest that the firm is making up the orders in the factory on receipt of the order, rather than taking from stock. With some of the orders came instructions about making which again suggests the factory is making on receipt of the order: 12/01/1909, "...128 pairs, all wide; no doeskin linings. When ready May 1st..."; 15/11/1908 "...7 pairs. AW jnr. to see before go to work...[sic]"; 22/02/1909 "...65 pairs. WA jnr. to see before work tickets go to clicking room and at each stage..."

10 F.W. Wheldon, *A Norvic Century* (1947) p. 122-23, and K .B. Brooker "*Cecil Colman 1878-1954*". D.B.B. Vol.1 (1984) p. 747-49.

contrast to the reactive nature of a pure commercial traveller system, the two processes merged together provided a proactive method of meeting final customer need quickly.

Use was also made of independent selling agents, particularly in overseas trade, where even quite modest firms utilised their services. For example Pollard & Sons of Northampton developed a wide trade in Australia and New Zealand. A local merchant acted as an important intermediary between the firm and retailers in these countries. This trade was conducted without any of the firm's people ever travelling to these countries. Some overseas agents carried the risks of credit loss and were given considerable discretion regarding selling prices. Agents were common amongst smaller manufacturers wishing to be relieved of marketing and sales responsibilities, so that very limited financial assets could be devoted exclusively to production. Retained on a commission basis, they worked closely with the manufacturers often over a long period of time: they had complete responsibility for sales. The agent often strongly influenced the firm's footwear style and design. In the shoe industry some agents acted for one firm, but given the small scale of many manufacturing operations, the majority carried a range of manufacturers' products. Footwear manufacturers in a more substantial way of business would have directly employed manufacturers' agents.

However, it was the footwear manufacturers increasing dominance of retail distribution from the 1870s through multiple trading, branding and advertising that was also significant. The considerable range of marketing and merchandising activities became increasingly utilised by both elite and volume producers. Retailing accompanied by the use of trade-marked goods, advertising and marketing techniques reached far into the wholesale industry at this time. Increasing use of these techniques was being made by domestic consumer industries in Britain and Europe and the USA generally. Indeed, the use of trade-marked goods became ubiquitous in the footwear industry, and both the Arnold companies widely traded such goods. The skill and ingenuity demonstrated by larger firms was noticeable, as was the scale of these operations: A. E. Marlow pioneered promotional advertising, whilst William Barratt began a mail order and boots-by-air service.[11] Multiple shop operations, however, were more clearly the province of the Northampton elite, not least because of the capital and operating costs involved with such chains. Nevertheless, a number of smaller

11 Kay's run the only significant mail order operation in Britain at this time: they handled 1,200 orders a day (R. Coopey & D. Porter, *"Agency Mail Order in Britain 1900-2000"* in J. Benson & L. Urgolini, *A Nation of Shopkeepers* (2003) p. 228). US mail order was more developed; Sears of Chicago were handling 100,000 orders daily early in the twentieth century: A. D. Chandler, *Scale & Scope: the Dynamics of Industrial Capitalism* (1990) p. 61.

manufacturers operated a small number of retail outlets, very often in London, but some were to be found in other provincial centres too. A pioneering example was the chain developed by Manfield. Initially doing business under the banner Cash & Co., the chain very quickly grew in number and included branches in Europe and the USA.

Multiple shop trading allowed wholesale manufacturers to take advantage of increased productivity and scale economies associated with machine production. These shops quickly offered low retail prices afforded by the bulk stocking of standardised lines. Working on small profit margins, multiple shops dispensed with traditional credit transactions in favour of cash trading. A modest service level was provided, together with the sale of related goods and a factory repair service. A key requirement was the selection of prime retail sites. Initially concentrating upon the expanding working class market, wholesalers sought worker neighbourhoods for their shops and gave emphasis to working boots and cheaper grades of footwear. But by the turn of the century there was a spread of these shops into the middle class shopping districts, once the domain of the bespoke shoe, as increasing volumes of good quality ready-made footwear potentially offered wholesalers higher margins. Both John Sears and William Barratt became known for their ability to select prime sites at keen prices. This ability was regarded as the key to the phenomenal success of the two companies. Both were regarded from their early days in the trade primarily as retailers rather than manufacturers: both came from retail shoemaker families.

The retailing developments first initiated by footwear manufacturers in the 1870s and 1880s constituted a major contribution to the retailing revolution in the economy generally. The trend laid down in the 1880s, expanded multiple shop operations at the expense of the independent retailer, to emerge as one of the most significant retail developments of the new century. The urban working class formed a new and ready market for cheap, often badly made shoes and clothing and the footwear was an early promoter of multiple trading in Britain. In 1870 there were ten footwear firms with more than ten branches and by 1880 there were eleven more. The statistics of this multiple shop boom tells the story. In 1880 there had been 1,564 multiple shop branches, and of these one third (521) were selling footwear. By 1905, the number of multiple shops had grown to 15,242 and by 1914 to 25,000. Of these, one sixth (4,170) were to be found in the footwear industry.[12] At 1914 the retail revolution was far from complete, but the pattern for the future established.

---

12 Jeffereys *op. cit.* p. 357: Cf. C. Fulop *op. cit.* (1964) p. 71, a multiple chain is where "…ten or

The increased localisation of production by wholesale manufacturers and their growing domination of retail distribution resulted in the gradual decline of local master retail shoemakers from 1870. The 1851 Census Enumerators' Returns shows how persistent small master production was in many locations: it was still not uncommon for the apprentice and journeymen to live in with the master's family in the time honoured way.[13] In terms of craft and cultural affinities, many masters were still bound closely to their employees. As late as 1869 it was noted that many were "... but a shade better off than the men... "and that "... we still retain the genuine cobbler who stitches away at old shoes and talks radical politics..."[14] The local shoemaker as lawyer, teacher, scribe and political polemicist to his neighbours, may have lived on in the popular imagination,[15] but the reality was more prosaic, as John Butcher, a Leicester manufacturer, noted:

> ...The number of men employed was limited and the man who could keep employed 10 or 12 hands was considered in a large way of business. It was almost a universal custom for people in the country to be measured for their boots and pay for them once a year... It was seldom that a shoe-maker employed more than two or three hands, and these men had to undertake every description of work...[16]

The penetration of the regional and local footwear markets began in the late 1860s as Leicester and Northampton wholesalers started to flood the market with cheap ready-made boots. Within a few years the intensity of competition resulted in the decline of experienced local retail shoemakers. Village shoemakers were the first to cease trading, followed by shoemakers in market towns. Those that survived ceased making as the wholesale ready-made trade grew: so retail shoemakers became footwear retailers: '...in many instances (amongst small masters) home manufacture is only pretence; their chief income being derived from profits in machine sewn (i.e. ready-made) articles...'[17]

As machine-made footwear increased in quality and costs fell, so manufacture passed to the wholesaler. And as quality improved, their

---

more shops are in the same ownership, with central direction of a number of branches, as distinct from an aggregation of separate shops..." No footwear chains were to match food chains: Liptons 449 stores, Maypole Dairy Company 977 stores, and Meadow & Perks Dairy Company 762 shops.

13 Census Enumerators' Returns in Northampton for 1851 provide a number of examples, including the households of Richard Turner and John Gibbs, that are referred to elsewhere in the introduction.

14 *Saint Crispin*, I, 6/2/1869 p. 7, and 8/5/1869, p. 249.

15 See *E. J. Hobsbawm* 'Political Shoemakers' P.P. 89 (1980) *passim*.

16 *B.S.T J.*, 28 /4/18/1888, p. 337.

17 B.&S. 30/3/1878 p. 23.

market for bespoke work, a mainstay of independent shoemaker retailers, declined also. The growing scarcity of skilled hand-sewn men, a function of low pay and technical change, merely added to the collapse of the retail shoemakers' competitive advantage. Contemporary observers advocated that local masters should safeguard their retail role by becoming agents selling wholesale manufacturers' branded goods instead of clinging to their craft principles. This conservatism had already led to drapers, grocers and other shopkeepers retailing footwear, whilst in larger towns and cities, the department store and the Cooperative store were already successfully competing with independent shoe retailers. By 1891, most of the remaining estimated 21,000 retail shoemakers continued to make at least some goods to order: '…it is no uncommon thing for a country boot maker to have special patterns and lasts for at least half of his customers, and…a ready means of closing his own special work…'[18] Within another decade the penetration of wholesale manufactured goods into the home market was complete.

1887-1895 Development of an integrated machinery capability

Industrial transformation in the footwear industry required both technical and organisational change. Initially technical changes were absorbed into the existing outwork structure. But as technical maturity was reached, manufacturer ascendency in the workplace achieved and price competition in the marketplace intensified, the impetus for a final shift to factory production was reached. There now took place a shift from outworking to integrated factory production. Emphasis has been placed upon the incursions of wholesale manufacturers into the domestic retail market being driven by the increased productivity from the beginnings of machine introduction and gradual changes in the manufacturers' approach to production. Many of these machines were often individually fitted into the existing production cycle as required. Few of them required a power source. The other characteristic of technical change in this period was that machine solutions were primarily applied to cheaper grades of work and so the extent of change in high quality centres like Northampton was slower than that witnessed in lower grade centres like Leicester. As a result there was a perpetuation in Northampton of the handwork processes associated with medium and high grades of footwear. This has led some accounts of industrial transformation within the industry to argue that centres making the lower grades of footwear were more progressive than centres like Northampton. The reality is, however, that prior to *c.* 1886 mechanisation was only economically attractive for those firms making poorer grades of work. Thus, in these first years of mechanisation, the

---

18 *B.S.T.J.* 14/6/1884 p. 9.

relatively unsophisticated machinery-assisted hand technology was
absorbed into the existing outwork structure of the industry: handwork
remained as important as the machine work that was ultimately to
supersede it.

Organisationally the transitional phase led to a considerable extension
in the numbers of small producers, together with new small producer
roles: roles that were created by the very process of technical change
itself. Thus, a small master presence continued, was re-defined, and
underpinned the development and expansion of the industry generally.

The townscape at this time was a rich mix of industrial buildings, which
reflected the variety of production models being used by the town's
footwear firms. At the heart of this was the relationship between
manufacturer and employees: some were in-door workers, but many
more remained as outworkers. Whilst machine use had proliferated, its
adoption was ultimately dependent upon its utility to a manufacturer;
hand work remained common. The shoe warehouse predominated
within the town during the transition period. Classically, these premises
provided a firm's base for holding stocks of materials and finished
goods; for housing key workers like clickers and packers; as well as
acting as a counting house and a place where outworkers gathered
materials and deposited finished goods. But by this time, some
warehouses had also begun to house machinery where manufacturers
had decided to bring a process "indoors". And additionally, the first
true factories could be seen; places were a firm was focusing its
production. Alongside the shoe warehouse, the town had many
outwork workshops and small premises where small masters and
component manufacturers operated.

The patchwork development of footwear technology in the generation
before 1887 gave rise to an organisational structure based on outwork,
which combined factory operation with domestic outwork. This
resulted in a variety of outworking forms persisting. And an important
effect was to produce as many new grades of hand-working as of
machine working: clicking, lasting, and finishing were to remain
substantially hand processes until the 1890s. Indeed, outwork, and with
it artisan skills and customs, retained a firm hold on the Northampton
industry.[19] The strong move to factory working after 1895 resulted in
the numbers of outworkers finally declining. As William Arnold's early
working life was spent as an outwork riveter it is interesting to look at

19 The local Medical Officer of Health figures for the five year period 1906-10 puts the
   numbers at 1906 = 886; 1907 = 1154; 1908 = 1248; 1909 = 747; 1910 = 600. Many of these
   workers were hand-sewn men. The 1901 Census records 15,474 people engaged in the
   industry, and in 1911 16,961.

the nature of this way of working in some more detail.

Up to 1887 market expansion was met by the extensive growth of production, in which manual outwork and small master production were as important as factory production. Technical change was dominated by the adoption of simple labour intensive machines. Hand or treadle powered, they easily fitted into the existing organisational structure of the industry: there was little need for a fixed power source and the resultant centralised work place. Although technical constraints largely determined Northampton's slow centralisation, manufacturers do appear to have centralised handwork operations, either in warehouse factories or in nearby manufacturer-owned workshops, where this was practicable. It is probably true to state that only new grades of hand-workers, rural men new to the industry, accepted this policy. This process of centralisation went furthest amongst best practice firms. A press report on the industry locally in 1886 stressed the mixed systems of hand and machine working necessary for a centre making better grades of footwear in the transition period. The article highlights the work of ten of the town's leading manufacturers. It and stresses that varying patterns of jobbing and variety production remained the norm: all second rank firms were described as utilising only traditional craft methods.

Everywhere in the industry these extensive growth patterns reinforced and perpetuated outwork operations. From the outset, outworking had underpinned the development of the Northamptonshire wholesale industry. There were two elements to this system of production: its organisational structure, and the geographical divisions that developed between different shoe centres within the industry. During the transitional phase, this structure of production was to become more entrenched and complex.

The nature of early geographical divisions within the wholesale industry was based upon the basket-work system of production, whereby ready-cut materials were sent into Northamptonshire by London merchants to be made up. Manufacturers from other centres had work made in the town, with strong links being made between Leicester factors and local sub-contractors. Manufacturers from other centres had branch factories too: Derham Brothers of Bristol; S. T. Midgley & Sons of Leeds; and J. N. Brown of Birmingham. Additionally, Stafford and Kettering firms used agents in Northampton. All took advantage of the lower wage rates and levels of collective action amongst Northampton shoemakers, which was combined with their high skill level. The basket-work system began to break down from the 1860s as a result of early mechanisation. Thomas Wright notes that the old system was eclipsed, '…because of William Hickson who settled as a manufacturer in Northampton…(&)…the basket work method gave place to the exhibition system – the first showplace in London being Hickson's warehouse in Smithfield…'[20] Within a short period, this innovation gave rise to an increasing trend whereby several London merchants established branch factories in Northampton, where goods were made in their entirety. Several of these London men came to reside in the town, and were soon to become members of the industry locally. Ebenezer Homan became the most prominent. Relatively lower wages, high operative skills and weaker levels of unionisation compared to London continued to see Northampton utilised by London merchants. A fresh wave of such migrations was experienced in the late 1880s and early 1890s.[21] One such firm, Samuel Smith & Co, also had a branch factory at Long Buckby: the firm's local agent was William Dickens of Daventry, who employed William Arnold as a young man. In addition to this, local manufacturers continued to undertake sub-contract work for London houses, and most established a warehouse-showroom from which to conduct their important London business.

Production within the county also revealed similar geographical divisions. From the earliest days, Northampton manufacturers had used country shoemakers as a surplus, reserve labour force that could be readily expanded and contracted according to seasonal shifts in activity and in times of heavy demand. Low levels of economic activity in the county caused by the decline of textile industries in the early nineteenth century and economic difficulties in agriculture later in the century (Table 10) resulted in an overstocked rural labour market together with lower local wages and lower levels of labour organisation. This gave rise to poor wage rates, and whilst current information concerning shoe industry wage rates is very sketchy given the prevalence of piecework payments, it may be safely assumed that they tended to be in excess of those prevailing in agriculture locally.[22] Traditional textile industries, with agriculture, had formed the core of the county's old industrial base.[23] Many of the rising East Northamptonshire shoe centres had suffered periods of economic decline and distress earlier in the century

---

20 T. Wright, *The Romance of the Shoe* (1920) p. 162.

21 *S.L.R.* 28/7/1888 p. 92 listed those London firms with branch factories in Northampton as being: James Branch, John Branch, J. Dawson & Sons, Davy Bros. (a branch of A. Salomon & Co), Hickson & Sons, Richard Mountford & Co, E. Parrish & Son, Henry Sharman, Stubbs & Grimsdell, and S. Smith & Co.

22 Able-bodied agricultural labourers in Northamptonshire received 11/- to 12/- per week in the 1860s, with perquisites adding possibly another 2/- or 3/-. Country shoemaker wages were above this level, but below those prevailing in the main centres: see *K.O.* 23/12/1885 p. 8, where it was noted Kettering shoemakers "…are paid at miserably poor wages compared with such towns as Northampton and Leicester…". Wage rates were fixed here in *c*.1872 and remained in force until the early 1890s.

23 These were the making of worsteds, silk, plush, linen, pillow lace, ribbon weaving and

Table 10: Shifting job opportunities in Northamptonshire (outside Northampton) in four principal occupational groups

Occupational group	Males			Females		
	1851	**1871**	**1891**	**1851**	**1871**	**1891**
Agriculture	26,274	23,268	17,685	2,014	313	182
Textiles	539	89	16	10,628	6,377	741
Footwear	10,759	15,026	25,796	3,950	4,562	10,338
Iron manufacture & quarries	227	1,421	2,176	–	–	–
Indoor domestic service	763	573	564	9,091	11,076	11,022

Source: Registrar General Printed Census Reports 1851-1891

Notes:
1. Agriculture – traditional employment: employment declining, but remaining important
2. Textiles – old industrial base that collapsed as mechanised factory-based capacity emerged in West Yorkshire (wool) and Nottinghamshire (lace)
3. Footwear – rising, dominant industrial employment sector
4. Iron – emerging sector, but provides relatively smaller employment pre-1914
5. Domestic service – dominant female employment sector

prior to the upsurge of footwear manufacture from 1870.[24]

Along with ironstone quarrying, iron making and foundry work, clothing and corset making, footwear manufacture paved the way for an economic restructuring of the area signalled by rising job opportunities particularly suited to former weavers and cloth makers (Table 11).[25] As the industry grew, so the spread of outworking, followed by manufacturing in country areas, increased. This consolidation of the industry in the east of the county after 1860 was based on increased market demand, the opening of the Leicester-Hitchin railway and the entry of semi-skilled labour permitted by early mechanisation. The two main types of centre, then, were outworking villages that remained on the periphery of production, providing manufacturing centres with surplus labour; and small manufacturing towns that emerged as manufacturing centres in their own right. For some, like Towcester and

wool combing. The working of wool was already in decline by the 1790s-1800s: for Kettering, see *VCH Northamptonshire* iii p. 219 and H. A. Randall, "The Kettering Worsted Industry of the Eighteenth Century" *N.P.P.* Vol. iv: 5 & 6 (1970 and 1971). And although wool stapling at Towcester continued to the 1890s, silk, plush and ribbon weaving was in full decline by the 1850s and hand pillow lace-making by the 1860s to be gradually replaced by boot making for Northampton masters.

24 E. J. Swaysland, *Boot and Shoe Manufacture as a Village Industry* (1902) *passim.*

25 East Northamptonshire centres only emerge as important footwear centres from the 1860s. Kettering is a case in point after a generation of industrial malaise. This pattern of mid-nineteenth century economic development was common to the midland region generally: For example, for Norfolk, A.W. Bayne, *History of Norwich* (1868) p. 568-605, and Coventry, A.R. Prest, *Industrial Revolution in Coventry* (1960) *passim.*

Table 11: Demographic movements in Northamptonshire 1851-1891

Registration district	Population movement	% change 1891 compared with 1851	Comment
Brackley	-2,117	-15.4%	Agricultural area
Towcester	-846	-6.6%	Minor footwear activity declining: wool stapling
Daventry	-4,278	-19.5%	Declining footwear activity: agriculture
Brixworth	-2,585	-17.5%	Agriculture: small outwork and quarries
Oundle	-2,774	-17.7%	Agriculture area
Pottersbury	+2,960	+30.2%	Agriculture
Northampton	+45,460	+134.3%	Footwear manufacture: foundry work
Hardingstone	+1,935	+22.3%	Northampton suburbs in north: small outwork
Wellingborough	+22,286	+104.3%	Footwear manufacture: iron works and quarrying
Kettering	+17,409	+96.2%	Footwear manufacture: iron works and quarrying
Thrapston	+1,741	+13.6%	Footwear manufacture: iron works and quarrying
Peterborough	+16,345	+56.6%	Railway, brickmaking, agricultural marketing
Northamptonshire	**+70,638**	**+33.2%**	

Source: Registrar General Printed Census Reports 1851-1891.

Daventry, expansion in the transition period fell away later in the century, whilst others, like Kettering, Raunds and Burton Latimer, witnessed urban development as the industry became more firmly established: by the Edwardian period these centres were vigorously competing in Northampton's medium grade footwear markets.

This shift in the county's economic base was particularly reflected in the differing scale of demographic changes at centre in known Northampton satellite settlements (Table 11). The Census Reports between 1851 and 1891 reveal rural depopulation in those Registration Districts unaffected by the new industrial base. By contrast urban districts particularly experienced rising population as the industry shifted away from many of the outworking villages. A closer analysis of Northampton's satellite shoe villages reveals a tendency for population to increase early in the transition period when job opportunities were increasing, only to fall later as the industry began to centralise production in the main manufacturing centres. Of shoe districts losing population, Towcester, Daventry and Long Buckby (older established manufacturing towns outside the main shoemaking belt), only the latter continued to flourish. Yet even in the new industrial districts, the essential rural, agricultural character of the county was never entirely eradicated. Of the districts experiencing population growth, only Cogenhoe and Peterborough were not reliant upon these new manufacturing developments.

The transitional period also witnessed a network of satellite outworking villages centred round each main footwear town emerging.[26] Of the forty parishes within a five mile radius of Northampton, concentrations of footwear activities are recorded to have occurred in 44% of them (Table 13). Some villages were particularly associated with one manufacturer, who became the dominant employer. In this way, Manfield & Sons can be linked to Harpole; Simon Collier & Sons to Kislingbury; and Pollard & Son to Long Buckby. Whilst at other places several Northampton firms undertook outwork operations; thus at Towcester, Hornby & West, Cove & West, J. Harrison & Co, and later, Church & Co, all relied heavily upon shoe workers there. The centres recorded in Table 12 refer to places where evidence can be adduced of an outworker concentration. Undoubtedly some of the remaining parishes contained smaller and scattered numbers of outworkers, but these places will only be traced by a very detailed scrutiny of sources, such as Enumerators' Returns. Happily, the outwork ledgers of one firm, F. W. Pollard & Son, are extant, and these list outworkers, either singularly or a small number, in the following additional parishes: Moulton, Hardingstone, Wood Burcote, Towcester, Greens Norton, Roade, Bugbrooke, Whiston and Brafield on the Green. In fact, within the shoe belt some villages came under the influence of more than one major centre: e.g. Earls Barton shoemakers made for both Northampton and Wellingborough; and Great Doddington shoemakers made for Wellingborough, Northampton, Rushden and Higham Ferrers. In addition, scattered references record that Northampton outwork was completed at Kettering in the mid-century; at Higham Ferrers; and more generally throughout the period to 1914 at Daventry and Long Buckby. However, where a firm carried out very extensive operations, the network of outworkers stretched farther out into the county. And in the case of Turner Brothers and Hyde, who employed *c.* 4,000 in the 1870s, outworkers were to be found in neighbouring counties.[27] Generally, these were places in which commoner grades of work were executed.[28]

26 D. Bythell *op. cit.* p. 114-5 suggests that in wholesale shoe areas outside the East Midlands outworking was "largely an urban phenomenon".

27 Wright *op. cit.* p. 228-30: Turners sent work into Bedfordshire and Buckinghamshire.

28 Northampton's low grade work was seen as being made up in adjacent country areas, where wages were lower, under the control of shoe agents: *V.C.H Northamptonshire* ii p. 319; S.L.R. 22/3/1890 p. 386.

Table 12: Population movements in Northampton footwear outwork parishes 1851-1911

Parish	1851	1861	1871	1881	1891	1901	1911
[1] rising population							
Dallington	714	686	1,051	1,610	2,233	4.852	5,451
Duston	563	1,162	1,640	2,497	2,963	3,528	4,513
Kingsthorpe	1,586	1,906	2,409	3,054	7,697	14,099	15,476
Earls Barton	1,277	1,557	1,905	2,337	2,602	2,914	2,556
Cogenhoe	374	360	367	345	447	467	485
[2] downward fluctuation							
Abthorpe	500	541	559	460	433	338	324
Astcote	*						
Denton	595	578	619	547	487	439	416
Doddington, Great	493	580	626	592	551	508	482
Grendon	558	610	532	542	536	412	416
Hackleton	497	535	475	378	381	327	346
Harpole	778	833	824	829	910	915	870
Houghton, Great	317	365	369	330	303	303	267
Houghton, Little	558	578	575	510	504	433	414
Kislingbury	690	723	669	695	725	649	609
Long Buckby	2,341	2,500	2,493	2,548	2,267	2,147	2,467
Pattishall	775	885	965	914	890	860	882
Piddington	559	567	572	508	523	387	377
[3] falling population							
Daventry	4,430	4,124	4,051	3,859	3,939	3,780	3,516
Holcot	508	517	404	377	341	343	289
Towcester	2,665	2,715	2,677	2,834	2,775	2,371	2,349

Source: Registrar General Printed Census Reports 1851-1891.

The making of better grades was concentrated within Northampton itself, where outwork patterns of employment also prevailed. Long Buckby, along with scattered evidence relating to a small number of other villages like Cogenhoe and Pattishall, provide exceptions to this general pattern: here first quality hand-sewn footwear was turned out.

As has been noted above, as the century passes the tendency to centralise production increased, and with it the role of these outworking villages declined. The organisation of this work has been little considered by shoe historians and is deserving of more attention. All work was executed by the piece, with shoe workers providing their own tools and incidental materials, known in the industry as grindery: this prevailed in Northampton also. The only machine commonly employed by outworkers working on their own premises was the sewing machine which was generally purchased on an instalment plan from either a machinery company, or the employer. The supply of materials and control of outworkers was effected by four methods within Northamptonshire:

where there were small concentrations of outworkers in a parish, outworkers tramped into the shoe centre once a week to shop work and collect a fresh stock of materials to be made up (distances of up to 15 miles have been recorded). Such outworkers were largely self-managing.

where there was a greater concentration of outworkers, the employer engaged a resident shoe agent to dispense work, collect it in, and generally look after his interest locally. Available written evidence points to a wide use of such men, but the directory analysis at Table 14 to some extent belies this. Census Enumerators' Returns for 1861 and 1871 reveal larger numbers of shoe agents in residence. Some were in the employ of a manufacturer, whilst others acted on a subcontracting basis: several became manufacturers. Agents maintained tight control of outworkers and there is evidence that suggests both country agents and shoe manufacturers exploited this outwork force by the systematic evasion of the Truck Acts. Tommy shops operated in some villages and led to the establishment of the Northamptonshire Productive Boot and Shoe Society at Wollaston.[29]

in addition, carriers were utilised to transport materials to outworkers and return the finished boots. It is probable that in places where there was no resident shoe agent, the carrier acted for the manufacturer.

lastly, small sub-contracting manufacturers emerged in large outworking settlements, particularly at Astcote, Pattishall and Towcester. Again, little is known of their activities beyond some scattered references in the trade press. This appears to have been a much more common practice in Leicestershire, being adopted from what had been common practice in the hosiery industry.

A point to stress, however, is that despite the small amount of hand-sewn work which continued to be handled by the larger firms, special hand-sewn orders and repairs did not cease altogether; as neither did outwork. In 1906-7 Manfield's range of styles still included four hand-sewn styles.[30]

This transitional character of industrial organisation and manufacture changed significantly from the late 1880s, when both the pace and character of change escalated following the 1887 strike at Northampton. William Arnold regarded this as the crucial catalyst of change:

...Since (the 1887 strike) the shoe trade has undergone the greatest

29 B. Jones, *Cooperative Production* Vol. II (1894), Chapter X1X *passim*.
30 N.R.O. Manfield Papers: Costing Books 1906-7. Church & Co company papers show a similar pattern.

Table 13: Known concentration of outworkers in county areas employed by Northampton wholesale manufacturers 1864-1894

Parish	Outworker concentration	Resident shoe agent	Small master or factory operations
[1] Small manufacturing outwork centres			
Daventry	X	X	X
Earls Barton	X	X	X
Long Buckby	X	X	X
Towcester	X	X	X
[2] Outwork villages			
Abthorpe	X	X	
Astcote	X	X	X
Cogenhoe	X	X	
Dallington [1]	X		X
Denton [1]	X	X	
Duston [1]	X		
Great Doddington	X		
Grendon	X		
Hackleton	X	X	X
Harpole	X	X	X
Houghton, Great	X	X	X
Houghton, Little	X		
Holcot	X	X	
Kingsthorpe [1]	X		
Kislingbury	X	X	X
Pattishall	X		
Piddington	X		X

Sources: Northamptonshire Notes & Queries; trade directories; trade press; VCH Northamptonshire; Northampton Public Library: village files.
Note: Parishes marked [1] amalgamated with Northampton to form Northampton County Borough in 1901.

change it has experienced since it was an industry and I am sure it can never undergo such a change again. It has been a trying and critical time for manufacturers and, although dozens have gone under, I have been fortunate enough to keep my head above water... [31]

Nor was this change confined to Northampton, but engulfed the entire industry. Thus, a 1901 review of the industry's progress, nationally, over the preceding fifty years noted: "...the greatest progress has been affected within the last ten or fifteen years..."[32]

As competitive pressures grew, the need to achieve centralised factory-

31 *Autobiography* p. 125; A. E. Marlow agreed with this view: "...Thirty years ago shoemaking in Northampton was just emerging from the domestic stage into that of a highly organised industry..." (S. & L. Supplement 1916 p. Ii).
32 *B.S.T.J.* 5/1/1901 p. 2.

Table 14: Northamptonshire footwear agents 1864-1914

Centre	1864	1869	1877	1885	1890	1894	1898	1903	1910	1914
Abthorpe			1	1	1	1	1	1		
Astcote				1	1	1	1	1	1	
Bozeat	1	1	1							
Brackley	1	1								
Burton Latimer	2	2	3	3	2	1	1			
Cogenhoe								1		
Denton					1					
Earls Barton				1	1					
Finedon	1	1								
Hackleton				2	1	1	1			
Harpole					6	9	8	8	5	3
Higham Ferrers			4	2	2	1	1	1		
Holcot									2	
Houghton						1				
Kettering		1								
Kislingbury							1	1		
Northampton				1	1					

Source: Northamptonshire Trade Directories 1864-1914.

based integrated production utilising machinery for medium and high grade footwear increased. It was at this time that technical solutions were found for two longstanding issues. The first was the production both of a machine-made product with the wearing and durability characteristics of a hand-made item, and of reaching a stage where it was possible to apply machinery to all processes and grades of work. This was achieved as engineers finally developed adequate lasting machinery, sole-sewing machinery, and the development of a suite of finishing machines to mechanise the stages of footwear manufacture. The second barrier scaled was the coordinated use of a series of sub-divided machine processes to give a balanced, synchronised output capacity across the different factory departments: the production of co-ordinated batch production. This was a systemised way of making a product where making was reduced to a series of discrete hand or machine processes, each of which was synchronised to give some balance between the output volumes of each process. For the first time, using these early flow techniques, footwear manufacturers had the capability of producing a pre-determined level of production both economically and efficiently.

1895-1905 Development of manufacturer control over production capability
With owners' ascendancy assured, the years 1895 to 1905 (when William Arnold was laying down his manufacturing success following his early business failure) witnessed the final stage of industrial transformation. Control of workplace organisation now enabled the achievement of the full introduction of integrated machine systems. For machine working

to become a reality, manufacturers faced the organisational problem of gaining shoe workers' acceptance of new working arrangements required to begin effective batch production. They needed to have control of production in their workplaces; something that had traditionally lain with the shoe worker.

Gaining control took a number of years and involved considerable labour disruption. There were many small stoppages and meetings regarding the re-negotiation of piecework rates. In 1887, disruption escalated into a centre-wide stoppage in the town. The Manufacturers' Association success in resolving this dispute gave the impetus to push ahead re-equipping factories with sufficient assurance that owners would be able to overcome shoe-worker hostility to change in working practices. This change process is encapsulated in the leadership prominent manufacturers gave to the development of shoe machinery companies and the sharp rise in factory building. The early 1890s, nevertheless, was a period of continued industrial tension, witnessing a number of small factory disputes which came to a climax in the 1895 dispute. Good quality centres like Northampton now had a set of unassailable commercial drivers for a more comprehensive process of change. Local manufacturers sought to gain greater controls over the work process by curtailing out-working and ending the working independence of shoe workers. The favourable settlement of the 1895 dispute enabled owners to introduce a new factory culture by asserting work discipline and work practice controls in their factories.

Some historians have sought to explain the adoption of factory production in wholesale centres of the industry as substantially the result of the late 1890s American-led import boom into British home markets.[33] Increased imports were concentrated in medium grade footwear markets that were benefiting most from rising disposable incomes. British manufacturers successfully met the challenge of rising cheap imports by the adoption of American systems of manufacture. But the reason for rising imports in the first place, it was argued, was manufacturer conservatism; especially the attitudes of Northampton manufacturers, the leading makers of medium grade footwear, towards modern machine manufacture. Yet the previous slowness of modernis- ation was not driven by a straightforward resistance to change. This was based on:

Different resource mix costs in the quality footwear areas like Northampton: the presence of abundant low cost labour in the county, and the slow

33 See R.A. Church "The Effect of the American Export Invasion on the British Boot & Shoe Industry 1885-1914" J. E.H. XXVIII (1968); P. Head 'Boots & Shoes' in D. H. Aldcroft (ed.), *The Development of British Industry & Foreign Competition: 1875-1914* (1968).

evolution of machine solutions for the production of quality footwear gave rise to the long transition period in the industry. *Customer resistance in quality footwear markets*: the character and nature of customer expectations and taste influenced manufacturers, giving rise to two sets of issues. Within civil markets until machine production could provide products with the wear, durability and style of hand-sewn goods, many customers insisted upon hand sewn goods (ready-made or bespoke). Within the government "army boot" market the War Office continued to insist upon hand-sewn boots until the late Edwardian period. Only the experience of the durability of military personnel kit in the Boer War brought forth a re-evaluation by the War Office and the Admiralty about the standards of footwear for military personnel.

Rather than being seen as conservative, Northampton and North-amptonshire manufacturers should be regarded as strategic rationalists. The Northampton trade, although diverse, was largely based on medium and above quality footwear in ready-made and bespoke wear particularly for metropolitan markets. Production costs on the one hand and customer expectations and taste on the other drove their decision making. Once credible cost efficient production solutions were available manufacturers actively moved to establish factory-based machine production. As suitable machinery and machine systems for medium grade work became available in the mid 1880s, the critical issue standing in the way of progress was workforce acceptance. The rise in imports a decade later provided manufacturers with the degree of leverage they required to meet that workforce resistance.

But the product of the new machine systems still had to meet customer expectation and taste. The British market for medium and above grade work remained unreceptive to change and relatively impervious to new invention. The extant order books of Northampton firms reveal that independent shoe retailers and other wholesale customers required more variation in terms of size additions and fit, changes to the shape, and additional embellishments than could be provided by a limited range of standardised product styles. In order to retain custom, these order books suggest that firms like William Arnold's was required not only to keep a more complex range of styles, fits, and sizes, but be prepared to make detailed changes according to a customer request than his US counterpart would have done.[34] Many of these new machines and industrial organisation methods had originated in the USA. With these innovations there also came new footwear styles, fit and materials. As the British trade press in Britain gave prominence to

34 N.R.O. *A. & W. Arnold Order Book 1907-09, op. cit.*

these innovations from the 1880s, so some manufacturers and retailers took them up. Thus, H. E. Randall Ltd set up American-style retail shops for the sale of imported American footwear. He soon incurred the ire of US manufacturers who had signed agreements to give his shops the only outlet for their footwear. This effectively prevented them from developing their own UK chains.

Yet the British market retained a strong preference for established styles. Customer preferences resulted in the retention of a wider diversity of shoe products: hand-sewn, various qualities, and the manufacture of complimentary items like spats, etc. This product diversity not only gave rise to niche markets and an array of footwear, but to the retention of more hand work in British footwear factories then in American. Not only was hand-made capacity retained, albeit on a small scale, but hand finishing and other operations became part of the machine systems used in this country. Increasingly from 1887 it was to be stressed that the machine was now dominant, but always this qualification should be borne in mind. In his report on the industry G. M. Butnam[35] included an appendix showing the weekly production of Northampton's fifty leading firms. It will be noticed that hand-sewn work was still present, despite the ascendancy of machine-made work:

Machine-welted work	61.8% of total weekly production
Machine-sewn work	35.7% of total weekly production
Hand-sewn work	1.2% of total weekly production
Hand-sewn nursery & turn-shoe	1.3% of total weekly production

Although British manufacturers adopted small batch production techniques, they never fully embraced the production of a small range of standardised lines at a standard price on the American model. American-style footwear certainly sold in Britain, and though it introduced new styles and novelty, many found it to be too flimsy and lacking in wearing qualities. It was persistently argued that footwear fashion amongst a significant portion of the British wearers of medium and above grades of footwear remained essentially conservative; not the manufacturers. Some contemporaries would have dismissed this conclusion, as British manufacturers were not ready to positively change market conditions in their favour, by imposing a restricted product range at standard prices, as American manufacturers had done. Yet, the American markets for which the new integrated machine systems were built were large and expanding on the back of significant population growth and large-scale immigration from Europe, together with the colonisation of the western part of the country. These market

35 G. M. Butnam, *Shoe & Leather Trade in the United Kingdom* (1912).

conditions enabled American footwear manufacturers and merchants to dictate product style and price to the market in a way that British manufacturers argued was not possible in their more established and diverse home markets.

Thus, by 1905, the British footwear industry had become concentrated in a limited number of regional centres, where production was increasingly dominated by a small group of large, oligopolistic footwear manufacturers. At regional wholesale centres, production was now focused on machine-made footwear produced by batch production techniques. And this technical change fuelled by increasing production costs finally caused manufacturers to end worker control over the means of production.[36]

Northampton Footwear Industry Business Community 1840-1914

Although technical and trading changes gave rise to the dominance of large manufacturers, there was no inevitability about the terminal decline of the smaller manufacturer and sub-contractor in this highly seasonal industry: some small producers continued to have a role. The business community within the town was made up of all sorts and conditions of business person and William Arnold's business career reflects this complexity. From tentative beginnings as a small producer, his *Autobiography* well illustrates a career path that many of his fellow manufacturers had followed. Unfortunately, too few of the existing historical studies of the industry reveal the rich diversity of business persons who were active in Northampton and other centres of production in the latter part of the nineteenth century. To understand more about the changing business position of Arnold's career and the footwear manufacturers that he represents, there is a need to know something more about the character of the town's footwear business community.

The developing pattern of mechanised production had a profound impact on Northampton producers and the footwear trade generally. And wholesale manufacturers and masters were the driving force behind industrial development there, and in this period there were three classes of manufacturer and master in the local trade:

1. *Wholesale manufacturers*, who became the leaders of the modern shoe industry.

---

36 On some of the aspects of the end of worker control in the workplace, see K. B. Brooker *N.P.P.* (1980) *op. ci,t;* Jeffery Porter, "The Northampton Boot & Shoe Arbitration Board Before 1914" *N.P.P.* (1979) Vol 2 p. 93-99; A. Fox (1957) *op. cit.*

2. *Wholesale component producers*, who in addition to the manufacture of component parts for the industry, also made specialist products and carried out sub-contract work for larger firms. This type of business opportunity was a function particularly of the long transitional phase where machine processes were grafted on to the outwork structure: their numbers fell quickly as the trend for integrated factory production increased.

3. *Master retail shoemakers*, a group of more craft-based small producers, making more traditional footwear for a largely local market.

In the fifty years after 1856 the size and nature of each of these three business groups changed in response to the wider changes happening in the industry. The most universal and unrelenting change was the gradual elimination of small producer firms from the industry, although they were never to be entirely displaced. A small producer firm had only one layer of management; where the owner manages the work force without any intermediary management. Other points of reference could be used, such as production levels and numbers of people employed, but both raise difficulties when looking at the footwear industry. In terms of employment, it would be expected that small master shoemakers would frequently employ fewer than 15 people and certainly not more than 30.

At an earlier point in the century, small producers were to be found in all three groups, but gradually they were progressively eliminated from the wholesale manufacturing sector after 1887.

Some idea of the nature of the changing trends in the internal shifts in shoe firm ownership can be had from the study of local trade directories. These give membership lists of business firms which can be used to provide turnover levels for the Northampton footwear industry (Table 15). Such analysis enables us to isolate two things. First, the underlying trend in the "real" number of firms that traded in the business community and its internal groups. Overall between 1840 and 1914, 1,123 wholesale manufacturing firms and 712 wholesale component firms were in business at Northampton. And secondly, a turnover analysis reveals the rapidity with which membership within the Northampton footwear business community changes over time. The results of the Northampton footwear firm turnover study reveal the following:

a secular expansion of business opportunity to 1893 followed by a contraction thereafter. Linked to this are the high levels of exit relative to entry after this date;

short run fluctuations in entry levels linked to the trade cycle can be observed. Here the extent of high exits linked to high entry rates in time of trade downturn is identifiable.

high entry rates matched to high exits of turnover over time are observable, which is suggestive of a high mortality of infant firms. Here, wholesale component firms appear to be particularly volatile. Constant endemic levels of mortality over time give prima facie support to such an assumption.

The single most glaring difference in business membership during the years that William Arnold traded was the gradual diminution in the opportunity for small men to enter every level in the trade. Small men certainly continued to pursue their dream of becoming successful masters and businessmen, and, equally, they continued to fail in realising this dream as high rates of business failure amongst them attests. The core challenge for many was the tension between business survival and the sustaining of small-scale production: those unable to exploit specialist niche markets had to grow their business to a viable size in order to assure long-term survival in the changing economic and training conditions. Thus, by the early years of the twentieth century, time was being called for many small wholesale masters.

Change was most complete amongst small wholesale manufacturers, whilst amongst wholesale component producers a small size of operation remained feasible due to the very nature of the service they provided to the wholesale trade. Nevertheless, the domination of integrated factory production also challenged the basis of this business too, with numbers of component producers trading over time declining. Wholesale sub-contractors similarly suffered to some degree as wholesale manufacturers took in-house all manufacturing to safeguard product quality as competition became more intense. They did continue, however, to selectively use smaller wholesale manufacturers to carry out sub-contract work during busy periods.

The experience of master retail shoemakers in the town was equally challenging (Table 15: III). The trading position of retail makers everywhere gradually became compromised in the wake of competition both from the domestic wholesale and overseas sources. As small men found in many businesses, the presence of cheaper, good quality goods in the marketplace gradually edged them out of business. Some were able to survive where the market for high-class and bespoke footwear remained strong. But one of the outcomes of the introduction of mechanised footwear was the excellence of medium grade machine-made goods and this bit deeply into small retail makers' markets. The

Table 15: Analysis of internal shifts in shoe firm owner internal group membership

Period	I Wholesale manufacturing				II Component manufacturing				III Retail making			
	Entry		Exit		Entry		Exit		Entry		Exit	
	No.	AA	No.	AA	No.	AA	No.	AA	No.	AA	No.	AA
1840	27	–	–	–	–	–	–	–	–	–	–	–
1841-47	57	11	28	6	–	–	–	–	74	11	52	7
1848-54	84	17	74	15	–	–	–	–	95	14	64	9
	141	**14**	**102**	**11**	**–**	**–**	**–**	**–**	**169**	**12**	**116**	**8**
1855-59	34	7	20	4	1	–	–	–	14	3	17	3
1860-64	118	24	106	21	34	7	7	1	99	20	73	15
1865-69	35	7	43	9	24	5	20	4	37	7	51	10
1870-74	93	19	61	12	117	23	22	4	39	8	37	7
1875-79	142	28	148	30	36	7	90	18	37	7	53	11
1880-84	88	17	50	10	110	22	36	7	81	16	14	3
	510	**17**	**428**	**14**	**322**	**11**	**174**	**6**	**307**	**10**	**245**	**8**
1885-89	114	23	71	14	58	12	158	32	61	12	86	17
1890-94	131	26	153	31	179	36	99	20	149	30	116	23
1895-99	62	12	74	15	63	13	93	19	69	14	87	17
1900-04	67	13	85	17	53	11	120	24	93	19	100	20
1905-09	46	9	43	9	13	3	26	5	74	15	77	15
1910-14	25	5	91	18	24	4	35	7	87	17	72	14
	445	**15**	**517**	**17**	**390**	**13**	**530**	**18**	**533**	**18**	**538**	**15**

Source: Northampton Trade Directories 1840-1914.

Note: AA = Annual average

position of the Northampton retail makers was, however, slightly different. Some of these small masters were in the habit of doing a small, selective wholesale trade. Others chose retail making as a retreat from the increasing rigours of trading in the wholesale sector. Some of these retailers can be found as listed in successive trade directories alternatively as retailers and manufacturers. An example of this type was the business of Frederick Thomas Tebbutt, a son of G. M. Tebbutt (qv). He traded from the early 1890s with a number of partners and suspensions. Retail making was initially more profitable for him than the rigours of manufacturing; his financial management was weak. After a third stoppage in 1910, a shift to manufacturing followed and a limited company formed: John Osborne joined as a director. Manufacturers like H. Manfield and C. Lewis gave capital, but despite this, the company went into voluntary liquidation in 1911. By contrast,

G. H. Kendall & Co and Isaac Bonhams, both prominent retail shoemakers, were able to successfully undertake periodic manufacturing. Kendall traded from 1854, and Bonhams from 1865 and on into the twentieth century.

William Arnold, then, was part of an energetic and striving manufacturer class. Whilst many could still claim lineage that went back into the small master craft, increasing numbers, like him, were shoe workers familiar with process work, the making of part of the shoe rather than having the ability to make a shoe in its entirety; whilst others were coming into the industry from more diverse business, commercial and professional backgrounds. The character of this business community was both complex and heterogeneous, underpinned as it was by small-scale production. Its business people were characterised by considerable diversity and breadth. Inevitably, their levels of skill and their approach to business differed markedly; as did their levels of wealth, social position and their view of society. Success accompanied the endeavours of the industry in the period up to 1914. But a visible feature was the high level of people who entered the ranks of business only to leave in a comparatively short time: high levels of turnover and of business failure were a commonplace feature. In reality, this resulted in many more business people – both men and women – being part of this long journey than the periodic lists of firms suggest. In terms of the time for which people traded, and thus able to have influence upon the trade, one can identify three types of firm:

> those that were trading in 1914 and had either traded all the way through the period 1884-1914 or mature firms who begun trading in the period

> firms that had traded for an extended period before ceasing to trade

> firms that traded for a much shorter period before failing

For many years the owner ranks had been open to large numbers of new entrants, but after 1887 there was a closing of entry coupled with a shake-out in the numbers of businessmen engaged in the trade. By 1914 there were 76 wholesale manufacturers in the town, compared with 195 thirty years previously.

As already noted, many men and women were involved in the industry's transformation (Table 16). In the period 1884 to 1914, 643 manufacturing firms entered the trade locally. Through the first ten years after 1884, 248 manufacturing firms joined the 195 firms already trading in that year, with a further 129 joining in the next ten years and

71 in the ten years after that. But of these, 567 firms had left the industry by the eve of the Great War. This reduction was a reflection of the long, very significant transformation in the British shoe industry already described, where hand production in small workshops typical of the mid-century gave way to the highly mechanised factory production and modern distribution techniques of fifty years later.

Table 16: Entry/exit configuration for Northampton wholesale manufacturers 1884 to 1914

Entry period	Entrants		Infant exits		Number of exits by five year periods						Present in 1914		
	No.	[i]	No.	[ii]	85/89	90/94	95/00	00/04	05/09	10/14	No.	[iii]	[iv]
1884	195	30.3	50	25.7	83[50]	34	12	16	5	22	25	12.8	32.9
1885/9	117	18.2	70	59.8	38[38]	43[32]	10	7	0	8	10	8.5	13.2
1890/4	131	20.4	85	64.9		76[76]	23[9]	10	3	10	9	6.9	11.8
1895/9	62	9.6	35	56.5			29[29]	15[6]	1	9	7	11.3	9.2
1900/4	67	10.4	37	55.2				37[37]	3	18	9	13.4	11.8
1905/9	46	7.2	31	67.4					31[31]	9	6	13.0	7.9
1910/4	25	3.9	15	60.0						15[15]	10	40.0	13.2
1884–1914	643	100.0	323	50.2*	121 [88= 72.2%]	153 [108= 70.6%]	74 [38= 51.4%]	85 [43= 50.6%]	43 [31= 72.1%]	91 [15= 16.5%]	76		100.0

Source: Northampton Trade Directories 1884-1914.

Northampton's wholesale manufacturers were the driving force behind the Industry's development. The dominant wholesale firms of the period can be grouped into three. There was a small elite formed of numerically small, but influential, relatively large-scale oligopolistic firms. Underneath was a range of second rank manufacturers, and lastly a group of small producers. Two contrasting yet inter-related features dominated: the contraction of the large, small-producer base, set against the progressive emergence of an industrial elite. A concentration of both production and of operating capital can be identified (Table 18). But whilst the period does witness the success of some firms, there were many that failed to achieve their objectives and goals. Both contemporary and later commentators make a broad distinction between men of substance, who were in the vanguard of factory production, and those insubstantial owners, who relied on outworking undertaken in small workshops and in small rooms in workers' homes.

Such small, economically unstable masters can be observed amongst component makers. Table 17 starkly captures their often precarious financial state: an inconsequential asset base matched by unsustainable levels of operating debt. The very nature of the development and growth of the industry in the transitional period encouraged this nature of trading on small capital. Yet these firms were not always an economic drag upon the industry, as they did provide a competitive means to manufacturers to buy components and getting seasonal orders completed. And although closers to the trade tended to operate at the scale of the small workshop, a small class of upper manufacturers flourished to satisfy the trade that developed for good quality ready-made uppers. Wellingborough became particularly noted for this class of trade and some firms there conducted business on a large scale.[37] But more generally, the social impact of component makers was potentially both negative and damaging, as has been noted elsewhere in the introduction.

Table 17: Sample of closers to the trade: liabilities and assets at suspension of trading

Date	Name	Liabilities [£]	Assets [£]
05/05/1888	S. Salter	177	62
27/10/1888	Jelley, Baker & Co	209	185
27/07/1889	Collins Bros	300	97
07/12/1889	Vigor & Son	456	130
21/10/1891	J. T. Farrell	200	53
24/03/1893	T. Clark	452	261
06/01/1897	J. Brovett	191	62
29/07/1899	E. J. Smith	360	12
24/01/1902	J. S. Francis	1,266	224
08/09/1905	E. Wills	165	94
15/09/1905	J. J. Gilbert	1,362	280
10/10/1906	Knightly & Adams	610	78
05/08/1910	J. K. Morgan	280	28

Source: Weekly business failure reports in *B.S.T.J.* and *S.L.R.* 1888 to 1910.

It would, however, be erroneous to view the industry as facing an inevitable shake-out of firms in the face of change. For this process was as much about the shifting qualities and strategies required by owners to sustain trading in changing circumstances as it was about failure. Those who remained in business faced a radical rationalisation of their organisation and of their attitude to business. In order to survive successfully they had to adopt new techniques, develop new business and management methods and accept new ideas and ways of thinking. The long transitional phase had both encouraged and relied upon an expanding small producer base in order to deliver growth in the

37 For example, the Wellingborough Boot & Shoe Co. Ltd. did a vast trade in ready-made uppers and employed 700 in this branch alone. At Northampton, typical of this group was Peach & Knightly. Founded by Edward Peach (1836-92), who lived in Billing Road and left personal effects of £2,287 at death.

industry. Their rise to prominence relied as much upon adapting established methods of outwork production, as on the machine and the factory. But in the later stages of these changes the smaller owners' position and function declined, unless individuals could find survival strategies to counteract the shift to large batch production and scale economies. These strategies can be grouped into two areas: the retention of quality hand-sewn work, and the adoption of some level of machine production. In the latter strategy, smaller manufacturers primarily engaged in variety production were assisted by the helpful machine leasing arrangements of the shoe machinery companies. And this enabled them to lay down modern machine systems and yet remain price competitive with larger, efficient firms, which produce almost exclusively standardised lines of shoes.

Table 18: Statistical summary of scale of the wholesale manufacturers' economic activity in 1914

Category	Weekly nominal factory production			No. factory production workers			Capital valuation (£)		
	Pairs	Mean	%	Number	Mean	%	Valuation	Mean	%
Elite producers	*71,450	10,207	44	**6,430	919	31	3,391,000	484,429	87.5
Volume producers	65,600	4,373	41	10,200	680	50	486,000	32,400	12.5
Small producers	24,400	581	15	3,900	98	19	n/a	n/a	–
Total	161,450	2,523	100	20,530	321	100	3,877,000	176,227	100

Notes: *In fact the production dominance of these firms was greater than these figures suggest as many of the volume producers and even some of the small producers produced for the oligarchs and as such were tied to them contractually.
** Additionally elite producers employed around 2,000 shop workers in their shop chains.

The contraction in the number of firms trading led to a gradual narrowing of business opportunity within the industry. At one end of the spectrum were successful firms able to survive over time; both elite firms, together with more diverse medium-sized volume producers and niche market small producers. Amongst this number can be counted formerly prominent firms from the generation prior to 1884; firms that could not face the challenge of change. They represented by the 1890s, older values of manufacturing and business conduct. At the other end of the spectrum were an economically unstable number of new, inexperienced firms and old established but inflexible firms, whose composition changed with remarkable rapidity. In part, the permanent reduction in firm numbers was a stark measure of the inability of these unstable firms to survive unscathed the change which swept the industry.

Given the degree of industrial concentration that change brought in its wake some closure of inefficient firms was inevitable, which tended to add to the toll from the traditionally high endemic level of 'normal' business mortality in the short term. As will be demonstrated below, a significant proportion of such mortality occurred amongst new infant firms; those that fail within the first five years of trading. The small master base itself was not fundamentally under threat until after 1893, but individually many small manufacturers, sub-contractors, retail-manufacturers had always found it difficult to survive: now small masters as a group found it difficult to continue trading in the face of fundamental change. Also under threat were mature firms that ceased trading because of an inability to manage the broader changes experienced within the industry.

Categorisation of Northampton Wholesale Manufacturing Firms in 1914

By 1914, the factory-based trade of the town was dominated by a group of just seven firms. All of them were managed by a combination of founder owners, second generation owners and professional manager control. Together they formed an industrial elite within the industry. Table 18 provides some basic statistical information concerning the size of the operations in 1914. Their dominance within the industry can be seen when this information is compared with that for volume producers (Table 19), and for small producers (Table 20).

A second internal group was made up of 15 firms that operated as significant producers of volume work. These producers were first and foremost manufacturers, makers of footwear, and this is their common uniting theme. The ability of a firm to be able to trade at or above the threshold level of efficient volume batch production was regarded as the economic baseline for membership to the group.[38] The technical literature concluded that a production layout with a nominal output of 3,000 pairs per week, employing *c.* 100 people is the smallest machine factory unit that was economically efficient for integrated production plant at this time. Of course, what differed was the productivity between individual firms, as Table 19 infers. The same predominance of standardised lines of footwear found amongst the elite was also a feature amongst them, but here there was more variety production too: this became a greater proportion of total production lower down the volume producer list, as did trading in lower grades of work. Some firms also ran specialist and novelty lines, just as some made hand-sewn work, both as bespoke and single order work. In this way, some echoed the production traits of small producer firms.

---

38 See the seminal textbook E. J. Swaysland, *Shoe Manufacture and Design* (1905), and G. P. Grant, "The Advantages of a Small Firm" *J.B.B.S.I.* Vol. 5, (1955).

Table 19: Listing of mature wholesale manufacturing firms at Northampton in 1914: elite producer firms

Firm	Production [1]	Production workers [2]	Capital valuation (£)
A. E. Marlow & Co	16,750	1,200	*c.* 275,000
C. & E. Lewis	15,000	1,200	*c.* 300,000
Sears & Co Ltd	12,500	1,000	350,000
Manfield & Sons	12,000	1,200	1,300,000
Crockett & Jones	7,000	1,100	*c.* 850,000
H. E. Randall Ltd	2,500 + factored stock	*c.* 300	212,000
F. Bostock & Co Ltd	6,000	450	104,000

Source: Butnam 1912; Trade press; company registration papers; company records.

Note: *Hornby & West Ltd – after Mounts Factory Co: 1909 failure – atrophy bought by A. E. Marlow – 1910 & Hornby & West share capital taken up = £10,000.

Table 20: Listing of mature wholesale manufacturing firms at Northampton in 1914: volume producer firms

Firm	Production [1]	Production workers	Capital valuation (£)
G. T. Hawkins & Co Ltd	6,250	*c.* 400	80,000
Padmore, Barnes & Co Ltd	6,000	350	44,000
John Marlow & Sons Ltd	6,000	400	38,000
James Branch Ltd	5,000	*c.* 400	42,000
A. & W. Church & Co	4,950	400	46,000
G. Swan & Co	4,300	250	n/k
A. & W. Arnold & Co	4,000	400	25,000
Arnold Bros & Co	4,000	400	25,000
J. Dawson & Sons	4,000	*c.* 300	42,000
Oakeshott & Finnemore	3,500	*c.* 350	22,000
S. Collier Ltd	3,000	*c.* 400	33,000
W. Barratt & Co Ltd	3,000	*c.* 350	40,000
A. Lee & Co	3,400	*c.* 350	18,000
H. Sharman & Co	3,200	*c.* 350	15,000
J. Robinson & Co	3,000	*c.* 350	16,000

Source: Butnam 1912; Trade press; company registration papers; company records.

Note: [1] Nominal production capacity.

The last internal group comprises 42 much smaller firms that operated on a more modest scale in terms of output and workers employed. For the most part these small producers carried on what contemporaries called a general high class trade. Some used machinery to make footwear, but many more of the group relied upon small-scale jobbing production using a mix of hand and machine work, short production runs, and the use of outworking as a dominant manufacturing system. In reality, outworking was never to entirely leave the industry. At various times in the twentieth century footwear firms were to resort to it both as a means of quickly expanding seasonal production and of making employment attractive to women with family commitments.

A greater use was made here of traditional hand techniques than was seen in the other two sub-groups. The majority of small producers, although aware of the economic realities of modern trading, tended to work in more traditional markets where profits were still to be found. They continued to adhere to the older, traditional norms of the small master world. Many worked very much more closely and directly with their workforce. It was much less likely that there was an intervening layer of managerial staff between them and their workers. Upon reaching this third group of wholesale manufacturers another threshold is crossed. A unifying characteristic was that their scale business was below the integrated manufacturing process threshold; the manufacturing standard of the day. These small producers had more in common with the retail master shoemakers of the town. And indeed there is some evidence that suggests that some of these more traditional producers traded intermittently between the retail and wholesale sectors. Some had fewer than 30 employees, whilst small 'mechanised factory' firms had less than 100: industrial writers have suggested that a shift in workshop relations is apparent when the number employed rises above thirty. The personal character which typifies relations between employer and employed steadily gives way to more formalised modes of contact and control. In addition, small independent artisan masters remained in the industry; men with varying degrees of dependence on merchants or their agents under the outwork system.

These owners are harder to summarise accurately, as their high-class trade ethos and attitude to trading was much more varied both in terms of the size of production and range of footwear produced. The majority of members of this internal group came out of a shared, small master/artisanal tradition, with values centred round the workshop, Nonconformity and liberal politics. This would also have once been true of many wholesale manufacturers, but during the long period of industrial and retail transformation as a group they were likely to embrace a new economic and social view of their world. And it is also clear that wholesale manufacturers needed the close collaboration between themselves and smaller producers to fuel the momentum of that transformation. As the introduction has shown, small-scale producers were present both amongst wholesale manufacturers and

Table 21: Listing of mature wholesale manufacturing firms at Northampton in 1914: small producer firms

Firm	Production
Roe Bros Ltd	2,000 pairs + factor stock + *c.* 250 factory workers
John Branch & Sons Ltd	2,400 pairs
G. M. Tebbutt & Sons Ltd	2,000 pairs + *c.* 100 factory workers
Crick & Company	2,000 pairs
R. Taylor & Sons	1,300 pairs
Allinson & Company	1,100 pairs + 100 factory workers
T. Singlehurst & Son	1,100 pairs
J. & W. Read	1,100 pairs
G. & W. Morton	1,100 pairs
W. B. Stevens & Co	1,000 pairs
G. H. Gainsford & Co	800 pairs
C. Gibbs & Company	700 pairs
Pollard & Son	700 pairs + 75 factory workers
J. Holmes & Company	700 pairs
George Green & Sons Ltd	*c.* 700 pairs
W. Beale & Company	600 pairs
Eales & Son	600 pairs + 50 to 150 workers
C. F. Tompkins & Company	400 pairs
W. J. Marks & Company	300 pairs
Conformable Boot Company Ltd	N/A
C. W. White & Company	300 pairs + 30 factory workers
R. Fisher & Company	N/A
F. Cook Ltd	N/A
J. Emmett Ltd	N/A: (1890s were 200 in Northampton & Towcester)
R. E. Tricker & Co	N/A

Source: Butnam 1912; Trade press; company registration papers; company records

Note:
Business information for the last 16 firms in the 1914 firms cohort is scanty: the basic bench mark of nominal weekly production capacity is not available to us and thus we have little information upon which to speculate about their size of operation.

These 16 firms are: W. P. Dalton & Company; G. H. Kendall & Son; C. E. Gubbins; J. J. McMain; The Pioneer Co-operative Boot Society Ltd; W. Bosworth & Company; E. De Loos & Sons; P. Frisby & Company; W. G. Garratt & Company; H. Gorbold & Company; Griffen & Fox; J. Jelley & Company; J. & J. Mann; T. Richardson & Company; W. Todd & Company; The I. L. P. Boot Society Ltd.

wholesale ancillary producers – sub-contractors and component producers – but whilst the latter owed their trading opportunities to the rise of machine shoemaking, the small producers were nearer in their origins and trading attitudes to the craft shoemaker. And the further down the listing one penetrates, the more one enters a producer world contemporaries described variously as "the general high class trade" or "the old world craftsman". Here, they were more likely to be operating a small order, singles, and bespoke trade, and be makers of specialist products; and to have close links with local master retail shoemakers.

Northampton also had a significant retail shoemaking capacity at this time and they too were affected by the larger changes happening in the industry. They faced the competition from the wholesale ready-made footwear. But unlike footwear retailers elsewhere, these men also had the opportunity of operating within the local wholesale trade too, either as small manufacturers or more commonly as sub-contractors or component manufacturers. In broad terms the increasing dominance of the wholesale trade is reflected in a downward trend in the numbers of small retailers. Their experience was similar in this regard to retail makers throughout the country noted above.

Business Failure in the Northampton Footwear Industry 1885-1914

Against a background of competitive pressures and import penetration, the footwear industry clearly successfully modernised. But '…despite the positive entrepreneurial response…mirrored by the successful development of large, integrated and efficient units of production, the traditionally high level of insolvency remained a central feature of the industry in this period of change…'[39] The judicious trading on credit had long been a fundamental axiom of good business practice, so the need of a means of legal redress against defaulting debtors was very real. The initial period of British industrialisation witnessed an ever increasing role for credit facilities. In the nineteenth century a series of statutes gradually broadened the method and scope of redress and the administration of insolvency law was simplified and speeded up. Three forms of redress evolved to meet commercial needs and practices:

1. *Bankruptcy* – a legal process brought against an individual, who had to cease trading.

2. *Composition* or scheme of arrangement – sanctioned by a court, it was an agreement to pay an agreed portion of the debt, as decided by a meeting of the creditors and debtor.

39 K .B. Brooker (1981) p. 7.

3. *Deed of arrangement* – an agreement reached by the parties as part of a private arrangement.

Many of the former harsh legal penalties had been mitigated and distinctions drawn between insolvency that was considered to be reasonably beyond the control of the debtor, and that resulting from recklessness, fraud, or dishonesty. But bankruptcy had two significant drawbacks: it necessitated the cessation of trading, and small debtors were too financially insignificant, given high legal costs, to be proceeded against under bankruptcy legislation. As a result many of the actions for the recovery of debts in the Northampton industry relied upon the last two remedies: composition and deed of arrangement.

Table 22: Longevity of wholesale footwear firms measured by approximate age at exit from trade directory lists: 1885-1914

Years after first directory entry in five year periods	Number of exits		As a % of total exits
0 – 5	323		57.0
6 – 10	113	261	19.9
11 – 15	51		9.0
16 – 20	35	86	6.2
21 – 25	15		2.6
26 – 30	30	45	5.3
Total exits 1884-1914	**567**		**100.0**

Source: [i] Northampton Trade Directories 1885-1914.

Historians and contemporaries have typically used business failure data as a barometer reading of the state of trade in the short run and of the vigour of the economy generally. In particular, contemporaries have argued that, given the sensitivity of consumer markets to trade cycle movements, footwear firms were particularly prone to trading pressures and failure in depression, as consumer durable purchases like footwear can be deferred by consumers during recession. But business failure data can also be used to give insights into the business behaviour of business owners. Such data from the Northampton footwear industry helps to give context to William Arnold's experience. Historically, the footwear industry has been regarded as an industry dominated by small firms.[40] This can be quantified for the Northampton footwear industry by using and analysing data from local trade directories, the longevity

40 K. B. Brooker (1981) *op. cit.* p. 8, the high turnover of firms in Northampton is shown by a trade directory analysis between 1874 and 1914. "...these list 402 separate footwear manufacturing firms. Of these, 239 (59.9%) only appear in one directory..."

of wholesale footwear firms in the period after 1884 can be observed (Table 21). Note the pattern of exits recorded amongst firms new to the industry: this is based on firms that leave within five years of their first listing in a trade directory. This early exit of infant firms has been repeatedly observed in studies of small firms. It is commonly recognised that young firms face considerable early trading difficulties commonly leading to business failure. This initial period of five years commonly witnesses failures running at the 70% level. As commercial maturity is reached the likelihood of failure recedes, only to return as firms reach old age, at which point a number of factors can trigger failure; hence the term 'mature atrophied failure'. William Arnold's failure was a classic infant firm failure. However, it should not be inferred that all exits of firms represent business failures. Some firms ceased to trade in the period as solvent companies able to meet their debts. Causes could vary and would certainly include the retirement of the principal from business. We obtain a similar result if we look at the entry of wholesale firms at fixed points in local Northampton trade directories over a longer period of time (Table 23).

Table 23: Entry configuration of wholesale manufacturing firms at 1854; 1884; 1914

Period of entry prior to year of listing	Number of firms in:					
	1854 list		1854 list		1914 list	
0–5 years	45	51.8%	84	43.1%	10	13.2%
6–10 years	25	28.7%	39	20.0%	6	7.9%
11–15 years	5	5.7%	28	14.3%	9	11.8%
15 years +	12	13.8%	44	22.6%	51	67.1%
Total number of firms	**87**	100.0%	**195**	100.0%	**76**	100.0%

Source: Northampton Trade Directories for 1854; 1884; & 1914.

Such high levels of firm exit starkly suggest that the path William Arnold and his partners embarked upon in 1889, far from being an easy option, was one that was laden with difficulty and problems. Initially, William Arnold remembers the easy confidence that he had at the beginning of the venture is modified after the suspension of trading when very aware of the business risk involved in the decision to mechanise the factory. At this point in his account there is the tension of his decision to mechanise and his wait with bated breath for the outcome. In this regard, he encapsulates the difference of attitude between infant and established firms.

This difference would have most clearly been observed in matters of business understanding and management: the risks associated with business. Such risks, and ways of guarding against them, were not always fully recognised and understood by those new to business, leading to early catastrophe. Established firms more readily guarded against and lessened such risks. The level of market information in this period was good and potentially enabled informed manufacturers to find out about emergent risks, to assess them, and to help mitigate against them:

How did they find out about risks and begin to evaluate them? – Their main sources were the Manufacturers Association, the local Chamber of Commerce and the flourishing trade press. These and Government trade and other industrial statistical sources enabled the informed Victorian businessmen to be "data aware and information wise".

How did they get hold of the data with which to inform risk? – Bank and government statistical information was beginning to provide some of the information they required. In turn the trade and daily press were providing a channel for making this information readily available. Once they had the information, they would need the skills to be able to interpret the information and make informed business decisions from that information.

How did they manage risk once aware of it? – Information could inform decisions relating to production and trading decisions. In the footwear industry, established firms used sub-contracting and outworking, though not without risk in itself, to alleviate operational and production risks. The risk was effectively passed on to the sub-contractors and outworkers.

How did they manage changes in production? – In addition to general information available on change, they would have the advice and practical support of machinery companies. These companies provided leasing arrangements; technical advice on installation and training operatives. In centres, local builders were experienced in constructing factories and re-modelling and extending existing buildings.

How did they make use of managers? – Firms could buy in the skills of managers and agents. This approach can be observed in the early days of A. & W. Arnold.

How did firms become "risk intelligent"? – In consumer industries like footwear, it was possible for aware firms to balance production and trading risks. The variations in production volume relating to the seasonal demand for footwear could be effectively managed by the use of sub-contracting, which placed the costs of low season lulls in demand onto the sub-contractor, and the use of making for stock in low seasons.

The approach to managing risk would have varied according to size and financial security of the firm. Of course it was not inevitable that a businessman had the necessary management skills, nor the attitude of mind to learn lessons from his business dealings. All that can be said with certainty is that young firms often had some hard lessons to learn if they were to survive. One of the key matters was the development of a business awareness of issues and behaviours and an approach to decision making needed to navigate through. Some issues were constantly recurring, for example the seasonality of trade or shifts in the trade cycle, whilst others less so, for example a change in manufacturing process. By using present-day ideas about assessing and mitigating business risks,[41] it is possible to make sense of the business world the late Victorian wholesale footwear manufacturer like William Arnold was called upon to manage. Table 24 summarises the main categories of business problem that confronted the footwear manufacturer, the likely impact and the risk they represented for the firm's continued trading.

The impact of risk on the business behaviour of different firms varied between new and older established firms. For new, infant firms there was a focus upon survival strategies and the need to understand the business world. They were grappling with emergent matters relating to understanding and establishing their place in the industry; few were able to develop without experiencing problems. As firms aged and matured they developed levels of experience and market knowledge that insulated them from failure. But, at some stage even the mature firm increased its exposure to failure unless it could refresh its business awareness and understanding of the marketplace. Moreover, their strategy and approach to business and to business risk varied according to the market sector they are operating in: ready-made footwear, hand-made, or bespoke.

Approaches to business risk also varied between family firms, according to whether they were family run, professionally managed, or had to take account of shareholders. For some pure survival was a significant issue, for others the needs of the members of family. Inherent in a purely family firm was the need to strike a balance between the continuation of the firm and the needs of the family: levels of security and trust lay

---

41 See, for example, R. Anderson & Associates, *Risk Management & Corporate Governance* (2010). What is presented here has been adapted from this source.

Table 24: Categories of business risk in the wholesale footwear industry: likelihood and impact

Major risk: Market and workplace management matters
Risks that are likely to have a major or catastrophic impact on business if not managed: • Short run market and financial risks   • Bad debts   • Sub-contracting and outwork are risk laden   • Transformation in production – for example, the transition from outworking to factory – imposed a critical change in worker management[1]   • Non-retention of talented and key workers during seasonal lulls in production and periodic downturns in trade
Moderate risk: Commercial and investment matters
Risks that are fairly likely to have a moderate impact on business: • Investment commitments   • Employment fraud (unfair dealing in wages and employment conditions)   • False accounting   • Failure to disclose information   • Theft of assets or of information
Minor risk: Asset management matters
Risks that are an unlikely occurrence and will have a minor impact on business: • Once the decision to mechanise is taken, the leasing of shoe machinery and the flexible use of property for manufacturing gave the manufacturer scope for …   • Commercial fraud; product fraud   • Theft of materials or skimping on retention for personal use of materials given to outworkers. Although this is going to happen, the probable level is not going to cause major difficulties if adequate supervision and inspection of completed work is carried out.   • Outworking work rate and quality of work of outworkers. Again, the key requirement is for there to be adequate supervision of outwork by enforcing hand in periods through use of fines and availability of future work
Insignificant risk: Government regulation matters
Risks that are unlikely and of insignificant impact: • Examples: Contraventions of building and other government regulations   • Contravention of laws relating to sanitary and public health nuisance regulations   • Contravention of local building planning and controls and regulations   • Contravention of Factory and Workshop Acts regulations   • Late or non-payment of local rating and other taxes
These matters can be rated insignificant, partly due to the rarity of action being taken and having a commercial impact on a firm, and partly due to the low levels of inspection and levying penalties

at the heart of operating such firms. But there are points where family needs at death or retirement potentially took capital out of the firm, acting as a significant drag on short-term business. In the final analysis, the risk profile was linked to the needs of the family. Moreover, approaches to risk by owners of family firms were mediated by both external trading circumstances and the internal family needs. Despite there being evidence of the provision of credit and loan facilities being made available by local banks – indeed there is circumstantial evidence of William Arnold funding the mechanisation of his factory in the mid-1890s in this way – significant reliance was still being based on retained profits, which lessened income to the family in the short term. In other types of business, the main capital stakeholders would have likewise affected the firm's approach to risk and to business generally. These institutional matters will be as significant in formulating the firm's business strategy and approach to risk such as the nature of the market and its growth; factor costs; labour issues. Whoever has made a financial stake in the firm will want a return on capital invested. In family firms, those family needs may be aspirational (for example, to buy a house in a better neighbourhood; or to fund a wedding); or to assure family succession or divide company capital on death of a member of the family; or extend the family educationally and culturally.

The categorisation set out above is useful when compared with the company failure information data in Table 24. As the volumes of and reasons for failure listed there are studied the different risk levels begin to make more sense. Thus, many cease trading because of their inability to keep records; a function that both allowed them to keep track of their expenditure and revenue, and provide the basis of information concerning future business planning. The two data elements provide a blueprint of the skills people, such as William Arnold, required to operate a successful business.

The available business failure evidence not only gives some quantitative idea of failure levels; from it we can also deduce some of the reasons for this large fallout of businessmen and particularly of those in the first years of their business career. Of the 643 manufacturing firms listed between 1884 and 1914, only 76 (11.8%) remained by the latter date, and in all 567 (88.2%) ceased trading. Such an observation raises a range of questions: what form and character did this failure take; what patterns of personal skill and qualities amongst manufacturers can one isolate, which contributed to failure; what macro factors affected mortality in the industry; how does a high turnover rate affect the industry overall? By raising these issues it is hoped, not only to place the high level of turnover into a sharper perspective, but also the ultimate, absolute decline of the industry's small master class.

Of the many wholesale Northampton footwear firms ceasing to trade in the period 1885 to 1914, a record of the failure exists for 305 of them. In some cases this record is an official one, but in many instances it is a trade press report, as was the case for Arnold's firm. The Victorian business community had redress to various legal procedures, of which bankruptcy

Table 25: Primary and secondary causes of business failure amongst Northampton wholesale footwear manufacturers 1885-1914

[1] Headline Summary

Cause of business failure	1885-1914		1885-1894		1885-1904		1905-1914	
	a	**b**	a	b	a	b	A	B
External factors	**96**	**40**	8	4	40	16	48	20
Internal factors	**290**	**260**	74	62	71	68	145	130
Total	**386**	**300**	82	66	111	84	193	150

Source: Weekly commercial intelligence reports of *Boot & Shoe Trades Journal* + *Shoe & Leather Record* 1885-1914.
Notes: (a) primary cause; (b) contributory cause

[2] Detailed causes of business failure

Cause of business failure	1885-1913		1885-1894		1885-1904		1905-1914	
	a	**b**	a	b	B	b	A	b
External factors								
1 *Business too small*								
insufficient turnover	4	6	1	0	1	3	2	3
want of capital	22	4	0	1	11	1	11	2
2 *Business activity changes*								
fall off in trade	18	6	0	0	9	3	9	3
competition	28	18	3	2	11	7	14	9
3 *Miscellaneous*								
fire	10	0	1	0	4	0	5	0
strike	4	2	1	1	1	0	2	1
demise of owner	4	0	1	0	1	0	2	0
debtor suspension	4	4	1	0	1	2	2	2
"genuine failure"	2	0	0	0	1	0	1	0
Group sub-total	96	40	8	4	40	16	48	20
Internal factors								
1 *Failure of business probity*								
poor costing*	74	84	18	18	19	24	37	42
failure to keep records	76	38	23	9	15	10	38	19
bad debts	70	44	20	11	15	11	35	22
excessive credit	0	2	0	1	0	0	0	1
borrowed capital	4	2	0	1	2	0	2	1
fixed capital depreciation	10	10	0	0	5	5	5	5
2 *Errors of judgement*								
knowingly selling below cost	14	40	3	13	4	7	7	20
knowingly insolvent	14	6	1	0	6	3	7	3
over extension: loss capital	10	8	1	1	4	3	5	4
recklessness	4	8	1	3	1	1	2	4
irregular bill transactions	2	8	1	3	0	1	1	4
no shoe trade experience	6	2	3	1	0	0	3	1
poor management	4	4	2	0	0	2	2	2
illiterate	2	4	1	1	0	1	1	2
Group sub-total	290	260	74	62	71	68	145	130
Total	386	300	82	66	111	84	193	150

Source: Weekly commercial intelligence reports of *Boot & Shoe Trades Journal* + *Shoe & Leather Record* 1885-1914.
Notes:
- (a) primary cause; (b) contributory cause
- Leading invariably to either weak profit, or a loss on trading

was only a final sanction. Bankruptcy left its official record, but a permanent record of many of the other forms of redress is now only to be found in the contemporary trade press of the day. Publication of these dealings was an important means of informing the trade of the viability of firms in difficulty. The frequency and detail found in these reports also serve to give us a glimpse of the extent of business failure in this period. Summary details of footwear firms ceasing to trade are set out in Tables 25 [1] and [2]. From these tables it can be concluded internal factors are the most significant set of causes for firm failure: they represent 24.9% of primary and 13.3% of contributory causes in the whole period. Nevertheless external factors are important and over time these significantly increase as the drive to modern factory working favours larger, efficient firms. A rise in external factors can be seen in the two periods after 1894: they rise by 500% in 1895-1905, and 600% in 1905-1914.

At first reading it could be argued that the level of failures in this, and indeed other towns, was disturbingly high. A common general feature emerging is that aspiring businessmen, like Arnold and his partners, may have had the practical skills required to run a manufacturing business but far fewer understood the nature of business and the skills required to adequately plan and manage a firm as a going concern over time. If the contemporary business failure reports in the Victorian press are to be believed, few indeed appear to have contemplated the business skills required before they started in business. The tradition in the industry of practical men "rising from the seat" was one that was to die only slowly as traditional craft workshop businesses were eclipsed by modern manufacturing techniques in the period.

The footwear industry and the role of entrepreneurship

A driver in recent historical enquiry about the performance of the British economy in our period relates to the positive link between that performance and the negative impact of cultural influences upon the business class.[42]

There has been a long debate amongst historians about the ways in which businessmen defined and translated their business success socially, culturally and politically. Few footwear manufacturers were to enter county society and seek to acquire a country estate.[43] It is difficult to make clear links between cultural life and business success. A study

---

42 These comments draw upon "Culture, wealth and the entrepreneurial spirit" in R. Floud & P. Johnson, *The Cambridge Economic History of Modern Britain*, Volume II (2012) p. 239 et seq.
43 On Northampton manufacturers see K. B. Brooker (2013) *passim*. T. Nicholas "Wealth making in the nineteenth and early twentieth century…", *Business History* vol. 42 p. 155-68.

by Tom Nicholas[44] has sought to analyse successful business performance by utilising lifetime rates of wealth accumulation as an index
of success. This study of the lifetime wealth accumulated from profits
and inherited wealth for a large sample of British entrepreneurs leads
him to conclude that "...industry, region and religious dissent cannot
explain performance differences. By contrast, education and entrepreneurial type are the important predictors..."[45] Wealth accumulation
by founders of firms was higher than that of subsequent generations.
The debate amongst historians regarding the cultural explanation for
poor business performance in Britain rests on some of the evidence used
in this introduction to place William Arnold in his social world. The
type of firm, the role of education, and the influence of religion are
central to the hypothesis of culturally induced economic decline in
Britain. It is useful to add in this introduction some commentary as to
ways in which this debate may influence the way in which William
Arnold's business contemporaries should be perceived.

For many years historians have tended to regard an inherent conservatism within family firms acting as a drag on economic performance
generally. Recruitment in family controlled firms "characterised by
patronage and nepotism in recruitment". This economic drag effect
showed itself as complacency and conservatism, together with a
preference for leisure over a competitive thrust of business. Behind this
analysis lies the resultant failure of both established and new technology
British industries to match the fast growing productivity of rising
American and German manufactures.

However, individual studies of firms do reveal individual differences
between individual firms that were technologically advanced and
profitable. One firm of this nature is Rowntree & Co, the chocolate
manufacturers of York. The success of this firm has been judged to one
that contradicts the classical stereotype of family-based entrepreneurial
lethargy. Here was a firm that used up-to-date management structures,
the recruitment of managers, and an "...advertising strategy based on
market research, product development, and branding..."[46] Leaving
aside the argument that firms might have sought economic outcomes
based on personal and family income goals, those patterns of business
activity seen in Rowntree's can also be observed in the footwear
industry. Here significant use was made by both best-practice firms and
the better average-practice ones, of new production technology and

44 T. Nicholas, "Businessman and land ownership in the late nineteenth century", *Ec.H.R.*
(1999) vol. 52 p. 27-44.
45 R. Floud & P. Johnson *ibid.* p. 241.
46 R. Floud & P. Johnson *ibid.* p. 240: on Rowntree & Co see R. Fitzgerald, *Rowntree & the
Marketing Revolution* (1995).

product lines, new marketing and retail developments, and the recruitment of a new class of professional manager. In effect is the real picture one of sectorial differences within the British economy? A situation where different sectors of British manufacturing industry achieved different economic results in the late nineteenth and early twentieth centuries? Like chocolate manufacture, footwear production was part of a burgeoning consumer industrial sector, embracing clothing, soap, bicycles, etc, that performed well in face of secular rising personal incomes. These industries were at the forefront of market developments and retailing in this period. By making this sectorial distinction, can we look at some of Britain's family firm owners in a different light? Be this as it may, it is nevertheless instructive to note that, whilst some footwear family firms were poor performers, a significant number were high performing manufacturing and retail concerns in the decades around the Great War.

Historians focus upon the role of education relates to the extent a public school/university classical education was detrimental to entre-preneurial performance. The gentlemanly focus of both public school and Oxbridge education led, it is argued, to the perceived inferior business performance of the period. Yet this argument, together with comparative assessments of British education to those in France and Germany, are inconclusive. Within the narrow confines of the North-ampton industry this debate does not help unduly as only 13% of the Northampton sample had a private, public school or university education. Of more moment in the Northampton sample is the stress that needs to be placed upon the positive utility of compulsory elementary education of the day; and even more pertinent is the utility of practical on-the-job training for young manufacturers; for this is an industry where many of the owners of firms came from a working background. Clearly, in one sense William Arnold's lack of education was a barrier to his early career, but his eagerness for business success assured that he sought training. And like many footwear manufacturers, he assured that his sons received both practical and managerial training before assuming control with the family firm.

Turning to religion, Northampton manufacturers as a group were influenced by religion and those prominent in church and chapel spent fulsomely both of their money and time. In this regard William Arnold stands as a good example. On a broad canvas, in recent years historians have sought to show a link between entrepreneurship and religion: to demonstrate the personal and group mechanisms used by religious groups to make their way in business life and to make their mark in the wider community. Earlier work laid stress upon the presence of religious groups in society who were outsiders: Jews and Quakers are the most obvious examples; important also were Non-conformist groups. In the Northampton sample, 45% of manufacturers were Nonconformists, compared to 27% being Anglicans, but such figures broadly match the religious affiliation patterns within the town's population. Nevertheless, it is possible that membership of a congregation could be a useful link to other manufacturers. William Arnold was not the only prominent manufacturer in the Kettering Road Primitive Methodist Church. And beyond this, there were close ties between this Non-conformist church and many others in the town. Yet, other historical studies have stressed that religious belief could positively hinder business activity. In Northampton, several manufacturers recruited their supervisors and foremen from amongst the congregation at their place of worship: Charles and Edward Lewis are the most prominent example of this practice. This practice was not only a closed method of selection that caused adverse comment in the town, but was not necessarily the method to assure the recruitment of the best supervisory staff. Another example relates to William Arnold's practice of giving 10% of his annual income to his church, and of making gifts and donations in addition. This practice, however laudable in itself, had the potential to syphon funds away from the family firm; reliant as it was on retained profit and unspent income for growth.

INDEX

This index contains references to people, firms, and places contemporary with William Arnold. Member of Arnold family in bold who was a first or second generation senior in either Arnold & Co; A. & W. Arnold & Co. Ltd; or Arnold Bros. & Co. Ltd.